ACCA

PRACTICE & REVISION KIT

Professional Paper 11

Tax planning (Finance Act 2000)

BPP Publishing
January 2001

First edition 1994
Ninth edition January 2001

ISBN 0 7517 0815 1 (Previous edition 0 7517 0855 0)

British Library Cataloguing-in-Publication Data
A catalogue record for this book
is available from the British Library

Published by

BPP Publishing Limited
Aldine House, Aldine Place
London W12 8AW

www.bpp.com

Printed in Great Britain by Ashford Colour Press

We are grateful to the Association of Chartered Certified Accountants for
permission to reproduce in this Kit the syllabus and the pilot paper questions of
which the Association holds the copyright.

We are also grateful to the Association of Chartered Certified Accountants, the
Chartered Institute of Management Accountants and the Institute of Chartered
Accountants in England and Wales for permission to reproduce past examination
questions. The answers to the past examination questions have been prepared by
BPP Publishing Limited.

CONTENTS

The headings indicate the main topics of questions, but questions often cover several different topics.

Tutorial questions, listed in italics, are followed by guidance notes. These notes show you how to approach the question, and thus ease the transition from study to examination practice.

A date alone (12/99, say) or 'pilot paper' after the question title refers to a current syllabus paper.

Questions preceded by * are **key questions** which we think you must attempt in order to pass the exam. Tick them off on this list as you complete them.

Handwritten: *accounting* ₚₐᵢₗₑ | Aᴄᵢₙₐₗ T.P.   AₐS-- CₐS.
Handwritten: *Schooner Ltd (12/98)* VAT – Eᵢ S – Scₕ.DI – FYA

PART C: CORPORATE TAXATION

PART D: OVERSEAS ASPECTS AND TAX PLANNING

BPP PUBLISHING

Recommended period of use	Elements of the BPP Effective Study Package
3-12 months before exam	**Study Text** Acquisition of knowledge, understanding, skills and applied techniques.

↓

| 1-6 months before exam | **Practice & Revision Kit**
Tutorial questions and helpful checklists of the key points lead you into each area. There are then numerous Examination questions to try, graded by topic area, along with realistic suggested solutions prepared by BPP's own authors in the light of the Examiner's Reports. June 2001 examinees will find the 2001 edition of the Kit essential for bringing them up-to-date for the Finance Act 2000. |

↓

| Last minute - 3 months before exam | **Passcards**
Short, memorable notes focused on what is most likely to come up in the exam you will be sitting. |

↓

| 1-6 months before exam | **Success Tapes**
Audio cassettes covering the vital elements of your syllabus in less than 90 minutes per subject. Each tape also contains exam hints to help you fine tune your strategy. |

↓

| 3-12 months before exam | **Breakthrough Videos**
These supplement your Study Text, by giving you clear tuition on key exam subjects. They allow you the luxury of being able to pause or repeat sections until you have fully grasped the topic. |

THE JUNE 2001 EXAM

Format of the June 2001 exam

	Marks
4 (out of 6) optional 25 mark questions	100

Time allowed: 3 hours

Pass rates

The pass rate for Paper 11 in recent sittings has been in the region of 40%-45%.

The examiner

The examiner for Paper 11 is David Harrowven. He has been setting the exams for many years. The exams can be time pressured and you must learn to be organised and disciplined in your approach to your work.

Mr Harrowven has a preference for examining topics in respect of which there has been a recent change and/or on which he has written a recent article in the *Students' Newsletter*. However, please note that because Finance Act 2000 will only be examinable for one sitting of the current syllabus, a number of changes to the Finance Act 2000 will not be examinable. The non examinable items are detailed below.

Core syllabus areas

The following are core syllabus areas:

* Overseas taxation, both corporate and personal including double taxation relief;
* Taxation of groups of companies including group relief and transfer of assets;
* Inheritance tax, including valuation of an estate, business property relief.

Other important areas of the Paper 11 syllabus are:

* Personal finance, including pension planning, individual savings accounts, the enterprise investment scheme and venture capital trusts;

* Schedule DI/II (including opening and closing year rules, change of accounting date and partnerships);

* Self assessment;

* Capital gains tax, particularly in business situations

* VAT is of increasing importance and you can now expect the VAT part of a question to be worth up to 15 marks.

Hot topics for the June 2001 exam

Given the examiner's track record and in the light of the 2000 exams, we believe there is a strong likelihood that the following 'hot topics' will come up in the June 2001 exam:

Inheritance tax	Partnerships
Overseas aspects	Groups (including capital gains groups)
CGT reliefs (including taper relief)	VAT (including groups)
Personal finance	National insurance contributions (including Class 1A
Benefits in kind	contributions)
Incorporation	

If you wish to concentrate on particular areas of the syllabus whilst maximising your chances of passing, you could start with the topics above. Questions on these are highlighted as 'key questions' in the Question and Answer Checklist on page (iv) ; we look at them in more detail on page (xi).

Disclaimer of liability

Please note that we have based our predictions of the content of the June 2001 exam on our long experience of the ACCA exams. We do not claim to have any endorsement of the predictions from either the examiner or the ACCA and we do not guarantee that either the specific questions, or the general areas, that are forecast will necessarily be included in the exams, in part or in whole.

We do not accept any liability or responsibility to any person who takes, or does not take, any action based (either in whole or in part and either directly or indirectly) upon any statement or omission made in this book. We encourage students to study all topics in the ACCA syllabus and the mock exam in this book is intended as an aid to revision only.

Examinable material

The Finance Act 2000 is examinable in June 2001. This Kit fully reflects the provisions of this Act.

In the July 2000 edition of the Student's Newsletter you will see that the examiner announced that he following topics will **not be examinable** in June 2001

- For people under 65, the married couples allowance and tax relief for maintenance payments

- The additional personal allowance and the widows bereavement allowance

- The Working Families tax credit and the Children's tax credit

- Tax relief for mortgage interest payments

- Stakeholder pensions

- Apportionment pre/post 6.4.2000 for CGT taper relief on non-business/business assets

- Relief for research and development expenditure

- The zero rate of NIC

- The all employee share scheme

- Enterprise management incentives

- The corporate venturing scheme

- Personal service companies

- A computational question involving the carry back/carry forward of excess foreign tax

- The Financial Services and Markets Bill

- The retirement relief limits available in 2000/01 will be examined but the limits applicable to other years are not examinable

Students' Newsletter

Students are advised to read the 'Exam Notes' published in the Students' Newsletter as these contain details of examinable legislation, changes in the syllabuses and other useful information. In particular, the notes state the Finance Act applicable to each examination session.

BPP PUBLISHING

REVISION

How to revise

This is a very important time as you approach the exam. You must remember three things.

> **Use time sensibly**
> **Set realistic goals**
> **Believe in yourself**

Use time sensibly

1 **How much study time do you have**? Remember that you must EAT, SLEEP, and of course, RELAX.

2 **How will you split that available time between each subject?** What are your weaker subjects? They need more time.

3 **What is your learning style?** AM/PM? Little and often/long sessions? Evenings/ weekends?

4 **Are you taking regular breaks?** Most people absorb more if they do not attempt to study for long uninterrupted periods of time. A five minute break every hour (to make coffee, watch the news headlines) can make all the difference.

5 **Do you have quality study time?** Unplug the phone. Let everybody know that you're studying and shouldn't be disturbed.

Set realistic goals

1 Have you set a **clearly defined objective** for each study period?

2 Is the objective **achievable?**

3 Will you **stick to your plan?** Will you make up for any **lost time?**

4 Are you **rewarding yourself** for your hard work?

5 Are you leading a **healthy lifestyle?**

Believe in yourself

Are you cultivating the right attitude of mind? There is absolutely no reason why you should not pass this exam if you adopt the correct approach

- **Be confident** - you've passed exams before, you can pass them again

- **Be calm** - plenty of adrenaline but no panicking

- **Be focused** - commit yourself to passing the exam

What to revise for the June 2001 exam

Ideally you should revise all areas of the syllabus thoroughly, using your BPP Study Text (and any notes you've made from it), this kit and, if you wish, the BPP Passcards. If your time is limited, however, you could concentrate on revising the areas covered by our hot topics highlighted on page (viii).

Topic	2000 Study Text Chapter/2001 Passcard Chapter	Key questions in this Kit	Key articles in Students' Newsletter
Inheritance tax	9, 10, 11	3, 9, 11, 12, 13, 14, 15	March 1999
Overseas aspects	28, 29	4, 7, 9, 13, 42, 43, 44, 46, 47	December 1998 and January 1999
CGT reliefs including taper relief	4, 7, 19	9, 11, 14, 15, 25, 27, 51	July 2000
Personal finance	3, 12	4, 7, 16, 18, 46	
Benefits-in-kind	2	2, 4, 6	
Incorporation	19, 30	16, 25, 26	
Partnerships	18	24, 26, 27	
Groups (including capital gains groups)	27, 20	35, 36, 37, 38, 39	July 2000
VAT (including groups)	20, 21	23, 24, 25, 31, 38, 39, 44, 48, 49	February 1999 April 1999, July 2000
National Insurance contributions (including Class 1A contributions)	2, 18	3, 4, 6, 23, 26	July 2000

Note that although the above articles are very useful, they are not all up to date for the Finance Act 2000. The examiner wrote an article covering Finance Act 2000 in the July 2000 edition of the Students' Newsletter.

BPP PUBLISHING

PRACTICE

Exam technique

Passing professional examinations is half about having the knowledge, and half about doing yourself full justice in the examination. You must have the right technique.

> **The day of the exam**

1. Set at least one **alarm** (or get an alarm call) for a morning exam

2. Have **something to eat** but beware of eating too much; you may feel sleepy if your system is digesting a large meal

3. Allow plenty of **time to get to the exam hall**; have your route worked out in advance and listen to news bulletins to check for potential travel problems

4. **Don't forget** pens, pencils, rulers, erasers

5. Put **new batteries** into your calculator and take a spare set (or a spare calculator)

6. **Avoid discussion** about the exam with other candidates outside the exam hall

---

> **Technique in the exam hall**

1. *Read the instructions (the 'rubric') on the front of the exam paper carefully*

   Check that the exam format hasn't changed. It is surprising how often examiners' reports remark on the number of students who attempt too few - or too many - questions, or who attempt the wrong number of questions from different parts of the paper. Make sure that you are planning to answer the **right number of questions**.

2. *Select questions carefully*

   Read through the paper once, then quickly jot down key points against each question in a second read through. Select those questions where you could latch on to 'what the question is about' - but remember to check carefully that you have got the right end of the stick before putting pen to paper.

3. *Plan your attack carefully*

   Consider the **order** in which you are going to tackle questions. It is a good idea to start with your best question to boost your morale and get some easy marks 'in the bag'.

4. *Check the time allocation for each question*

   Each mark carries with it a **time allocation** of 1.8 minutes (including time for selecting and reading questions). A 25 mark question should be completed in 45 minutes. When time is up, you *must* go on to the next question or part. Going even one minute over the time allowed brings you a lot closer to failure.

5. *Read the question carefully and plan your answer*

   Read through the question again very carefully when you come to answer it. Plan your answer to ensure that you **keep to the point**. Two minutes of planning plus eight minutes of writing is virtually certain to earn you more marks than ten minutes of writing.

6. *Produce relevant answers*

   Particularly with written answers, make sure you **answer the question set**, and not the question you would have preferred to have been set.

7 *Gain the easy marks*

Include the obvious if it answers the question and don't try to produce the perfect answer.

Don't get bogged down in small parts of questions. If you find a part of a question difficult, get on with the rest of the question. If you are having problems with something, the chances are that everyone else is too.

8 *Produce an answer in the correct format*

The examiner will **state in the requirements** the format in which the question should be answered, for example in a report or memorandum.

9 *Follow the examiner's instructions*

You will annoy the examiner if you ignore him or her. The **examiner will state** whether he or she wishes you to 'discuss', 'comment', 'evaluate' or 'recommend'.

10 *Lay out your numerical computations and use workings correctly*

Make sure the layout fits the **type of question** and is in a style the examiner likes.

Show all your **workings** clearly and explain what they mean. Cross reference them to your solution. This will help the examiner to follow your method (this is of particular importance where there may be several possible answers).

11 *Present a tidy paper*

You are a professional, and it should show in the **presentation of your work**. Students are penalised for poor presentation and so you should make sure that you write legibly, label diagrams clearly and lay out your work neatly. Markers of scripts each have hundreds of papers to mark; a badly written scrawl is unlikely to receive the same attention as a neat and well laid out paper.

12 *Stay until the end of the exam*

Use any spare time **checking and rechecking** your script.

13 *Don't worry if you feel you have performed badly in the exam*

It is more than likely that the other candidates will have found the exam difficult too. Don't forget that there is a competitive element in these exams. As soon as you get up to leave the exam hall, *forget* that exam and think about the next - or, if it is the last one, celebrate!

14 *Don't discuss an exam with other candidates*

This is particularly the case if you **still have other exams to sit**. Even if you have finished, you should put it out of your mind until the day of the results. Forget about exams and relax!

Practising tutorial questions

A total of 6 tutorial questions are included in the Question Bank. If you read through the revision topics and feel confident that you know what they are about, try to produce at least a plan for the tutorial questions, using the guidance notes to ensure your answer is structured so as to gain a good pass mark.

BPP PUBLISHING

Practising exam standard questions

Once you are confident with the revision topics and the tutorial questions, you should try as many as possible of the exam standard questions; at the very least, you should attempt the 'hot topic' questions identified in the Question and Answer Checklist. Try to produce full answers under timed conditions; you are practising exam technique an much as knowledge recall here.

Doing the Mock Exam

The Mock Exam includes the style and content of the questions we think are most likely to be set in the June 2001 exam. You should attempt the paper under exam conditions, so that you gain experience of selecting and sequencing your questions, and managing your time, as well as of writing answers. Applying our marking scheme will help you get an idea of how you will fare in your exam.

ANALYSIS OF PAST PAPERS 1998-2000

The analysis below shows the topics which have been examined in the six most recent sittings of the syllabus.

December 2000

1   CGT and IHT implications on disposal of business. Income tax losses
2   Income tax, CGT and IHT implications of various gifts. Trusts
3   Corporation tax: groups and overseas aspects. Income tax: overseas aspects
4   VAT. Employment v self employment
5   ISAs, Pensions, EIS and Schedule A
6   Partnerships. Change of accounting date

Examiner's comments were not available at the time of printing this Kit.

June 2000

1   Corporation tax: overseas aspects. Quarterly payments regime. Loss reliefs
2   Income tax computation. Self assessment
3   Investments. Financial Services Act 1986
4   IHT: Domicile. BPR. Gift with reservation. DTR. Sale of assets after death
5   Purchase of own shares. Benefits in kind
6   Income tax losses. VAT registration. Farmers averaging

Examiner's comments

Although not up to the standard for the two previous diets, the performance at this diet was quite satisfactory. A number of candidates achieved pass marks in the seventies and eighties, and maximum marks were frequently awarded for questions 1, 2, 4 and 5. Those candidates that did not achieve a pass mark generally indicated a lack of knowledge and poor examination technique. Questions 1, 2 and 4 were all relatively straightforward, and these gave well prepared candidates that chance to obtain a pass mark without too much difficulty. The three questions dealt with the corporate taxation for a group of companies, the self-assessment system for individual taxpayers, and IHT in respect of lifetime transfers and on death. These are all important areas of the syllabus. It was particularly noticeable at this diet that poor examination technique often resulted in the failure to obtain a pass mark.

Examiner's comments

The performance at this diet was very encouraging, with many candidates achieving pass marks in the seventies and eighties. The overall performance is reflected in the high pass percentage, and it was apparent that may candidates had benefited by studying my series of articles in the *Students' Newsletter*. Those candidates that did not achieve a pass mark generally indicated a lack of knowledge and poor examination technique.

Examiner's comments

The performance at this diet was very encouraging, with many candidates achieving pass marks in the seventies and eighties. The overall performance is reflected in the high pass percentage, and it was apparent that may candidates had benefited by studying my series of articles in the *Students' Newsletter*. Those candidates that did not achieve a pass mark generally indicated a lack of knowledge and poor examination technique.

December 1998		*Question reference in this Kit*
1	IHT and income tax for a non-domiciled individual.	13
2	Income tax self-assessment. Personal pension scheme.	20
3	Corporation tax: groups and capital gains. VAT group registration.	39
4	CGT: retirement relief. Partnership. Income tax losses	27
5	VAT. Raising finance. Schedule D profits.	31
6	Schedule E and Schedule A for individuals.	6

Examiner's comments

It was disappointing that the performance at this diet was not up to the standard of recent sittings. this was largely due to the number of candidates who did not appear to have prepared themselves sufficiently to answer four questions at a pass standard. Typically marginal fail candidates answered two or three questions at the required standard but were then unable to obtain a pass mark because of a poor attempt at the final question.

June 1998		*Question reference in this Kit*
1	Capital allowance and CGT aspects of the relocation of the business, sale and purchase of assets	–
2	Income Tax and CGT aspects of working overseas plus proposed sales and gifts of assets	43
3	Corporation tax group of companies with loss relief	Mock exam
4	Sole trader commencing in business; income tax and VAT consequences. Employed versus self employed discussion. Annual accounting scheme and consequences of late VAT returns	Mock exam
5	Investments; tax consequences of various investments plus discussion of tied adviser and independent adviser and ACCA Statement of Principle on standards expected of an authorised person	18
6	IHT and CGT on lifetime gifts and death estate. Purchase of own shares	11

Examiner's comments

Considering that this paper included relatively straightforward questions on overseas personal tax, group taxation and personal finance, all of which are regularly examined, those candidates who failed to achieve a pass mark can only blame a lack of adequate preparation.

Question 1 dealt with a number of recent changes covered in a Students' Newsletter article. It was therefore disappointing that answers to this question were considerably below the standard of the other five.

Questions 2, 3 and 6 were popular with reasonably good answers. Question 5 was also fairly popular but the answers were not as good as expected for what is an important topic that is regularly examined.

Question 4 was not a popular question but when attempted it was reasonably well answered.

BPP

THE OFFICIAL JUNE 2001 SYLLABUS

Aim of Paper 11

To equip students with the ability to solve unstructured problems which draw on the interaction of taxes between income, profits and capital.

On completion of this paper students should be able to:

- display an awareness of the impact of all major taxes on the transactions of individuals, partnerships and companies
- apply that knowledge to practical situations involving computation, explanation, discussion and advice
- appreciate the importance of taxation in personal and corporate financial planning and decision making
- demonstrate an understanding of the regulations associated with the provision of suitable investment advice to individuals
- identify opportunities to minimise potential tax liabilities by making full use of available options, reliefs and exemptions
- demonstrate the skills expected at the Professional Stage

Syllabus

Below is reproduced the detailed syllabus as published by the ACCA.

---

1   Overview of personal business taxation

(a)   Interactions between different taxes in a range of situations or transactions

(b)   Tax planning; the application of tax planning measures appropriate to the particular situation

2   Capital gains tax

Application of capital gains tax to individuals and corporate taxpayers, with emphasis on business situations.

3   Inheritance tax

(a)   Principles and scope.

(b)   Rules, basis and application.

(c)   Calculating the tax due by clients.

(d)   Minimising/deferring tax liabilities by identifying/applying relevant exemptions, reliefs and allowances.

4   Trusts

Application to trusts of income tax, capital gains tax and inheritance tax.

5   Value Added Tax

The application of Value Added Tax to transactions and other activities of corporate taxpayers.

6 Corporate taxation

(a) Groups and consortia.

(b) The provisions covering liquidations and areas such as disincorporations, purchases of own shares, sales and acquisitions of subsidiaries and share for share amalgamations.

(c) Implications of a company being classed as an investment or close company.

7 Overseas activities giving rise to taxation liabilities

(a) Definition of residence, ordinary residence and domicile.

(b) The taxation of UK income and gains of non-domiciled individuals.

(c) Overseas income and gains: the UK tax treatment of overseas income and gains of UK resident individuals and companies, including relief for double taxation.

(d) Overseas persons, the UK tax treatment of income and gains arising within the UK to non resident individuals and companies.

(e) The inheritance tax position regarding overseas assets of UK individuals and UK assets of non resident individuals.

(f) Business structures, including a UK branch/subsidiary of a foreign company/group and a foreign branch/subsidiary of a UK company/group.

(g) Anti-avoidance legislation relating to overseas activities, income or persons.

8 General

(a) Inter-relationship of taxes: the effect of any of the taxes in a given situation or on a particular transaction.

(b) Anti-avoidance: appreciation of the main areas of anti-avoidance legislation and of the enquiry and investigation procedures of the Inland Revenue and Customs and Excise.

9 Personal finance

(a) Assisting clients in the determination of personal financial objectives, taking into account such factors as individual circumstances, expectations and the economic environment.

(b) Determining financial needs of clients (how much, when, for how long, and for what purpose?).

(c) Regulations affecting investment advisers, and ethical considerations, including the definition of investment business.

(d) Advising on sources and costs of different forms of finance and their applicability to different circumstances including:

   (i)   bank borrowing;
   (ii) finance houses;
   (iii) mortgages;
   (iv) money and capital markets.

(e) Advising on investment of clients' personal funds.

    (i)   Insurance policies
    (ii)   Pension funds
    (iii)   Unit and investment trusts
    (iv)   TESSAs
    (v)   PEPs
    (vi)   Equity shares
    (vii)   Gilt edged securities and other bonds
    (viii) Real property
    (ix)   Banks and building societies
    (x)   National savings

Standard of the paper

The standard of the paper is comparable to that required in the examinations for the second year of a three year UK honours degree course.

Prerequisite knowledge

A thorough understanding of Paper 7 *Tax Framework* is essential for the study of Paper 11.

Paper 11 builds on topics introduced in Paper 7 by:

- applying the knowledge of income tax to tax planning problems for personal and business situations
- interacting knowledge of National Insurance with other taxes
- extending the coverage of corporation tax to include groups and consortia, liquidations and investment and close companies
- applying capital gains tax to individuals and corporate taxpayers, with emphasis on business situations
- applying VAT to transactions and other activities of corporate taxpayers

The teaching guide for Paper 11 assigns the revision of basic areas covered in Paper 7 (income tax, capital gains tax, corporation tax and VAT) to self study to allow sufficient contact time to be allocated to the more advanced subject matter.

In addition, Paper 11 introduces some new areas - overseas considerations, inheritance tax, trusts and personal finance.

List of excluded topics

National Insurance

- The calculation of directors' NIC on a month by month basis
- For the purposes of Class 4 NIC: the offset of trading losses against non-trading income
- Social security: the areas of benefit
- The zero rate of NIC

Income tax

- Profit related pay schemes

- The working families tax credit and the children's tax credit

- Stakeholder pensions

- Detailed computations in respect of share options, share incentives, profit sharing and profit related pay. An employee share ownership plan (ESOP) will not be examined in its own right

- A detailed knowledge of the conditions which must be met to obtain Inland Revenue approval for an occupational pension scheme

- All employee share schemes: Enterprise management incentives

- Computations in respect of a non-qualifying life assurance policy or a qualifying policy which is surrendered within ten years

- Additional personal allowance

- Widows bereavement allowance

- Retirement annuities

- The married couples allowance for those under 65

Capital gains tax

- The rules applicable to assets held on 6 April 1965

- The grant of a lease or sub-lease out of either a freehold, long lease or short lease

- A detailed knowledge of the statements of practice on partnership capital gains

- A question would not be set in respect of a principal private residence where the taxpayer was not in occupation on 31 March 1982

- A detailed question will not be set on the pooling provisions for shares (post 6/4/98 acquisitions)

- Reinvestment relief

- A detailed question will not be set on the relief available where gains are re-invested in enterprise investment scheme shares or in venture capital trusts.

- Capital sums derived from the loss, destruction or damage to a non wasting asset

- Small part disposals of land

Inheritance tax

- A detailed knowledge of gifts with reservation

- Double grossing up on death

- Valuation of an interest in possession trust where there is an annuity and requiring the use of higher and lower income yields

- Double tax relief calculation involving $\dfrac{A}{A+B} \times C$ formula

- An accumulation and maintenance trust ceasing to qualify

- Conditional exemption for heritage property

- Woodlands relief

- A question will not be set involving the computation of a principal or an exit charge for a discretionary trust (note that a written question could be set on the principles involved)

- The relief on BPR/APR given to exempt legacies

Trusts

- Tax liabilities arising during a period of administration
- The 'tax pool' where insufficient 34% income tax has been paid by a discretionary trust
- The IHT implications of adding property to discretionary trust
- Retirement relief
- The residence of trusts
- The overseas aspects of trusts

Value Added Tax

- The special VAT schemes for retailers
- The capital goods scheme
- In respect of property and land: leases, do-it-yourself builders and demolition
- A detailed knowledge of penalties (apart from the default surcharge, serious misdeclarations and default interest)

Corporation tax

- Advance corporation tax (ACT)
- A question will not be set on the interaction of consortium relief and group relief, although this does not preclude the situation where a (loss making) company has both a (profit making) 75% subsidiary and is also a consortium member (re a profit making consortium company)
- The definition of a close company (although the consequences of being a close company are examinable)
- Demergers and reconstructions (other than share for share amalgamations). On disincorporations, a question is unlikely to be set on the sale of a trade or business in return for shares. A question involving a double charge to CGT would not be set
- On liquidations, a question would not be set on the more complex areas such as the different types of liquidation, the preference of debts, or income and expenses arising during the liquidation. A question involving a double charge to CGT would not be set
- A computational question involving the carry back of a loss arising from a loan relationship for non trading purposes
- Relief for research and development expenditure
- Corporate venturing
- Personal service companies

Overseas activities

- A detailed knowledge of double tax agreements
- A computational question on the carryback / carry forward of double tax relief
- Migration of UK resident companies

General

- The names of cases or a detailed knowledge of the judgements, although a knowledge of the principles derived from the leading cases is required

- A question will not be set requiring a knowledge of anti-avoidance legislation (eg artificial transactions in land). However, a question might be set requiring comment as to the Inland Revenue's possible attitude towards a particular transaction/situation taking into account the principles from decided cases

BPP
PUBLISHING

NEW SYLLABUS FROM DECEMBER 2001

The last sitting of the current ACCA syllabus is June 2001. The first sitting of the new syllabus is December 2001. All students registered on the current examination (ie those who registered before 1 January) will automatically be transferred to the new scheme in August 2001.

Transfer arrangements between current and new syllabus

CURRENT SYLLABUS			NEW SYLLABUS	
Foundation Level				
MODULE A				
Paper 1	Accounting Framework	→	Part 1	1.1 Preparing Financial Statements
Paper 2	Legal Framework	→	Part 2	2.2 Corporate and Business Law
MODULE B				
Paper 3	Management Information	→	Part 1	1.2 Financial Information for Management
Paper 4	Organisational Framework	→	Part 1	1.3 Managing People
Certificate Level				
MODULE C				
Paper 5	Information Analysis	→	Part 2	2.1 Information Systems
Paper 6	Audit Framework	→	Part 2	2.6 Audit and Internal review
MODULE D				
Paper 7	Tax Framework	→	Part 2	2.3 Business Taxation
Paper 8	Managerial Finance	→	Part 2	2.4 Financial Management and Control
Professional Level				
MODULE E				
Paper 9	Information for Control and Decision Making	→	Part 3	3.3 Performance Management (optional)
Paper 10	Accounting and Auditing Practice	→	Part 3	2.5 Financial Reporting
Paper 11	Tax Planning	→	Part 3	3.2 Advanced Taxation (optional)
MODULE F			Part 3	3.5 Strategic Business Planning and Development (core)
Paper 12	Management and Strategy	→		
Paper 13	Financial Reporting Environment	→	Part 3	3.6 Advanced Corporate Reporting (core)
Paper 14	Financial Strategy	→	Part 3	3.7 Strategic Financial Management (core)

Optional papers 3.1 (Audit and Assurance Services) and 3.4 (Business Information Management) do not have direct equivalents under the current syllabus.

OXFORD BROOKES DEGREE IN APPLIED ACCOUNTING

The standard required of candidates completing Part 2 is that required in the final year of a UK degree. Students completing Parts 1 and 2 will have satisfied the examination requirement for an honours degree in Applied Accounting, awarded by Oxford Brookes University.

To achieve the degree, you must also submit two pieces of work.

- A 5,000 word **Research and Analysis Project** on a chosen topic, which demonstrates that you have acquired the necessary research and IT skills.

- A 1,500 word **Key Skills Statement**, indicating how you have developed your analytical and communication skills.

BPP has been selected by the ACCA to produce the official text *Success in your Research and Analysis Project* to support students in this task. The book pays particular attention to key skills not covered in the professional examinations.

> AN ORDER FORM FOR THE NEW SYLLABUS MATERIAL, INCLUDING THE OXFORD BROOKES PROJECT TEXT, CAN BE FOUND AT THE END OF THIS KIT.

BPP
PUBLISHING

TAX RATES AND ALLOWANCES

A INCOME TAX

1 *Rates*

	1999/00	%	2000/01	%
	£		£	
Starting rate	1 - 1,500	10	0 – 1,520	10
Basic rate	1,501 - 28,000	23	1,521 – 28,400	22
Higher rate	28,001 and above	40	28,401 and above	40

In 2000/01 savings (excl. Dividend) income is taxed at 20% if it falls in the basic rate band. Dividend income in both the starting rate and the basic rate bands is taxed at 10%. Dividend income within the higher rate band is taxed at 32.5%.

2 *Allowances and tax reducers*

	1999/00 £	2000/01 £
Personal allowance	4,335	4,385
Personal allowance (65 - 74)	5,720	5,790
Personal allowance (75 and over)	5,980	6,050
Married couple's allowance – minimum amount	1,970	2,000
Married couple's allowance (65 - 74)	5,125	5,185
Married couple's allowance (75 and over)	5,195	5,255
Income limit for age-related allowances	16,800	17,000
Blind person's allowance	1,380	1,400

3 *Car fuel scale charges*

	2000/01 Petrol £	Diesel £
Cars having a cylinder capacity		
1,400 cc or less	1,700	2,170
1,401 cc to 2,000 cc	2,170	2,170
More than 2,000 cc	3,200	3,200
Cars not having a cylinder capacity	3,200	3,200

4 *Fixed profit car scheme - 2000/01 rates*

	On first 4,000 miles	On each mile over 4,000
Size of car engine		
Up to 1,000 cc	28p	17p
1,000 cc - 1,500 cc	35p	20p
1,501 cc - 2,000 cc	45p	25p
Over 2,000 cc	63p	36p

5 *Personal pension contribution limits*

	Maximum percentage %
Age	
Up to 35	17.5
36 – 45	20.0
46 – 50	25.0
51 – 55	30.0
56 – 60	35.0
61 or more	40.0

Subject to earnings cap of £90,600 for 1999/00 and £91,800 for 2000/01

6 *Capital allowances*

	%
Plant and machinery	
Writing down allowance★	25 p.a.
First year allowance (acquisitions 2.7.97 - 1.7.98)★★	50
First year allowance (acquisitions after 2.7.98)	40
First year allowance (information and communication technology equipment - period 1.4.00 - 31.3.03)	100
Industrial buildings allowance	
Writing down allowance: post 5.11.62	4
pre 6.11.62	2
Agricultural buildings allowance	
Writing down allowance	4

[handwritten: Reducing. —]
[handwritten: is also available if bought on H.P... see p158]
[handwritten: For small a Medium sized c]
[handwritten: see equipment p158]
[handwritten: Straight line basis]

★ 6% reducing balance for certain long life assets.

★★ 12% for certain long life assets. *[handwritten: → 97/98 only - not for 98 + .. 97/98 only.]*

B   **CORPORATION TAX**

1   *Rates*

Financial year	Full rate %	Small companies rate %	Starting rate	Marginal relief Fraction	Lower limit for starting rate £	Upper limit for starting rate £	Upper limit for SCR £	Lower Limit for SCR £
1994	33	25	-	1/50	-	-	1,500,000	300,000
1995	33	25	-	1/50	-	-	1,500,000	300,000
1996	33	24	-	9/400	-	-	1,500,000	300,000
1997	31	21	-	1/40	-	-	1,500,000	300,000
1998	31	21	-	1/40	-	-	1,500,000	300,000
1999	30	20	-	1/40	-	-	1,500,000	300,000
2000	30	20	10	1/40	10,000	50,000	1,500,000	300,000

[handwritten: NEW]

2   *Marginal relief*

$(M – P) \times I/P \times$ Marginal relief fraction

[handwritten: Retirement relief - first 150 - 100%. Next 450 - 50%]

C VALUE ADDED TAX

1 *Registration and deregistration limits*

	To 31.3.00	*From 1.4.00*
Registration limit	£51,000	£52,000
Deregistration limit	£49,000	£50,000

2 *Scale charges for private motoring*

2000/2001 (VAT inclusive)

	Quarterly	
	Petrol	*Diesel*
Up to 1400 cc	256	232
1401 to 2000 cc	325	232
Over 2000cc	478	295

D INHERITANCE TAX

6.4.97 - 5.4.98	*6.4.98 - 5.4.99*	*6.4.99 – 5.4.00*	*6.4.00 onwards*	*Rate*
£1 - £215,000	£1 - £223,000	£1 - £231,000	£1 - £234,000	Nil
Excess	Excess	Excess	Excess	40%

E RATES OF INTEREST

Official rate of interest: 10% (assumed)

Rate of interest on unpaid/overpaid tax: 10% (assumed)

F CAPITAL GAINS TAX

1 *Lease percentage table*

Years	Percentage	Years	Percentage	Years	Percentage
50 or more	100.000	33	90.280	16	64.116
49	99.657	32	89.354	15	61.617
48	99.289	31	88.371	14	58.971
47	98.902	30	87.330	13	56.167
46	98.490	29	86.226	12	53.191
45	98.059	28	85.053	11	50.038
44	97.595	27	83.816	10	46.695
43	97.107	26	82.496	9	43.154
42	96.593	25	81.100	8	39.399
41	96.041	24	79.622	7	35.414
40	95.457	23	78.055	6	31.195
39	94.842	22	76.399	5	26.722
38	94.189	21	74.635	4	21.983
37	93.497	20	72.770	3	16.959
36	92.761	19	70.791	2	11.629
35	91.981	18	68.697	1	5.983
34	91.156	17	66.470	0	0.000

(2) *Retail prices index (January 1987 = 100.0)*

	1982	1983	1984	1985	1986	1987	1988	1989	1990
Jan		82.6	86.8	91.2	96.2	100.0	103.3	111.0	119.5
Feb		83.0	87.2	91.9	96.6	100.4	103.7	111.8	120.2
Mar	79.4	83.1	87.5	92.8	96.7	100.6	104.1	112.3	121.4
Apr	81.0	84.3	88.6	94.8	97.7	101.8	105.8	114.3	125.1
May	81.6	84.6	89.0	95.2	97.8	101.9	106.2	115.0	126.2
Jun	81.9	84.8	89.2	95.4	97.8	101.9	106.6	115.4	126.7
Jul	81.9	85.3	89.1	95.2	97.5	101.8	106.7	115.5	126.8
Aug	81.9	85.7	89.9	95.5	97.8	102.1	107.9	115.8	128.1
Sept	81.9	86.1	90.1	95.4	98.3	102.4	108.4	116.6	129.3
Oct	82.3	86.4	90.7	95.6	98.5	102.9	109.5	117.5	130.3
Nov	82.7	86.7	91.0	95.9	99.3	103.4	110.0	118.5	130.0
Dec	82.5	86.9	90.9	96.0	99.6	103.3	110.3	118.8	129.9

	1991	1992	1993	1994	1995	1996	1997	1998	1999	2000*	2001*
Jan	130.2	135.6	137.9	141.3	146.0	150.2	154.4	159.5	163.4	167.5	173.5
Feb	130.9	136.3	138.8	142.1	146.9	150.9	155.0	160.3	163.7	168.0	174.0
Mar	131.4	136.7	139.3	142.5	147.5	151.5	154.4	160.8	164.1	168.5	174.5
Apr	133.1	138.8	140.6	144.2	149.0	152.6	156.3	162.6	165.2	169.0	175.0
May	133.5	139.3	141.1	144.7	149.6	152.9	156.9	163.5	165.6	169.5	175.5
Jun	134.1	139.3	141.0	144.7	149.8	153.0	157.5	163.4	165.6	170.0	176.0
Jul	133.8	138.8	140.7	144.0	149.1	152.4	157.5	163.0	165.1	170.5	176.5
Aug	134.1	138.9	141.3	144.7	149.9	153.1	158.5	163.7	165.5	171.0	177.0
Sept	134.6	139.4	141.9	145.0	150.6	153.8	159.3	164.4	166.2	171.5	177.5
Oct	135.1	139.9	141.8	145.2	149.8	153.8	159.6	164.5	166.5	172.0	178.0
Nov	135.6	139.7	141.6	145.3	149.8	153.9	159.6	164.4	166.7	172.5	178.5
Dec	135.7	139.2	141.9	146.0	150.7	154.4	160.0	164.4	167.3	173.0	179.0

* Estimated figures.

(3) *Annual exemption (individuals)*

	£
1996/97	6,300
1997/98	6,500
1998/99	6,800
1999/00	7,100
2000/01	7,200 ✓

(4) Taper relief: Disposals after 6 April 2000

Number of complete years after 5.4.98 for which asset held	Business assets % of gain chargeable		Non business assets % of gain chargeable	
0	100	0	100	
1	87.5	12.5	100	
2	75	25	100	
3	50	50	95	5
4	25	75	90	10
5	25	75	85	15
6	25	75	80	20
7	25	75	75	25
8	25	75	70	30
9	25	75	65	35
10 or more	25	75	60	40.

(xxix)

G NATIONAL INSURANCE (NOT CONTRACTED OUT RATES) 2000/01

Class 1 contributions

£

Employee

	£
Primary threshold	3,952 (£76 pw)
Upper earnings limit (UEL)	27,820 (£535 pw)

Employer

	£
Secondary threshold	4,385 (£84 pw)

Employee contributions	10% on earnings between the primary threshold and the UEL (8.4% if contracted out)
Employer contributions	12.2% on earnings above secondary threshold (Reduced rates on earnings between secondary threshold and UEL if contracted out)

Class 1A and Class 1B contributions

Rate 12.2%

Class 2 contributions

Rate	£2.00 pw
Small earnings exception	£3,825 pa

Class 4 contributions

Rate	7%
Lower earnings limit	£4,385
Upper earnings limit	£27,820

Question
bank

DO YOU KNOW - PERSONAL COMPUTATIONS, EMPLOYMENT AND INVESTMENT INCOME

- *Check that you can fill in the blanks in the statements below before you attempt any questions. If in doubt, you should go back to your BPP Study Text and revise first.*

- In a personal computation, we must add up the individual's income from all sources and deduct charges to arrive at ...., and then deduct the personal allowance to arrive at ....

- Income from employment is taxed under Schedule E, on a .... basis.

- Expenses are generally deductible only if they are incurred ...., ... and .... in the performance of the duties of the employment.

- The general measure of a benefit for an employee earning £8,500 or more per annum or a director is the ....

- For employees earning £8,500 or more per annum and directors:

  ° The taxable benefit for cars is cost × a % (35%, 25% or 15%) which depends on the number of .... miles travelled × a factor (1 or $^3/_4$) which depends on the ...... of the car. A partial contribution by the employee .... the benefit.

  ° There is a set scale benefit for fuel for private motoring. A partial contribution by the employee .... the benefit.

  ° Loans may give rise to taxable benefits based on the official rate of interest, but there is an exemption for loans under ....

  ° The taxable value of assets made available for use is the higher of

    (i)   ....% of the asset's ...., and

    (ii)   any .... paid by the employer

  ° The first .... of any benefit arising in respect of the private use of computer equipment is exempt.

  ° If ownership of an asset is subsequently transferred, the benefit is based on the higher of ....,   and ....

- Accommodation can give rise to a taxable benefit for .... employees

  ° The basic benefit is the .... of the property.

  ° There is an additional benefit where the accommodation cost over .... There is an exemption for .... accommodation.

- There is a .... exemption for termination payments.

- Employees pay .... NICs. Employers pay .... NICs, and also .... NICs on most benefits and Class 1B NICs.

- Most interest income is received net of ....% tax and is taxed in the year of .... Basic rate taxpayers have ...... further liability.

- Dividends are received net of a .... tax credit. The tax credit can be offset against a taxpayer's tax liability but it cannot be repaid to a non taxpayer.

- Income from renting out land and buildings is taxed under Schedule A, on an .... basis as if the owner were running a business.

TRY QUESTIONS 1 TO 7

BPP
PUBLISHING

(margin notes, handwritten):
STI
T+I

WEN

CAR
M A 7

LOAN

Asset
es.
~Furniture

C

Accomo
BB AA
JRA

R

DID YOU KNOW - PERSONAL COMPUTATIONS, EMPLOYMENT AND INVESTMENT INCOME

- *Could you fill in the blanks? The answers are in bold. Use this page for revision purposes as you approach the exam.*

- In a personal computation, we must add up the individual's income from all sources and deduct charges to arrive at **statutory total income**, and then deduct the personal allowance to arrive at **taxable income**.

- Income from employment is taxed under Schedule E, on a **receipts** basis.

- Expenses are generally deductible only if they are incurred **wholly**, **exclusively** and **necessarily** in the performance of the duties of the employment.

- The general measure of a benefit for an employee earning £8,500 or more per annum or a director is the **cost to the employer of providing it.**

- For employees earning £8,500 or more per annum and directors:

  - The taxable benefit for cars is cost × a % (35%, 25% or 15%) which depends on the number of **business** miles travelled × a factor (1 or $^3/_4$) which depends on the **age** of the car. A partial contribution by the employee **reduces** the benefit.

  - There is a set scale benefit for fuel for private motoring. A partial contribution by the employee **does not reduce** the benefit.

  - Loans may give rise to taxable benefits based on the official rate of interest, but there is an exemption for loans under **£5,000**.

  - The taxable value of assets made available for use is the higher of

    (i)   **20%** of the asset's **market value,** and

    (ii)   any **rent** paid by the employer

  - The first **£500** of any benefit arising in respect of the private use of computer equipment is exempt.

  - If ownership of an asset is subsequently transferred, the benefit is based on the higher of **the original cost of the asset less amounts already taxed**, and **the market value at the date of transfer.**

- Accommodation can give rise to a taxable benefit for **all** employees

  - The basic benefit is the **annual value** of the property.

  - There is an additional benefit where the accommodation cost over **£75,000**. There is an exemption for **job related** accommodation.

- There is a **£30,000** exemption for termination payments.

- Employees pay **primary Class 1** NICs. Employers pay **secondary Class 1** NICs, and also **Class 1A** NICs on most benefits and Class 1B NICs.

- Most interest income is received net of **20%** tax and is taxed in the year of **receipt**. Basic rate taxpayers have **no** further liability.

- Dividends are received net of a **10%** tax credit. The tax credit can be offset against a taxpayer's tax liability but it cannot be repaid to a non taxpayer.

- Income from renting out land and buildings is taxed under Schedule A, on an **accruals** basis as if the owner were running a business.

TRY QUESTIONS 1 TO 7

1   **TUTORIAL QUESTION: CAR AND TRAVEL**

R Robb was appointed Sales Director of Wirral Widget plc, a UK company, on 1 April 2000, at a salary of £20,000 a year. The company also provided him with the following.

(a)   A new petrol engined company car, a 2,500 cc model, costing £17,000. Mr Robb's annual mileage is 25,000 miles, of which 20% is non-business. Total annual expenditure on the car, paid by the company, is £2,800 including all fuel.

(b)   Company-owned computer equipment for both business and private use. The equipment cost the company £3,300 on 6.4.00.

He contributes 4% of his salary (excluding benefits in kind) to an approved superannuation scheme.

In the three months to 30 June 2000 Mr Robb was primarily working from the company's offices in Aberdeen. However, he was, from time to time, required to work at a client's premises in Inverness. The company reimbursed Mr Robbs travel expenses of £800 which was the full cost he incurred in travelling directly from his home to the client's premises. The cost of travelling from the company's offices in Aberdeen to Inverness would have been £600.

On 1 July 2000 he flew from London to Egypt on the first stage of a sales visit from which he returned to London on 12 September 2000. For the month of August 2000 he was joined by his wife Sally and their young son. The company reimbursed him £1,600 for their fares and £1,000 for their accommodation.

On 1 November 2000, the company made him a loan of £25,000 at 4% a year, with interest payable monthly in arrears, to assist his purchase of a new home. He has no other mortgage. Assume an official rate of interest of 10%.

He has a pension of £750 a year from a German company for whom he worked in Africa for ten years.

Required

Compute R Robb's taxable income for 2000/01. Do not calculate tax payable.

Guidance notes

1   When a taxpayer receives several benefits, you can take them one by one. Your first step should be to jot down the benefits (car, computer equipment, etc) and then search the question for relevant information on each one. You should also note separately other information, such as pension contributions.

2   You can then work out the value of each item of income separately. Do not try to do two things at once. Get each item right and then move on to the next one.

3   You can then combine all the components of income to arrive at statutory total income and then at taxable income.

2   **LANDSCAPE LTD (12/99)**   *45 mins*

Landscape Ltd is an unquoted trading company that operates a nationwide chain of retail shops. Landscape Ltd is a close company.

(a)   Landscape Ltd employed Peter Plain as a computer programmer until 31 December 2000. On that date he resigned from the company, and set up as a self-employed computer programmer. Peter has continued to work for Landscape Ltd, and during the period 1 January to 5 April 2001 has invoiced them for work done based on an hourly rate of pay. Peter works five days each week at the offices of Landscape Ltd, uses their computer equipment, and does not have any other clients. The computer function is an

5

integral part of Landscape Ltd's business operations. Peter now considers himself to be self-employed but Landscape Ltd's accountant is not sure if this is the correct interpretation.

(b) Landscape Ltd operates an Inland Revenue approved company profit sharing scheme whereby employees receive fully paid up ordinary shares in the company free of charge. On 1 January 1998 Richard Rosland, the personnel manager, received the maximum entitlement of shares allowed under the scheme based on his salary of £36,000 pa. At that date the shares were worth £1.50 each. He sold half of these shares on 30 June 2000 for £2,800 and the other half on 31 January 2001 for £3,200.

(c) On 15 March 2001 Landscape Ltd dismissed Simon Savannah, the manager of their shop in Manchester, and gave him a lump sum redundancy payment of £55,000. This amount include statutory redundancy pay of £2,400, holiday pay of £1,500, and £5,000 for agreeing not to work for a rival company. The balance of the payment was compensation for loss of office, and £10,000 of this was not paid until 31 May 2001.

(d) Trevor Tundra is one of the Landscape Ltd's shareholders, but is neither a director nor employee of the company. On 6 April 2000 Landscape Ltd provided Trevor with a new motor car with a list price of £14,000. No private petrol was provided, and Trevor did not drive any business mileage during 2000/01. On 1 July 2000 Landscape Ltd made an interest free loan of £40,000 to Trevor. He repaid £25,000 of the loan on 31 August 2000, and the balance of the loan was written off on 31 March 2001.

(e) On 1 October 2000 Landscape Ltd opened a new shop in Cambridge, and assigned three employees from the London shop to work there on a temporary basis.

   (1) Ursula Upland is to work in Cambridge for a period of 18 months. Her ordinary commuting is a daily total of 90 miles, and her daily total from home to Cambridge is 40 miles. She uses her private motor car for business mileage.

   (2) Violet Veld was initially due to work in Cambridge for a period of 30 months, but this was reduced to a period of 20 months on 1 January 2001. Violet walks to work whereas the cost of her train fare from home to Cambridge is £30 per day. This is paid by Landscape Ltd.

   (3) Wilma Wood is to work in Cambridge for a period of six months. Her ordinary commuting is a daily total of 30 miles, and her daily total from home to Cambridge is 150 miles. Wilma passes the London shop on her daily journey to Cambridge. She uses her private motor car for business mileage.

All three employees worked at Cambridge for 120 days using 2000/01. Landscape Ltd pays a mileage allowance of 36 pence per mile for business use. The relevant rates under the fixed profit car scheme are 45 pence per mile for the first 4,000 miles, and 25 pence per mile thereafter.

Required

Explain the income tax implications arising from the payments and benefits that have been made or provided by Landscape Ltd to Peter, Richard, Simon, Trevor, Ursula, Violet and Wilma. Your answer should be confined to the implications for 2000/01.

Marks for this question will be allocated on the basis of:

6 marks to (a)
4 marks to (b)
4 marks to (c)
4 marks to (d)
7 marks to (e)   **(25 marks)**
Assume that the official rate of interest is 10%

3   CLIFFORD JONES (12/94)   *45 mins*

Clifford Jones and Dinah Smith, both of whom are divorced, are to marry on 30 April 2000. You should assume that today's date is 15 April 2000. Clifford is aged 68, whilst Dinah is aged 62. They have asked for your advice, and the following information is available:

(a)   Clifford and Dinah are both self-employed practitioners in alternative medicine. Clifford's practice is in London, and he makes tax adjusted profits of £74,000 pa. Dinah's practice is in Glasgow, and she makes tax adjusted profits of £20,000 pa. Clifford's business is valued at £125,000, whilst Dinah's is valued at £80,000. They will continue to run both practices once they are married although they are unsure as to whether or not it would be beneficial to do so in partnership with each other.

Each year, Clifford and Dinah both contribute the maximum possible amounts qualifying for tax relief into personal pension schemes. Neither receives any pension benefit at the moment

(b)   Clifford and Dinah jointly own a holiday cottage in Scotland worth £80,000, which produces taxable income of £5,000 pa. The cottage is 75% owned by Clifford and 25% by Dinah.

(c)   Dinah plans to sell a number of assets during March 2001, and this will result in chargeable gains before taper relief of £6,500, £4,200 and £9,000, and an allowable loss of £2,400. The gains of £6,500 and £4,200 will arise on non-business assets whilst the gain of £9,000 and the loss will arise on the disposal of business assets. All of the assets were acquired before 17 March 1998. Neither Clifford nor Dinah will dispose of any other chargeable assets during 2000/01.

(d)   Clifford has £50,000 in a building society deposit account, which will produce interest of £1,920 (net) during 2000/01.

(e)   Clifford and Dinah have other assets worth £95,000 and £10,000 respectively.

(f)   Clifford and Dinah will both draw up new wills when they get married. Clifford is to leave the cash in his building society deposit account to his son, with all of his remaining assets passing to Dinah, or his son if Dinah predeceases him. Dinah is to leave all of her assets to her daughters.

Clifford and Dinah do not feel that they are wealthy enough for either of them to make any substantial lifetime gifts of assets to their children. They are both concerned that their own children should ultimately inherit the majority of their respective assets.

Required

(a)   Advise Clifford and Dinah of the income tax implications arising from their forthcoming marriage on 30 April 2000.   (5 marks)

(b)   Advise Clifford and Dinah of tax planning measures that they could take following their marriage on 30 April 2000. Your answer should be confined to the implications of income tax, capital gains tax and NIC and should include a calculation of their tax liabilities for 2000/01 prior to your advice. You are not expected to advise on tax-free investments such as ISAs.   (8 marks)

(c)   Briefly discuss the inheritance tax implications arising from Clifford and Dinah's proposed new wills. Your answer should outline tax planning measures that they could take in order to reduce their potential IHT liability.   (5 marks)

(d)   Clifford is concerned that should Dinah outlive him, his son should inherit upon her death any assets that Clifford has bequeathed to Dinah under the terms of his will. Explain how this could be achieved by the use of an interest in possession trust. Your

7

answer should include a brief description of how such a trust would be subject to income tax, capital gains tax and IHT up to, and including, the time that its assets are distributed to Clifford's son. (7 marks)

(25 marks)

4   **CHARLES CHOICE (6/97)**   *45 mins*

Charles Choice, aged 47, is an assistant manager with the Northwest Bank plc on a gross annual salary of £23,500.

You should assume that today's date is 2 April 2001, and that the tax rates and allowances for 2000/01 apply throughout. You are *not* expected to take the time value of money into account in any of your answers.

(a)   As from 6 April 2001, Charles will be required to drive 8,000 miles each year for business purposes. The Northwest Bank plc have offered him a choice of either a company car or a cash alternative, as follows.

   (i)   A new 1298cc diesel powered motor car with a list price of £14,400. All running costs, including private fuel, will be paid for by the Northwest Bank plc. Charles will be required to contribute £50 per month towards the private use of the motor car, of which £15 will be partial reimbursement of private fuel. Under this alternative, Charles would not run a private motor car.

   (ii)   Additional salary of £2,800 pa. Charles would then use his private motor car for business mileage. The private motor car is leased at a cost of £285 per month, and has a list price of £11,500. The annual running costs including fuel, are £1,650. He will drive a total of 12,000 miles per year. The Northwest Bank plc pays a business mileage allowance of 23 pence per mile for the type of car run by Charles. The relevant rates allowed under the fixed profit car scheme are 35 pence per mile for the first 4,000 miles, and 20 pence per mile thereafter.

   Required

   Advise Charles as to which of the two alternatives will be the most beneficial from his point of view. Your answer should include:

   (i)   calculations of the additional tax liabilities that will arise under each alternative, and

   (ii)   a comparison of a claim for business expenditure and a claim based on the fixed profit car scheme. (13 marks)

(b)   Charles joined the Northwest Bank plc four years ago, but has not joined the company's Inland Revenue approved occupational pension scheme. He has been offered the chance to join on 6 April 2001.

   Before joining the Northwest Bank plc, Charles regularly changed employers. He has therefore saved for a pension by contributing into a personal pension plan. For 2000/01 he made the maximum amount of tax deductible contributions based on his salary of £23,500.

   Under the Northwest Bank plc's occupational pension scheme, Charles would contribute 6% of his salary (you should assume that this is £23,500), and the company would contribute a further 6%. The benefits payable on retirement will be based on final salary. Assume the rules applying to pensions in 2000/01 also apply in later years.

   Required

   (i)   Advise Charles of the factors that he will have to take into account when deciding whether or not to join the Northwest Bank plc's occupational pension scheme. (5 marks)

(ii)   Charles is concerned that if he joins the Northwest Bank plc's occupational pension scheme, his tax deductible contributions will be less than under a personal pension scheme.

Advise Charles of how he could make additional voluntary contributions in order to increase his entitlement to a pension.   (2 marks)

(c)   David Spence is resident, ordinary resident and domiciled in the UK. On 1 June 2000 he left the UK and went to work in Australia. David expects to return to the UK in March 2005.

David is considering selling a French holiday cottage whilst he is absent from the UK. This sale would result in a gain for capital gains tax purposes of £100,000.

Required

Advise David on whether the gain arising on the sale of the holiday cottage will be subject to UK CGT if he sells the cottage in (i) March 2001 or (ii) September 2001.

(5 marks)

(25 marks)

5   **WILLIAM WILES (6/97)**   *45 mins*

(a)   William Wiles acquired three houses on 6 April 2000. Houses 1 and 2 were acquired freehold, and are let as furnished holiday accommodation. House 3 was acquired on a 25 year lease, and is let furnished. During 2000/01 the houses were let as follows.

House 1 was available for letting for 42 weeks during 2000/01, and was actually let for 14 weeks at £375 per week. During the 10 weeks that the house was not available for letting, it was occupied rent free by William's sister. Running costs for 2000/01 consisted of business rates £730, insurance £310, and advertising £545.

House 2 was available for letting for 32 weeks during 2000/01, and was actually let for eight weeks at £340 per week. The house was not available for letting for 20 weeks due to a serious flood. As a result of the flood, £6,250 was spent on repairs. The damage was not covered by insurance. The other running costs for 2000/01 consisted of business rates £590, insurance £330, and advertising £225.

House 3 was unoccupied from 6 April 2000 until 31 December 2000. On 1 January 2001 the house was sub-let on a four year lease for a premium of £8,000, and a rent of £8,600 pa payable annually in advance. William had paid a premium of £85,000 for the 25 year lease. During 2000/01 he paid the rent of £6,200 due annually in advance on 6 April 2000, and spent £710 on redecorating the property during June 2000.

Immediately after their purchase, William furnished the three houses at a cost of £6,500 per house. With the exception of the 10 week rent-free letting of house 1, all the lettings are at a full rent.

During 2000/01 William also rented out one furnished room of his main residence. he received rent of £4,600, and incurred allowable expenditure of £825.

Required

(i)   Briefly explain why both house 1 and house 2 qualify to be treated as a trade under the furnished holiday letting rules. State the tax advantages of the houses being so treated.   (5 marks)

(ii)   Calculate William's allowable Schedule A loss for 2000/01, and advise him as to the possible ways of relieving the loss.   (14 marks)

9

(b) On 30 June 2000 William permanently separated from his wife. William is aged 66 and his wife is aged 55, and they have a son, aged 15, who is in full-time education. The son spends an average of two days each week living with William. Since 1 July 2000 William had been paying his wife maintenance of £475 per month. He has also been paying his son's school fees of £1,800 per term. Until 31 December 2000, these payments were made voluntarily, but on 1 January 2001 they were confirmed by a written agreement as part of the divorce settlement. Under the agreement, William made a lump sum payment of £25,000 to his wife, and will continue the regular payments until the son completes his full-time education in three year's time.

Required

(i) Explain the tax implications arising in 2000/01 from the payments made by William to support his wife and son

    (1) voluntarily between 1 July 2000 and 31 December 2000, and

    (2) under the divorce settlement from 1 January 2001 onwards.   (4 marks)

(ii) State what personal allowances William will be entitled to for 2000/01.

    (2 marks)

(25 marks)

6   **DUNCAN MCBYTE (12/98)**   *45 mins*

Duncan McByte is a computer programmer currently living in Scotland. Duncan's services are in great demand, and he has recently accepted the offer of a contract of employment with Mainframe plc for a period of three years commencing on 1 July 2000 and ceasing on 30 June 2003. Duncan will be based in London during the period of the contract. The remuneration package comprises:

(1) A salary of £65,000 pa together with a termination bonus of £40,000 upon satisfactory completion of the three year contract.

(2) Mainframe plc is providing accommodation for Duncan in London. This is an apartment that was purchased in 1989 for £94,000, and was improved at a cost of £35,000 during 1997. The apartment has a rateable value of £6,700 and is currently valued at £170,000. The furniture in the apartment cost £21,000 and Mainframe plc is paying for the annual running costs of £6,200.

(3) Duncan using his private motor car for business mileage. The motor car is leased at a cost of £380 per month, and the annual running costs, including fuel, are £1,800. He drives a total of 1,200 miles per month, of which 1,000 miles are for business purposes. Mainframe plc pays a mileage allowance of 40 pence per mile for business mileage. The relevant rates allowed under the Fixed Profit Car Scheme are 63 pence per mile for the first 4,000 miles, and 36 pence per mile thereafter.

(4) On 1 July 2000 Mainframe plc provided Duncan with a loan of £60,000 that he has used to purchase a holiday cottage in France. The loan has an interest rate of 4% pa. and will be repaid by six half-yearly instalments of £10,000 commencing on 31 December 2000.

(5) Mainframe plc will pay for Duncan's annual subscription of £125 to the Institute of Chartered Computer Consultants, a sports club membership of £800 pa, an annual premium of £650 for liability insurance, and £1,200 pa. for computer training courses that will keep him up to date with the latest software developments. These amounts will all be paid during January of each year.

(6) On 1 July 2000 Duncan was granted options to purchase 15,000 £1 ordinary shares in Mainframe plc at their value on that date. The options were provided free, and will be exercised by Duncan upon the termination of his contract on 30 June 2003. Mainframe plc's shares were valued at £1.75 on 1 July 2000, and are forecast to be worth £5.00 by 30 June 2003.

Duncan's options have been granted under the Inland Revenue approved company share option scheme that is operated by Mainframe plc.

From 1 July 2000, Duncan has rented out his main residence in Scotland as furnished holiday accommodation. The forecast rental income for 2000/01, based on 32 weeks letting is £21,000, of which 22.5% will be paid to a letting agency. Running costs will amount to £900. The house was furnished at a cost of £24,000 during June 2000. Duncan has a mortgage of £60,000 on which interest of £5,400 will be paid during 2000/01.

Required

(a) Explain the income tax and NIC implications arising from the remuneration package that Mainframe plc has given to Duncan.

Your answer should include calculations of the amounts assessable under Schedule E for 2000/01. Assume the official rate of interest is 10%.   (17 marks)

(b) Explain why it was beneficial for Duncan's share options (see note (6)) to be granted under an Inland Revenue approved company share option scheme.   (3 marks)

(c) Advise Duncan of the Schedule A profit that he will be assessed on for 2000/01.

                                                                        (5 marks)

                                                                   (25 marks)

7   **HAROLD AND WILMA CHAN (6/99)**   *45 mins*

Harold and Wilma Chan are a married couple aged 66 and 55 respectively. Following Harold's retirement from full-time employment on 31 March 2000, the couple have become aware that there may be tax planing measures that they could take in order to reduce their combined income tax liability. Harold and Wilma have the following income and outgoings for 2000/01.

(a) Harold receives an annual pension of £16,000.

(b) Wilma is employed on a gross annual salary of £45,000. She contributes 6% of her salary into her employer's Inland Revenue approved occupational pension scheme. Wilma is not planning to retire for several years.

(c) Wilma receives building society interest of £3,600 (net) pa, interest of £2,400 (gross) pa from UK government stocks, and interest of £900 (gross) pa from index linked National Savings Certificates.

(d) Wilma owns a property situated in the UK that is rented out unfurnished. The annual Schedule A profit is £4,800.

(e) Harold and Wilma jointly own a property situated overseas. The annual profit is £2,300 (gross), and this is subject to overseas tax at the rate of 35%.

Harold and Wilma have made full use of TESSAs. They both have fully funded follow up TESSAs maturing on 15 March 2002 and 30 September 2002 respectively.

Harold and Wilma have heard that they could make additional tax efficient investments by investing in individual savings accounts (ISAs). Neither of them currently have any ISA investments but they wish to consider making them. They are, however, concerned that they might wish to withdraw their money at short notice and they would like to know how this will affect the tax status of their investment.

Required

(a) (i) Before taking account of any tax planning measures, calculate the income tax liability of Harold and Wilma for 2000/01. (8 marks)

   (ii) Advise Harold and Wilma of tax planning measures that they could have taken in order to reduce their overall income tax liability for 2000/01. Your answer should include an explanation of any suggested proposals, and a calculation of the amount of income tax that could have been saved. (8 marks)

(b) (i) Advise Harold and Wilma of the maximum amounts they the could invest in ISAs and the types of ISAs that are available for them to invest in. (6 marks)

   (ii) Advise Harold and Wilma of the tax advantages enjoyed by ISAs and whether or not it would be possible to withdraw any amounts from their ISAs without affecting the tax status. (3 marks)

(25 marks)

Assume 2000/01 tax rates and allowances continue to apply.

DO YOU KNOW? - CAPITAL GAINS TAX AND INHERITANCE TAX

- *Check that you can fill in the blanks in the statements below before you attempt any questions. If in doubt, you should go back to your BPP Study Text and revise first*

- The basic CGT computation is: proceeds – cost – indexation allowance = gain.

- The indexation allowance cannot create or increase a .... For individuals the indexation allowance is not available after 6 April 1998, instead a .... relief is available.

- Losses brought forward are deducted before taper relief. However, brought forward losses should only be deducted to the extent that the .... is not wasted.

- Special rules apply to assets acquired before 31 March 1982.

  - Two computations are done, one deducting cost and the other deducting the 31 March 1982 value.

  - The indexation allowance is based on the .... of cost and March 1982 value

  - The final result is the .... gain, the .... loss or (if there is one gain and one loss) ....

  - A global election to use only .... values may be made.

- Enhancement expenditure is deductible if it is reflected in the ....…..... at the time of disposal.

- On a reorganisation, the original cost of shares is apportioned to new types of capital using the .... of the new capital on the first day of quotation after reorganisation

- Wasting chattels are .... (unless capital allowances were available on them). For other chattels, both gains and losses may be restricted. The key figure is ....

- On a part disposal cost/March 82 value must be apportioned using the formula ....

- A non-domiciled individual is only taxable on foreign gains to the extent that they are .... to the UK.

TRY QUESTION 8

- Inheritance tax (IHT) is charged on the amount which an individual or a trust loses through giving property away, or selling it for less than its value. This is known as the .... principle. Transfers are cumulated for .... years.

- The charge on an individual is basically on all his property at death. IHT is also charged on amounts given away in the .... years before death. Tapering relief reduces the tax charged on gifts made more than .... years before death.

- Practically all gifts during lifetime which are not exempt for other reasons (as, for example, gifts to charities are), and are not to discretionary trusts, are potentially exempt transfers. If the donor survives for seven years after a PET, it is ....; otherwise it is ....

- An annual exemption of .... is available each year. Unused annual exemption may be carried forward .... year. The current year annual exemption is used .... the annual exemption brought forward.

- Business property relief (BPR) is available on businesses, partnership shares and shareholdings. The rate of relief is ....% or ....%. Agricultural property relief (APR) applies to the .... value of farmland. It is at ....%.

TRY QUESTIONS 9 TO 15

DID YOU KNOW? - CAPITAL GAINS TAX AND INHERITANCE TAX

- *Could you fill in the blanks? The answers are in bold. Use this page for revision purposes as you approach the exam.*

- The basic CGT computation is: proceeds – cost – indexation allowance = gain.

- The indexation allowance cannot create or increase a **loss**. For individuals the indexation allowance is not available after 6 April 1998, instead a **taper** relief is available.

- Losses brought forward are deducted before taper relief. However, brought forward losses should only be deducted to the extent that the **annual exemption** is not wasted.

- Special rules apply to assets acquired before 31 March 1982.

  ° Two computations are done, one deducting cost and the other deducting the 31 March 1982 value.

  ° The indexation allowance is based on the **higher** of cost and March 1982 value

  ° The final result is the **lower** gain, the **lower** loss or (if there is one gain and one loss) **no gain/no loss.**

  ° A global election to use only **31 March 1982** values may be made.

- Enhancement expenditure is deductible if it is reflected in the **state and nature of the asset** at the time of disposal.

- On a reorganisation, the original cost of shares is apportioned to new types of capital using the **market values** of the new capital on the first day of quotation after reorganisation

- Wasting chattels are **exempt** (unless capital allowances were available on them). For other chattels, both gains and losses may be restricted. The key figure is **£6,000.**

- On a part disposal cost/March 82 value must be apportioned using the formula $\dfrac{A}{A+B}$.

- A non-domiciled individual is only taxable on foreign gains to the extent that they are **remitted** to the UK.

TRY QUESTION 8

- Inheritance tax (IHT) is charged on the amount which an individual or a trust loses through giving property away, or selling it for less than its value. This is known as the **diminution in value** principle. Transfers are cumulated for **seven** years.

- The charge on an individual is basically on all his property at death. IHT is also charged on amounts given away in the **seven** years before death. Tapering relief reduces the tax charged on gifts made more than **three** years before death.

- Practically all gifts during lifetime which are not exempt for other reasons (as, for example, gifts to charities are), and are not to discretionary trusts, are potentially exempt transfers. If the donor survives for seven years after a PET, it is **exempt**; otherwise it is **chargeable**.

- An annual exemption of **£3,000** is available each year. Unused annual exemption may be carried forward **one** year. The current year annual exemption is used **before** the annual exemption brought forward.

- Business property relief (BPR) is available on businesses, partnership shares and shareholdings. The rate of relief is **100%** or **50%**. Agricultural property relief (APR) applies to the **agricultural** value of farmland. It is at **100%.**

TRY QUESTIONS 9 TO 15

8   **TUTORIAL QUESTION: A CHATTEL, LAND AND SHARES**

Price supplied the following information in order that his accountant could compute his capital gains tax position for 2000/01.

(i)   He sold a vase on 1 August 2000 for £10,900 which he had purchased for £8,400 on 31 March 1982.

(ii) He sold a piece of land on 5 July 2000 for £54,000. He had purchased the land as an investment on 6 December 1974 for £2,000, and had improved it on 1 June 1984 for £3,000. Incidental costs of sale were £985. The market value on 31 March 1982 was £15,000.

(iii) He sold 12,000 shares in Index plc (a quoted company) on 1 July 2000 for £42,000. He had acquired and sold shares in the company on the following dates.

Purchases	Number of shares	Cost
		£
1 May 1981	10,000	9,000
1 March 1982	2,000	2,000
1 May 1999	2,000	5,314

The market value of Index plc shares at 31 March 1982 was £1.40 per share.

(iv) On 10 September 2000 he sold a property for £60,000, which he had purchased for £25,000 on 1 February 1984. The property had always been used in Price's business.

Price is a single man aged 40, and his income for 2000/01 comprises salary of £6,000 and dividends of £16,875 net.

Required

(a)   Compute his income tax and capital gains tax position for 2000/01.
(b)   State the due date for payment of capital gains tax for 2000/01.

Guidance notes

1   This question involves a number of separate disposals. They should be dealt with one at a time, and any gains and losses only combined at the end.

2   Indexation is only given to individuals to April 1998.

3   The vase is a chattel (tangible movable property). Special rules apply to non-wasting chattels, based on their value. What are the value-based rules, and how (if at all) do they affect this case?

4   The land was acquired before 31 March 1982 so two calculations are needed.

5   Shares acquired after 6.4.98 are not pooled. After this date each acquisition is dealt with separately.   *after 31.3.98*

6   The amount of taper relief available depends on the number of years of ownership of the asset. There is an additional year of relief for non-business assets held at 17 March 1998.
                    BONUS

9   **ARTHUR RICH (6/99)**   *45 mins*

Arthur Rich, aged 62, has asked for your advice regarding the following gifts that he has made during 2000/01.

(a)   On 20 May 2000 Arthur gave 100,000 of his 200,000 ordinary shares in Legacy Ltd, an unquoted trading company, to his son. Legacy Ltd has an issued share capital of 500,000 ordinary shares. His wife also owns 100,000 shares in the company. On 20 May 2000 the relevant values of Legacy Ltd's shares were as follows.

Shareholding	Value per share
	£
60%	5.50
40%	3.75
20%	3.40

Arthur has been a full-time working director of Legacy Ltd for eight years, and has owned his shares for six years. The cost of his total shareholding of 200,000 shares (indexed to April 1998) prior to the gift was £189,200.

(b) On 30 June 2000 Arthur made a gift of a freehold property worth £275,000 into a discretionary trust for the benefit of his children. Arthur purchased the property on 1 July 1982 for £47,600, and occupied the house as his main residence until 31 December 1990. Since then it has been rented out as furnished accommodation.

(c) On 28 November 2000 Arthur gave 24,000 ordinary shares in Grant plc, a quoted company, to his granddaughter as a wedding gift. On that day the shares were quoted at 304 – 320, with recorded bargains of 288, 310, 315 and 326. Arthur originally purchased 15,000 shares in Grant plc during 1991 and the cost of these shares (indexed to April 1998) prior to the gift was £27,600. Arthur also bought 10,000 shares on 30 June 2000 for £23,700, and has subsequently bought 2,000 shares on 16 December 2000 for £6,500 and 32,000 shares on 5 January 2001 for £10,350. Grant plc has an issued share capital of 1,000,000 ordinary shares.

(d) On 8 December 2000 Arthur signed a legally binding agreement that transferred the ownership of a vintage Aston Martin motor car worth £125,000 to his son. Arthur purchased the motor car in August 1983 for £26,500. Under the terms of the agreement the motor car is garaged at Arthur's main residence, and may be driven by him when he pleases.

Arthur is a 40% taxpayer, and has not previously made any lifetime transfers of assets. He is to pay any CGT and IHT liabilities arising from the above gifts.

Required

(a) Advise Arthur of the CGT and IHT implications arising from the gifts made during 2000/01. Your answer should be supported by appropriate calculations, and should include an explanation of any reliefs that are available. You should ignore the effect of annual exemptions both for CGT and for IHT. (20 marks)

(b) (i) The trustees of the discretionary trust set up on 30 June 2000 wish to purchase an insurance policy to cover against any IHT liability that may arise as a result of Arthur's death. Advise the trustees as to the maximum amount of insurance cover that they should obtain. You should ignore tapering relief.

(3 marks)

(ii) Briefly explain any other circumstances in which the discretionary trust will be liable to IHT. (2 marks)

(25 marks)

10   **ABC LTD** *45 mins*

ABC Ltd is an unquoted trading company that is under the control of three sisters, Agnes, Betty and Chloe, and is a close company. The share capital of ABC Ltd consists of 100,000 £1 ordinary shares, of which Agnes owns 20,000, Betty 40,000 and Chloe 40,000. Agnes and

Betty are full-time working directors of the company, but Chloe is neither a director nor an employee.

Agnes is 57 years old, and is to retire on 31 December 2000. She will sell her 20,000 shares in ABC Ltd to Betty and Chloe for £20 per share. ABC Ltd's shares are currently worth £30 each for a minority shareholding. Agnes acquired her shares at their par value on 1 July 1992, the date of ABC Ltd's incorporation. She became a full-time working director of ABC Ltd on 1 July 1993 having not previously worked for the company. The market value of ABC Ltd's assets at 31 December 2000 is forecast to be as follows.

	£
Goodwill	500,000
Freehold property - factory and warehouse	1,050,000
Plant and machinery (costing more than £6,000 per item)	400,000
Investments in quoted companies	700,000
Motor cars	100,000
Current assets	750,000
	3,500,000

Agnes personally owns a freehold office building that is used rent free by ABC Ltd. This cost £78,000 on 1 June 1993, and is to be sold to Betty and Chloe for its current market value of £200,000 on 31 December 2000.

ABC will make an interest free loan of £200,000 to Chloe in order to help her finance the acquisitions from Agnes. This loan will be repaid over the next four years. ABC Ltd has an accounting date of 30 September and is expected to have profits chargeable to corporation tax of £800,000 for the year ended 30 September 2001. No dividends will be paid during the year. This is similar to its level of profits in the prior year.

Agnes, Betty and Chloe are all 40% taxpayers. Agnes has not made any lifetime gifts of assets, and has an estate (excluding the above assets and the consideration to be paid by Betty and Chloe) valued at £400,000 which she has left to her children.

Required

(a) Calculate Agnes' CGT liability for 2000/01. Your answer should include an explanation of the amount of retirement relief that will be available to Agnes. You should assume that holdover relief is *not claimed* in respect of the gift of business assets.   (11 marks)

(b) Calculate the IHT liabilities that would arise if Agnes were to die on 30 June 2003. You should assume that the shareholding in ABC Ltd is still owned by Betty and Chloe at that date, and that the market values and tax rates for 2000/01 apply throughout.

(7 marks)

(c) Briefly advise both ABC Ltd and Chloe of the tax implications arising from the provision of the interest free loan of £200,000.   (4 marks)

(d) As an alternative to Agnes selling her shareholding in ABC Ltd to Betty and Chloe, it has been suggested that the shareholding should instead be purchased by ABC Ltd for £20 per share. The purchase will not qualify for the special treatment applying to a company's purchase of its own shares, and will therefore be treated as a distribution.

Advise Agnes of the tax implications for her arising from the company making a distribution.   (3 marks)

(25 marks)

11   BLUETONE LTD (6/98)   *45 mins*

Bluetone Ltd is an unquoted trading company that manufactures compact discs. The company has four full-time working directors, each of whom owns 25% of its share capital of 200,000 £1 ordinary shares. These are currently valued as follows:

Shareholding	Value per share £
15%	9.00
25%	11.00
35%	12.50
50%	15.00

Melody Brown

Melody has recently been appointed a director after inheriting her father's 50,000 shares in Bluetone Ltd. Melody's father purchased the shareholding on 12 November 2000, but died on 15 February 2001. At the date of his death he also owned the following assets:

(a)   42,000 50p ordinary shares in Expanse plc quoted at 312 - 320, with bargains of 282, 288, 306 and 324.

(b)   26,000 units in World-Growth, a unit trust. The bid price was 80 and the offer price was 84.

(c)   Building society deposits of £32,000 of which £3,000 was in an ISA.

(d)   His main residence valued at £125,000 with an outstanding repayment mortgage of £42,000.

(e)   A life assurance policy on his own life with an open market value of £53,000. Proceeds of £61,000 were received on 4 March 2001.

On 15 February 2001, Melody's father had an income tax liability of £6,600 and gambling debts of £1,200. Funeral expenses came to £3,460. Under the terms of his will, Melody was left the shares in Bluetone Ltd. The shares are to bear their own IHT. Melody wants to retain the full 25% holding so she is to personally account for the IHT liability. The residue of the estate was left to Melody's brother. Melody's father made the following lifetime gifts:

(a)   On 10 February 1997 he made a wedding gift of £30,000 to Melody.
(b)   On 4 June 1997 he made a gift of £164,000 into a discretionary trust.

Liam and Opal White

Liam and Opal, a married couple aged 37 and 32 respectively, have been directors and shareholders of Bluetone Ltd since its incorporation on 1 October 1991 when they acquired their shares at par. On 20 March 2001 Liam is to sell 30,000 of his shares in Bluetone Ltd to their son for £75,000. Liam is a 40% taxpayer, and has not previously made any lifetime gifts of assets.

Noel Green

Noel is aged 52 and has been a director and shareholder of Bluetone Ltd since its incorporation on 1 October 1991. For the past two years he has disagreed with the other directors of Bluetone Ltd over the company's business policies. He is therefore to resign as a director on 31 March 2001, and it has been agreed that Bluetone Ltd will purchase his shareholding for £550,000. The Inland Revenue has given advance clearance that the purchase qualifies for the special treatment applying to a company's purchase of its own shares, and can therefore be treated as a capital gain.

Noel acquired the shares at par, and is a 40% taxpayer.

For the year ended 31 March 2001 Bluetone Ltd is forecast to have profits chargeable to corporation tax of £1,100,000. The company has no chargeable non-business assets.

Required

(a) Calculate Melody's IHT liability and state when this will be due.   (10 marks)

(b) Advise Liam of the CGT and IHT implications of selling the 30,000 shares in Bluetone Ltd to his son. You should assume that reliefs are claimed in the most favourable manner on the basis that Liam wishes to defer gains where possible.

(9 marks)

(c) Advise both Bluetone Ltd and Noel of whether it will be beneficial to have the purchase of Noel's 25% shareholding treated as a capital gain under the special treatment, rather than as a distribution by Bluetone Ltd.   (6 marks)

The rates and allowances for 2000/01 should be used throughout.

(25 marks)

12 **MONTY NOBLE (12/97)**   *45 mins*

Monty Noble, aged 72, died on 15 July 2000. You should assume that today's date is 31 October 2000. At the date of his death Monty owned the following assets.

(a) His main residence valued at £255,000.

(b) Three holiday cottages valued at £55,000 each.

(c) Building society deposits of £285,000

(d) 20,000 50p ordinary shares in Congo Ltd, an unquoted trading company. The shares were acquired by Monty on 1 May 2000 and on 15 July 2000 were valued at £3.50. Congo Ltd has 20% of the value of its total assets invested in property which is let out.

(e) Agricultural land and buildings valued at £225,000, but with an agricultural value of £180,000. Monty purchased the land on 1 January 1992, and it has always been let out to tenant farmers. The most recent tenancy commenced on 1 January 2000.

Monty was survived by his wife, Olive, and their two children Peter and Penny. Penny has three children aged 6, 15 and 17. Under the terms of his will, Monty left all of his estate to Olive. She is aged 70 and does not own any assets. Olive is not in good health, and does not expect to live past 31 December 2003. Under the terms of her will, Olive has left all of her estate to Peter and Penny. The Noble family appreciate that Monty's estate has not been distributed in a tax efficient manner, and had therefore agreed the following plan.

(a) The three holiday cottages are to be sold on 10 December 2000. The expected selling prices are £47,500, £58,100 and £54,400. Professional fees of £500 will be incurred in respect of each sale.

(b) A field adjoining the existing farmland and buildings is to be purchased for £27,000 on 18 December 2000. Professional fees of £600 are included in the purchase price.

(c) The terms of Monty's will are to be varied so that Olive is left the main residence and £270,000 in cash. The agricultural land and buildings, together with the field purchased on 18 December 2000, will be put into a trust for the benefit of Penny's children. Under the terms of the trust, the income will be used to pay the children's school fees, with the balance being accumulated until the youngest child reaches the age of 18. The assets of the trust will then be distributed as the trustees so decide at that date. The remaining assets will be left to Peter and Penny.

(d) On 25 December 2000, Olive will make a gift of the main residence to Peter. She will continue to live in two rooms of the house, but will pay Peter a commercial rent.

With the exception of the holiday cottages, the only asset which is likely to change in value before 31 December 2003 is the main residence which will then be worth £330,000. Neither Monty nor Olive have made any lifetime transfers of value prior to 15 July 2000.

Required

(a) Advise the Noble family of the inheritance tax implications of the proposed plan. Your answer should consist of:

(i)   a calculation of the inheritance tax that will be saved as a result of implementing the plan.   (16 marks)

(ii)   An explanation of the conditions that must be met for the plan to be valid for inheritance tax purposes.   (2 marks)

(iii) Advice as to any improvements that could be made to the plan.   (3 marks)

You should assume that Olive dies on 31 December 2003, and that the tax rates and allowances for 2000/01 apply throughout. You should ignore the instalment option.

(b) Explain whether or not the proposed trust for the benefit of Penny's children will qualify to be treated as an accumulation and maintenance trust. Briefly state the tax advantages of the trust being treated as an accumulation and maintenance trust rather than a discretionary trust.   (4 marks)

(25 marks)

13 MING WONG (12/98)   *45 mins*

Ming Wong aged 63, was born in the country of Yanga, but has lived in the UK since 6 April 1986. Ming is a resident and ordinarily resident in the UK, but is not domiciled in the UK. Following her marriage to a UK citizen Ming is planning to become UK domiciled.

Ming is employed by the Yangan National Bank in London and was paid a salary of £29,000 during 2000/01. At 5 April 2001 Ming owned the following assets.

(1) A main residence valued at £245,000. This is situated in the UK, and has an outstanding endowment mortgage of £80,000.

(2) A house in Yanga worth £60,000, from which rental income of £7,500 (gross) was received during 2000/01. Yangan tax at the rate of 35% was paid on the rental income.

(3) 40,000 shares in Ganyan Inc., a company quoted on the Yangan Stock Exchange at 308-316. Dividends of £5,950 (net) were received during 2000/01, after the deduction of Yangan tax at the rate of 15%.

(4) Antiques worth £35,000. These were bought in Yanga, but are now situated in Ming's UK residence.

(5) Bank deposits of £50,000 with the Yangan National Bank of which £30,000 is held at the London branch and £20,000 at the main branch in Yanga. During 2000/01 interest of £1,680 (net) was credited to the account in London, and £1,530 (net of Yangan tax at the rate of 15%) was credited to the account in Yanga.

(6) An interest-free loan of £15,000 to Ming's brother who is resident in Yanga. The loan was used to purchase property situated in the UK.

(7) Ming has recently become the beneficiary of a trust set up by her father. Under the terms of the trust, she is entitled to receive all of the trust income, although no income

was actually received during 2000/01. The trust owns UK government stocks with a nominal value of 20,000, quoted at 92-94. Ming's father was domiciled in Yanga at the time of setting up the trust.

None of the income arising in Yanga has been remitted to the UK.

Under the terms of her will, Ming has left all of her assets to her three children. If she were to die, Yangan death duty of £48,000 would be payable in respect of the house situated in Yanga and the 40,000 shares in Ganyan Inc., irrespective of her domicile.

There is no double taxation agreement between the UK and Yanga. All of the above figures are in Pounds sterling.

Ming has not made any previous chargeable transfers.

Required:

(a)   Advise Ming of

 (i)   when she will be treated as domiciled in the UK for the purpose of IHT, and
 (ii)   how she could acquire domicile in the UK under general law.   (4 marks)

(b)   Advise Ming as to the potential increase in her liability to UK IHT if she were to become domiciled in the UK. Your answer should include an explanation of why Ming's assets are or are not subject to UK IHT.   (12 marks)

(c)   (i)   Calculate the UK income tax payable by Ming for 2000/01.

 (ii)   Calculate the additional UK income tax that would have been payable by Ming for 2000/01 if she has been domiciled in the UK as from 6 April 2000.

          (9 marks)

          (25 marks)

14   **JANE MACBETH (12/99)**   *45 mins*

(a)   Jane Macbeth, aged 61, died on 20 November 2000. At the date of her death Jane owned the following assets.

 (1)   A main residence valued at £235,000. This has an outstanding repayment mortgage of £40,000.

 (2)   Building society deposits of £87,000.

 (3)   10,000 £1 ordinary shares in Banquo plc. On 20 November 2000 the shares were quoted at 945-957, with bargains on that day of 937, 961 and 939. Jane inherited the shares as a specific gift on the death of her sister on 10 August 1998 when they were valued at £68,000. The sister's executor's paid IHT of £54,000 on an estate valued at £360,000.

 (4)   A life assurance policy on her own life. Immediately prior to the date of Jane's death, the policy had an open market value of £86,000. Proceeds of £104,000 were received following her death.

 (5)   Agricultural land valued at £168,000, but with an agricultural value of £110,000. The land was purchased during 1992, and it has always been let to tenant farmers. The most recent tenancy commenced on 1 January 2000.

Jane made the following gifts during her lifetime (any IHT arising was paid by Jane).

 (1)   On 28 November 1992 she made a cash gift of £76,000 into a discretionary trust.

 (2)   On 15 April 1996 she made a gift of 50,000 shares in Shakespeare Ltd, an unquoted trading company, to her son as a wedding gift. The shares were valued

at £155,000, and were originally acquired by Jane in 1991. Her son still owned the shares on 20 November 2000. Shakespeare Ltd has 20% of the value of its total assets invested in quoted shares.

(3)   On 10 March 1997 she made a cash gift of £240,000 into a discretionary rust.

Jane's husband Duncan is wealthy in his own right. Under the terms of her will Jane has therefore left a specific gift of £100,000 to her brother, with the residue of the estate being left to her children.

Required

(i)   Calculate the IHT that will be payable as a result of Jane's death.   (15 marks)

(ii)   State who is primarily liable for the tax; the due dates of the IHT liabilities; the amount of IHT that can be paid under the instalment option; and the amount of inheritance that will be received by Jane's children.   (4 marks)

Assume Finance Act 2000 tax rates have always applied.

(b)   Jane's husband Duncan is aged 58. He is in good health, and expects to live for at least ten more years.

The Macbeth family appreciate that Jane's estate may not have been distributed in a tax efficient manner. They have therefore agreed that the terms of her will are to be varied so that the entire estate is left to Duncan.

Duncan will then make gifts totalling £500,000 to the children and Jane's brother during 2001 and 2002.

Required

(i)   State the conditions that must be met in order that the variation of the terms of Jane's will is valid for IHT purposes.   (2 marks)

(ii)   Advise the Macbeth family of the IHT implications of the proposed plan. You are not expected to calculate the revised IHT liability or to consider anti-avoidance legislation.   (4 marks)

(25 marks)

15   **MICHAEL EARL (12/95)**   *45 mins*

Michael Earl, aged 48, died on 30 June 2000. At the time of his death, Michael owned the following assets.

(a)   50,000 £1 ordinary shares in Compact Ltd, an unquoted UK resident trading company with an issued share capital of 1,000,000 shares. Michael originally bought 100,000 shares for £400,000 in May 1999. He made a gift of 50,000 shares to his daughter, Jade, on 10 July 1999. Michael's wife, Naomi, also owns 50,000 shares in Compact Ltd, which she also acquired in May 1999. The relevant values of Compact Ltd's shares, as agreed by the Inland Revenue, are as follows.

	Value per share	
Shareholding	*at 10.7.99*	*at 30.6.00*
	£	£
5%	5.00	6.00
10%	7.00	8.40
15%	10.00	12.00

(b)   50,000 £1 ordinary shares in Diverse Inc, a quoted trading company with an issued share capital of 10,000,000 shares. The company is resident in the country of Gobolia. Michael originally bought 150,000 shares in March 1987. He made a gift of 100,000 shares into a discretionary trust for the benefit of his grandchildren on 19 August 1999.

Michael paid the IHT arising as a result of the gift. Diverse Inc's shares were quoted on the Gobolian Stock Exchange at 308 - 316 on 19 August 1999, with recorded bargains of 296, 320 and 328 for that day. On 30 June 2000 they were quoted at 279 - 287, with recorded bargains of 275 and 285. All of the above figures are in pounds sterling.

(c) Other UK assets valued for IHT purposes at £850,000. This figure is after providing for any tax liabilities outstanding at 30 June 2000.

Under the terms of his will, Michael left £200,000 in cash to his wife Naomi, and the residue of his estate to his daughter Jade. Michael and Jade are domiciled in the UK, but Naomi is domiciled in Gobolia.

Following Michael's death, the following occurred:

(a) On 5 September 2000 the executors of Michael's estate sold the 50,000 shares in Compact Ltd for £260,000, and the 50,000 shares in Diverse Inc for £120,000.

(b) On 10 December 2000 Jade sold her 50,000 shares in Compact Ltd for £285,000.

Up to the date of his death Michael was a 40% taxpayer. Jade is also a 40% taxpayer. Neither Michael nor Jade has ever been a director or employee of either Compact Ltd or Diverse Inc.

Gobolian death duty of £35,000 was paid as a result of Michael's death. There is no double taxation treaty between the United Kingdom and Gobolia.

Required

(a) (i)   Calculate the IHT liabilities arising as a result of Michael's death on 30 June 2000. Your answer should state who is liable for the payment of each liability, and should show the due date of payment. You should *ignore* the IHT annual exemption in your answer.

     (ii)   State what IHT reliefs will be available as a result of the disposals by the executors of Michael's estate on 5 September 2000, and advise them of whether or not a claim would be beneficial in each case. (Died on 30.6.00.)   (16 marks)

You should assume that tax rates and allowances for 2000/01 apply throughout.

(b) (i)   Assuming that holdover relief was *not claimed* in respect of the gift made by Michael to Jade on 10 July 1999, calculate Jade's CGT liability for 2000/01.

     (ii)   Advise Jade and the executors of Michael's estate as to the tax implications arising from making a claim for holdover relief in respect of the gift on 10 July 1999. You should assume that if a holdover relief claim is made, then the value of Michael's estate will increase by the amount of the CGT no longer payable.

You should *ignore* the CGT annual exemption in your answer.   (9 marks)

(25 marks)

DO YOU KNOW - INVESTMENTS AND FINANCE; TRUSTS

- *Check that you can fill in the blanks in the statements below before you attempt any questions. If in doubt, you should go back to your BPP Study Text and revise first.*

- Unused personal pension relief can be carried forward for .... years. A premium paid can be related back for relief in ....

- An investor should consider not only any exemptions from income tax and/or CGT (for example those available for ISAs) but also .... and ....

- When a business is selecting a source of finance, its main choice is between debt and equity. Interest is tax-deductible, unlike dividends, but a high level of debt increases the risk of insolvency.

- Rental income is taxed on an .... basis under Schedule A.

- The special rules for furnished holiday lets apply if a property is available for commercial letting to the public for at least .... days, is actually let for at least .... of those days and is not normally in the same occupation for more than 31 days for at least seven months.

- Interest in possession trusts are taxed at ....% on non-savings income and at ....% on savings income. Dividends are received net of a tax credit of 10%. Discretionary trusts are taxed at ....%.

- The rate of capital gains tax for all trusts is .... Chargeable gains may arise when assets enter or leave a trust.

- There are special inheritance tax charges on property in discretionary trusts. As well as charges on every .... anniversary of the creation of the trust and on property ...., transfers into the trust are chargeable (at half the normal tax rates) when made.

TRY QUESTIONS 16 TO 19

DID YOU KNOW - INVESTMENTS AND FINANCE; TRUSTS

- *Could you fill in the blanks? The answers are in bold. Use this page for revision purposes as you approach the exam.*

- Unused personal pension relief can be carried forward for **six** years. A premium paid can be related back for relief in **the previous year**.

- An investor should consider not only any exemptions from income tax and/or CGT (for example those available for ISAs) but also **risk** and **liquidity**.

- When a business is selecting a source of finance, its main choice is between debt and equity. Interest is tax-deductible, unlike dividends, but a high level of debt increases the risk of insolvency.

- Rental income is taxed on an **accruals** basis under Schedule A.

- The special rules for furnished holiday lets apply if a property is available for commercial letting to the public for at least **140** days, is actually let for at least **70** of those days and is not normally in the same occupation for more than 31 days for at least seven months.

- Interest in possession trusts are taxed at **22%** on non-savings income and at **20%** on savings income. Dividends are received net of a tax credit of 10%. Discretionary trusts are taxed at **34%**.

- The rate of capital gains tax for all trusts is **34%**. Chargeable gains may arise when assets enter or leave a trust.

- There are special inheritance tax charges on property in discretionary trusts. As well as charges on every **tenth** anniversary of the creation of the trust and on property **leaving the trust**, transfers into the trust are chargeable (at half the normal tax rates) when made.

TRY QUESTIONS 16 TO 19

BPP PUBLISHING

16   MING LEE (6/94)   *45 mins*

Ming Lee, a UK resident who was born on 9 June 1948, is a self-employed management consultant. For 2000/01 she will have Schedule D Case II profits of £95,000, and this level of profits is expected to remain the same for the foreseeable future. Ming has had the following taxable profits since she commenced self-employment during 1993/94.

Tax Year	Schedule D Case II profits
	£
1993/94	26,000
1994/95	34,500
1995/96	47,000
1996/97	53,000
1997/98	63,500
1998/99	70,000
1999/00	90,000

Because she operates from rented office accommodation, Ming's only chargeable business asset is the goodwill of the business which is currently valued at £250,000. She plans to sell her business and retire in three or four years time. However, due to the high level of her profits, Ming is considering the incorporation of her business in the near future.

Ming has funds surplus to her requirements of £140,000, which are presently invested in an ordinary deposit account at a building society. She would like to invest these funds in a way that will reduce her overall liability to income tax. Apart from building society interest of £8,700 (net) pa, Ming, who is single, has no other income. Her only outgoing is interest of £12,000 pa (gross) on her mortgage of £120,000. Ming's only previous payment of a personal pension premium was one of £20,000 during 1997/98.

Required

(a)   Calculate the maximum amount of tax deductible contributions that Ming could make into a personal pension scheme for 2000/01. Advise Ming of whether or not it would be beneficial for her to actually contribute this maximum amount, and whether or not this is a suitable investment for her.   (7 marks)

(b)   As an alternative to investing in a personal pension scheme, Ming is considering using her surplus funds as follows.

   (i)   Repaying some, or all, of her mortgage.

   (ii)   Purchasing National Savings Certificates.

   (iii) Investment in an enterprise zone trust which will itself invest in commercial properties situated in enterprise zones.

   Advise Ming of the suitability of each of these alternatives to her particular circumstances. Your answer should include an outline of the tax implications of each alternative.   (8 marks)

(c)   Outline the taxation factors that would have to be considered when deciding whether or not Ming should incorporate her business. You are *not* expected to include calculations in your answer, and you should *ignore* the implications arising from capital allowances and the private use of assets.   (10 marks)

You should assume that the tax rates and allowances for 2000/01 apply throughout.

(25 marks)

17   **MURIEL GRAND (6/96)**   *45 mins*

On 31 December 2000 Muriel Grand aged 52, made a gift of a house in London to her brother Bertie, aged 45. Muriel had bought the house on 1 April 1985 for £60,000. Surplus land adjoining the house was sold for £24,000 to a neighbour in June 1986, at which date the market value of the property retained was £72,000. The market value at 31 December 2000 has been agreed by the Inland Revenue as £320,000. Muriel occupied the house as her main residence until 30 September 1993, and then moved on to another house that she owned in Glasgow. Muriel elected for the house in Glasgow to be treated as her main residence from 1 October 1993 onwards.

Bertie is to rent out the house in London, either unfurnished or as furnished holiday accommodation. In either case, the roof of the house must be repaired at a cost of £24,000 before it will be possible to let the house. The roof was badly damaged by a gale on 5 December 2000. If the house is let unfurnished, then Bertie will have to decorate it at a cost of £3,500. The forecast rental income is £28,000 pa. If the house is let as furnished holiday accommodation, then the house will be converted into two separate units at a cost of £42,000. The total cost of furnishing the two units will be £9,000. This expenditure will be financed by a £50,000 bank loan at an interest rate of 12% pa. The total forecast rental income is £45,000 pa, although 22.5% of this will be deducted by the letting agency. Other running costs, such as cleaning, will amount to £3,500 pa in total.

Bertie plans to sell the house when he retires on 31 December 2005 aged 50, and anticipates making a substantial capital gain. Both Muriel and Bertie are 40% taxpayers. Muriel has a portfolio of investments valued in excess of £1 million, and has already utilised her CGT annual exemption for 2000/01.

Required

(a) Calculate the CGT liability that will arise from Muriel's gift of the house in London to Bertie.   (4 marks)

(b) Advise Muriel as to how it would be possible to roll-over the gain on the house in London by making an investment in EIS or VCT shares. State which of these investments will be the more risky and outline the other tax reliefs available.

(6 marks)

(c) Advise Bertie of the tax implications of letting out the house in London either:

(i)   unfurnished; or

(ii)   as furnished holiday accommodation. Your answer should include details of the tax advantages of letting the house as furnished holiday accommodation.

(13 marks)

(d) Advise Muriel as to where she could obtain independent financial advice.   (2 marks)

(25 marks)

18   **MARY MOLE (6/98)**   *45 mins*

You are a Chartered Certified Accountant who is authorised to conduct investment business under the Financial Services Act 1986. Mary Mole, a client, inherited £25,000 on 15 December 2000, and has asked for your advice regarding a number of recommendations that she has received as to how this sum should be invested. The recommendations are as follows.

(a) Mary's bank manager has suggested that she invest the maximum amount possible in a maxi ISA, with the balance invested in a unit trust aimed at capital growth. The bank offers each of these investments.

(b) An insurance salesperson has suggested that Mary contribute the maximum tax deductible amount into a personal pension scheme. Mary was born on 1 December 1961, and has not previously made any provision for retirement. She is a partner in a business that writes computer software, and her recent Schedule D Case I assessments are as follows.

	£
1993/94	4,600
1994/95	46,200
1995/96	12,600
1996/97 and 1997/98	Nil (studying at university)
1998/99	8,100
1999/00	18,300
2000/01	57,400

(c) One of Mary's business partners has suggested that she make an investment in a venture capital trust. He believes that unquoted companies will offer an attractive investment return over the next three to four years, and that using a venture capital trust will diversify the risk of holding unquoted shares.

(d) Mary's post office manager has given her a leaflet on government stocks. She understands that these offer a competitive return, and has read that it is possible to purchase government stocks ex div and then to sell them cum div so that interest is effectively turned into a capital gain.

Mary's investment criteria are as follows:

(a) She would like to reduce her income tax and Class 4 NIC liability that you have advised her will be payable in respect of the 2000/01 partnership profits.

(b) Capital growth is more important that additional income.

(c) She is prepared to take a moderate amount of risk.

(d) Some or all of the capital may be needed in nearly three years time when her daughter leaves home.

Required

(a) In respect of each of the four recommendations:

    (i) explain the potential income tax and CGT implications. Your answer should include details of the maximum amount that can be invested in each case assuming that each investment will be made in 2000/01;

    (ii) advise Mary as to the suitability of each recommendation in relation to her investment criteria. (21 marks)

(b) (i) Explain the difference between a tied adviser and an independent adviser.

    (ii) The ACCA has issued Statements of Principle which cover the standards expected of an authorised person. State briefly what these principles are.

(4 marks)

(25 marks)

19   **MR ROWE**   *45 mins*

At today's date (which you should assume is 1 July 2000), George Rowe, a single man aged 42, is expected to earn £63,000 from his employment as an oil company executive for the year ended 5 April 2001 (subject to PAYE of £18,150). During the year George expects to receive net dividends of £28,800 from his shareholdings.

On 6 April 2000, George had sold quoted shares in a multinational company Gong plc, which realised a capital gain of £90,000. He also intends to transfer further shares in Gong plc, with a value of £248,000, into a trust for his brother Bob on 5 April 2001. This transfer will realise a further capital gain of £35,000. Bob is aged 12 and lives with George who has maintained him since the death of their parents in 1996. George is unsure whether the trust for Bob should be an accumulation and maintenance trust or a discretionary trust (of which George would not be a beneficiary). George has made no previous gratuitous transfers of any assets. He will pay any taxes or costs associated with setting up the trust. George is in excellent health.

George had acquired a house in Derby, together with grounds of 0.4 hectare on 1 August 1981 for £280,000. There was no change in the value of the house up to 31 March 1982. Unfortunately it has recently been decided that a motorway is to be built close to the house and as a result it is currently worth only £200,000. George's history of occupation of the house is as follows.

1.8.81 - 30.6.82	Occupied
1.7.82 - 31.12.83	Sent by employer to Saudi Arabia
1.1.84 - 30.9.96	Occupied
1.10.96 - date	Working in various parts of the UK on a four year tour of duty

George intends to sell the house on 31 December 2000 but is unsure whether or not he should reoccupy the house between 1 October 2000 (when his UK tour of duty ends) and 31 December 2000. He will rent a flat in Brighton from 1 January 2001 at a rent of £400 per month payable in advance.

Required

(a)   Discuss the current and potential CGT and IHT implications for George of setting up:

    (i)   an accumulation and maintenance trust for Bob;

    (ii)   a discretionary trust for Bob.   (10 marks)

(b)   Compute George's income tax payable for 2000/01.   (8 marks)

(c)   Discuss whether George should occupy the house in Derby between 1 October 2000 and 31 December 2000. Show all supporting calculations.   (7 marks)

                                                                        (25 marks)

DO YOU KNOW - SELF ASSESSMENT AND PAYMENT OF TAX; SCHEDULE D CASES I AND II; PARTNERSHIPS; NATIONAL INSURANCE

- *Check that you can fill in the blanks in the statements below before you attempt any questions. If in doubt, you should go back to your BPP Study Text and revise first.*

- Under self assessment taxpayers must submit their tax return by the later of .... following the tax year and ....

- Payments on Account of income tax and Class 4 NICs are due on .... in the tax year and on the .... following. Final payments of income tax, Class 4 NICs and CGT are due on .... following the tax year.

- Interest may be charged on the late payment of tax.

- An initial surcharge of ...... is levied on unpaid income tax, CGT and Class 4 NICs which the taxpayer does not pay within ...... days of the 31 January following the tax year.

- There is a fixed penalty of .... for not making a tax return by the filing date when required to do so.

- The usual basis period for a tax year is the period of account ending ....

  ° In the first tax year we tax profits arising from the .... to the following..........................

  ° When an accounting date ends in the second tax year we tax the profits of .... or, if this is not possible, the profits of ....

  ° When no accounting date ends in the second tax year we tax ....

  ° In the third tax year we tax profits of the .... months to the accounting date ending in that year

  ° In the final tax year we tax profits arising from the .... to ....

- .... arise when profits are taxed twice in the opening years of a business. These may either be relieved on .... or on ....

TRY QUESTIONS 20, 21, 23 AND 25

- A trading loss may be carried forward against ....

- A loss may be set against total income of .... and/or total income of ....

- Losses of the final twelve months of trading may be relieved against trading profits of the final tax year and the .... preceeding years, ... years first.

- Losses of the first four years of a business may be set against total income of the .... preceding years, ... year first.

TRY QUESTION 22

- Partners are taxed on their share of partnership profits. When a partner joins or leaves, commencement or cessation rules apply to ....

- The self-employed pay .... (flat rate) and .... (profit related) national insurance contributions.

TRY QUESTIONS 24, 26 AND 27

DID YOU KNOW - SELF ASSESSMENT AND PAYMENT OF TAX; SCHEDULE D CASES I AND II; PARTNERSHIPS; NATIONAL INSURANCE

- *Could you fill in the blanks? The answers are in bold. Use this page for revision purposes as you approach the exam.*

- Under self assessment taxpayers must submit their tax return by the later of **31 January** following the tax year and **3 months after it was issued**.

- Payments on Account of income tax and Class 4 NICs are due on **31 January** in the tax year and on the **31 July** following. Final payments of income tax, Class 4 NICs and CGT are due on **31 January** following the tax year.

- Interest may be charged on the late payment of tax.

- An initial surcharge of **5%** is levied on unpaid income tax, CGT and Class 4 NICs which the taxpayer does not pay within **28** days of the 31 January following the tax year.

- There is a fixed penalty of **£100** for not making a tax return by the filing date when required to do so.

- The usual basis period for a tax year is the period of account ending **in the tax year.**

  - In the first tax year we tax profits arising from the **date of commencement** to the following **5 April**.

  - When an accounting date ends in the second tax year we tax the profits of **the twelve months to the accounting date ending in that year** or, if this is not possible, the profits of **the first twelve months**

  - When no accounting date ends in the second tax year we tax **the profits arising from 6 April to 5 April**

  - In the third tax year we tax profits of the **twelve** months to the accounting date ending in that year

  - In the final tax year we tax profits arising from the **end of the last accounting period** to **cessation**

- **Overlap** arise when profits are taxed twice in the opening years of a business. These may either be relieved on **change of accounting date** or on **cessation.**

TRY QUESTIONS 20, 21, 23 AND 25

- A trading loss may be carried forward against **future profits of the same trade.**

- A loss may be set against total income of **the year of the loss** and/or total income of **the preceeding year.**

- Losses of the final twelve months of trading may be relieved against trading profits of the final tax year and the **three** preceeding years, **later** years first.

- Losses of the first four years of a business may be set against total income of the **three** preceding years, **earliest** year first.

TRY QUESTION 22

- Partners are taxed on their share of partnership profits. When a partner joins or leaves, commencement or cessation rules apply to **that partner**.

- The self-employed pay **Class 2** (flat rate) and **Class 4** (profit related) national insurance contributions.

TRY QUESTIONS 24, 26 AND 27

20   **TONY TORT (12/98)**   *45 mins*

(a)   Tony Tort commenced self-employment as a solicitor on 6 April 1999. His tax adjusted
Schedule D Case II profit for the first year of trading to 5 April 2000 was £61,535, and
the income tax and class 4 NIC liability for 1999/00 based on this figure was £19,033.
The Inland Revenue issued a tax return for 1999/00 on 31 May 2000, but Tony did not
submit this until 15 April 2001. He has made the following payments of income tax
and class 4 NIC during 2001.

1999/00 Balancing payment	£19,033 paid 10 May 2001
2000/01 First payment on account	£2,500 paid 15 June 2001
2000/01 Second payment on account	£2,500 paid 31 July 2001

Because of cash flow problems, Tony claimed to reduce each of his payments on
account for 2000/01 from £9,516.50 to £2,500.

Tony's tax adjusted Schedule D Case II profit for the year ended 5 April 2001 (before
capital allowances) is £52,100. He purchased a new computer on 15 May 2000 for
£5,200 and new photocopier on 20 January 2001 for £4,400. The tax written-down
values of plant and machinery and Tony's motor car at 6 April 2000 were £13,600 and
£17,800 respectively. The private use of the motor car is 10%.

Prior to 6 April 1999 Tony was employed by a firm of solicitors. He is single, and has
no other income or outgoings.

Required:

(i)   Calculate the interest on overdue tax that Tony will be charged in respect of the
late payments of income tax and class 4 NIC made during 2001. You should
assume that the balancing payment for 2000/01 is made on the due date. Assume
an interest rate of 10%.

(ii)   Explain what surcharges and penalties Tony may be liable to.   (12 marks)

(b)   On 10 September 2001 Tony received written notice from the Inland Revenue that
they were to enquire into his tax return for 1999/00. The Inland Revenue gave written
notice of the completion of the enquiry on 5 December 2001, stating that he has
incorrectly claimed for entertaining expenditure of £4,500 in calculating his tax
adjusted Schedule D Case II profit for the year ended 5 April 2000.

No adjustment is required to Tony's tax adjusted Schedule D Case II profit for the year
ended 5 April 2001.

Required:

(i)   State the possible reasons why the Inland Revenue has enquired into Tony's tax
return for 1999/00.

(ii)   Explain the options open to Tony following the completion of the Inland
Revenue enquiry.

(iii)   Advise Tony of the interest on overdue tax, surcharges and penalties that he may
be liable to as a result of the Inland Revenue enquiry into his 1999/00 tax return.

(7 marks)

(c)   Tony is planning to make a contribution of £20,000 into a personal pension scheme on
15 February 2002. A claim will then be made to relate the contribution back so that is
it treated as paid during 2000/01.

Tony is aged 43, and prior to 6 April 1999 was a member of the occupational pension
scheme run by his employer.

32

Required:

Advise Tony of the implications of making the contribution into a personal pension scheme and claiming to relate it back to 2000/01. Your answer should include a calculation on the maximum tax deductible contribution that Tony could make into a personal pension scheme for 2000/01. Assume the rules about pensions in 2000/01 also apply in 2001/02. (6 marks)

(25 marks)

21   **CECILE GRAND (12/97)**   *45 mins*

(a) Cecile Grand has been a self-employed antiques dealer since 1989. Her income for 2000/01 was as follows.

	£
Adjusted Schedule DI profit	38,400
Dividends (net)	4,860
Schedule A profit	800
Capital gain before taper relief	7,800

The capital gain was in respect of a let property that was bought in 1986 and sold on 30 June 2000. The Schedule A profit is for the period 6 April 2000 to 30 June 2000. During 2000/01 Cecile paid a personal pension contribution of £3,500.

Her forecast income for 2001/02 is as follows.

	£
Adjusted Schedule DI profit	21,750
Dividends (net)	4,320
Capital gain before taper relief	14,300

The capital gain is in respect of quoted shares bought in December 2000 and sold on 30 July 2001. Due to the fall in profits, Cecile will not pay a personal pension contribution during 2001/02.

Required

(i)   Calculate Cecile's payments on account and balancing payment or repayment for 2001/02. You should assume that Cecile does not make a claim to reduce her payments on account. Assume 2000/01 rates and allowances apply throughout.

(10 marks)

(ii)   Based on the above figures, advise Cecile of the amount of the maximum claim that she could have made to reduce her payments on account for 2001/02.

(2 marks)

(b) Cecile's adjusted Schedule D Case I profit for 2001/02 is an estimated figure based on her provisional accounts for the year ended 31 March 2002. The actual figures will not be available until 31 August 2002, because of the difficulty that Cecile has in separating antiques acquired for business purposes, from those acquired for private purposes.

Required

(i)   Assuming that Cecile made the maximum claim to reduce the payments on account for 2001/02, explain the tax implications if her actual taxable income for 2001/02 is higher than the estimated figure. (2 marks)

(ii)   Advise Cecile of the powers that the Inland Revenue have with regard to enquiring into her tax return for 2001/02. (2 marks)

(iii) Briefly advise Cecile of the tax implications if the Inland Revenue enquire into her tax return for 2001/02, and decide that the Schedule D Case I profits for the year ended 31 March 2002 are understated. (2 marks)

(c) Cecile is planning to change her accounting date from 31 March to 30 September by preparing her next accounts for the six month period to 30 September 2002. The forecast profit for this period is £18,000.

Required

(i) State the qualifying conditions that must be met for Cecile's change of accounting date to be valid. (2 marks)

(ii) Explain the tax implications of Cecile changing her accounting date from 31 March to 30 September. Your answer should include a calculation of the Schedule D Case I profits that Cecile will be assessed to for 2002/2003. (2 marks)

(iii) Briefly advise Cecile of the advantages and the disadvantages for tax purposes, of changing her accounting date from 31 March to 30 September. (3 marks)

(25 marks)

22 FIONA FUNG (12/99) *45 mins*

You are the tax adviser to Fiona Fung, aged 59, and have the following information regarding her tax affairs for 2000/01.

(1) On 31 August 2000 Fiona retired as a director of Garments Ltd, an unquoted trading company manufacturing women's clothing. On that date she sold her entire holding of 100,000 £1 ordinary shares in the company for £650,000. Fiona had been a shareholder of Garments Ltd since its incorporation on 1 January 1989, when she subscribed for her shares at par. Fiona did not become a full-time working director of the company until 1 September 1991. Garments Ltd has a share capital of 400,000 £1 ordinary shares. The market value of its assets at 31 August 2000 was as follows.

	£
Goodwill	400,000
Freehold property (factory and warehouse)	760,000
Plant and machinery (costing more than £6,000 per item)	240,000
Motor cars	90,000
Investments in quoted companies	280,000
Net current assets	730,000
	2,500,000

You should assume that the quoted investments held by Garments Ltd do not preclude it from being treated as a trading company.

(2) Fiona used the proceeds from the disposal of her shareholding to set up in business on 1 October 2000 as a self-employed manufacturer of women's clothing. Her tax adjusted Schedule D Case I profit for the period ended 5 April 2001 is £25,400. This figure is before capital allowances, and before any adjustments that might be necessary as a result of the actions detailed in (4) below.

(3) On 1 October 2000 Fiona purchased a freehold factory for £338,000 (including land valued at £65,000). This was immediately brought into trade use. The factory was originally constructed at a cost of £229,000 (including land valued at £40,000), and was first brought into use on 1 April 1993. On 1 October 2000 Fiona also purchased plant

and equipment for £172,500, and a motor car for £22,000. The motor car has been used 20% for private mileage. None of the equipment was computer equipment.

(4) Because of concern about her high tax liability for 2000/01, Fiona took the following actions during the week ending 5 April 2001.

    (i)   Bonuses totalling £20,000 were given to the employees of the business in respect of the period ended 5 April 2001. The bonuses were not actually paid until June 2000.

    (ii)   A contract for the sale of goods that was due to take place on 5 April 2001 was postponed until the following day. The sale would have resulted in additional gross profit of £9,600. The relevant goods are included in closing stock.

    (ii)   Closing stock that cost £15,400 was written down to its net realisable value of £5,600.

(5) Fiona received director's remuneration of £17,500 from Garments Ltd during 2000/01. Her remuneration in previous years was £39,000 pa. Fiona is single, and has no other income or outgoings.

Required

(a) Calculate the chargeable gain (before taper relief) that Fiona will be assessed on for 2000/01.   (5 marks)

(b) Advise Fiona as to whether the actions that she undertook during the week ending 5 April 2001 are likely to be viewed by the Inland Revenue as tax avoidance or as tax evasion.   (3 marks)

(c) Assuming that the actions during the week ending 5 April 2001 are *not treated* as tax evasion:

    (i)   calculate Fiona's Schedule D Case I trading loss for 2000/01;   (6 marks)

    (ii)   explain why Fiona's most beneficial loss relief claim is under s 380 ICTA 1988 against total income for 2000/01, and then under s 72 FA 1991 against the chargeable gain of the same year;   (5 marks)

    (iii)   after taking account of the loss relief claim in (ii), calculate Fiona's income tax and CGT liabilities for 2000/01.   (6 marks)

(25 marks)

---

23   **BASIL NADIR** (12/95)   *45 mins*

Basil Nadir is a computer programmer. Until 5 April 2000, Basil was employed by Ace Computers Ltd, but since then has worked independently from home. Basil's income for his first 12 months of trading to 5 April 2001 is forecast to be £60,600, of which 50% will be in respect of work done for Ace Computers Ltd. His expenditure for the year will be as follows.

(a) Computer equipment costing £7,375 (inclusive of VAT) was purchased on 6 April 2000.

(b) Basil uses two rooms of his eight room private residence exclusively for business purposes. The cost of light, heat and insurance of the house for the year will amount to £1,800 (inclusive of VAT of £100).

(c) Basil's telephone bills currently amount to £250 per quarter. They were £100 per quarter up to 5 April 2000. Both figures are inclusive of VAT.

(d) Basil owns a two year old motor car which originally cost £15,000. It was worth £10,000 on 6 April 2000. His motor expenses for the year will amount to £3,500 (inclusive of

VAT of £400). Although Basil works from home, he has to visit his clients on a regular basis. His mileage for the year ended 5 April 2001 will be as follows.

Visiting Ace Computers Ltd	10,000 miles
Visiting other clients	10,000 miles
Private use	5,000 miles

Basil spends 50% of his time working for Ace Computers Ltd, and since 6 April 2000 has been working for them on a 12 months contract to develop a taxation program for accountants. He visits the company's offices twice a week in respect of this contract. Apart from Ace Computers Ltd, Basil presently has five other clients.

On 8 August 2000, Ace Computers Ltd was the subject of an Inland Revenue PAYE compliance visit, and Basil's self-employed status in respect of his contract with the company was queried. The Inland Revenue have stated that they consider Basil to be an employee of Ace Computers Ltd for the purposes of both income tax and NIC. Basil has agreed to refund Ace Computers Ltd for any tax liability that the company suffers if the Inland Revenue's view is upheld.

Basil has not yet registered for VAT. He has no other income or outgoings. You should assume that today's date is 15 August 2000.

Required

(a) Briefly discuss the criteria that will be used in deciding whether Basil will be classified as employed or self-employed in respect of his contract with Ace Computers Ltd. You answer should include:

   (i)   an explanation as to the likely reasons why the Inland Revenue have queried Basil's self-employed status; and

   (ii) advice to Basil and Ace Computers Ltd as to the criteria that they could put forward in order to justify Basil's self-employed status.   (9 marks)

(b) Calculate Basil's liability to income tax and NIC for 2000/01 if he is treated as self-employed in respect of his contract with Ace Computers Ltd, and advise him of by how much this liability will increase if he is instead treated as employed.

   You should *ignore* the implications of VAT, and should note that Basil's self-employed status in respect of his contracts with his other five clients is not in dispute. (10 marks)

(c) Assuming that Basil is classified as self-employed in respect of his contract with Ace Computers Ltd, state when he will have to compulsorily register for VAT. Explain the implications of being so registered, and advise him of whether or not it would be beneficial to voluntarily register before that date. You should assume that Basil's income accrued evenly throughout the year.   (6 marks)

(25 marks)

24   **BASIL PERFECT (12/99)**   *45 mins*

Basil Perfect commenced self-employment on 1 July 1998, and is involved in the provision of educational services. His wife Sybil commenced self-employment on 1 June 2000, and is also involved in the provision of educational services.

You should assume that today's date is 20 March 2001, and that the tax rates and allowances for 2000/01 apply throughout.

(a) Basil and Sybil are planning to combine their two businesses into a partnership on 1 April 2001. Basil's tax adjusted Schedule D Case I profits are as follows.

	£
Year ended 30 June 1999	38,640
Year ended 30 June 2000	49,920
Period ended 31 March 2001 (forecast)	47,700

Sybil's forecast tax adjusted Schedule D Case I profits for the ten-month period to 31 March 2001 are £11,100. The partnership is planning to have an accounting date of 31 March. Its forecast profit for the year ended 31 March 2002 are £80,000, and there are to be shared 75% to Basil and 25% to Sybil.

Required

(i) Calculate Basil and Sybil's Schedule D Case I assessments for 2000/01 and 2001/02. (5 marks)

(ii) Advise Basil and Sybil of the advantages and disadvantages of having an accounting date of 31 March as compared to an accounting date of 30 June.

(3 marks)

(b) Basil is registered for VAT. Sybil is not registered because she is below the VAT registration turnover limit and her supplies are all to the general public in a competitive market. Basil and Sybil are concerned that they will have to pay additional VAT as a result of forming a partnership on 1 April 2001, compared to operating as sole-traders. Their individual sales and expenses for the year ended 31 March 2002 are forecast to be as follows.

	Basil	Sybil
	£	£
Sales: Standard rated	170,000	47,000
Exempt	115,000	-
Expenses: Standard rated	160,000	26,000

25% of Basil's expenses directly relate to standard rated sales, 30% directly relate to exempt sales, with the balance not directly attributable. Basil's standard rated sales include a supply of £15,000 to Sybil. There are no expenses related to this supply. All of the above figures are *exclusive* of VAT where applicable.

Required

(i) Advise Basil and Sybil of the additional amount of VAT that will be payable for the year ended 31 March 2002 if they form the partnership on 1 April 2001, as compared to the position if they had remained as sole traders.

(8 marks)

(ii) Basil and Sybil understand that even if a partnership is not formed, they could still be required to account for VAT as a single taxable person if HM Customs and Excise make a direction under the disaggregation rules. Explain the circumstances in which such a direction will be made. (3 marks)

(c) Although they are planning to share the forecast partnership profits of £80,000 for the year ended 31 March 2002 on the basis of 75% to Basil and 25% to Sybil, the couple want to know if it would be beneficial to instead share profits 60% to Basil and 40% to Sybil. Basil is aged 54, and always makes the maximum amount of tax deductible contributions into a personal pension scheme. Neither Basil nor Sybil has any other income or outgoings.

Required

Advise Basil and Sybil of the income tax and NIC implications of the two alternative profit sharing arrangements. (6 marks)

(25 marks)

25   **ALEX ZONG (12/97)**   *45 mins*

(a)   Alex Zong, aged 38, commenced <u>self-employment</u> as a builder on 1 October 1997. The business has been quite successful, and Alex is therefore going to <u>incorporate his trade</u> into a new limited company, Lexon Ltd, on 31 December 2000. The following information is available.

(i)   Tax adjusted Schedule DI profits (before capital allowances) are as follows.

	£
Period ended 30.6.98	28,000
Year ended 30.6.99	44,000
Year ended 30.6.00	53,000
Period ended 31.12.00 (estimated)	29,000

The above figures are before capital allowances.

(ii)   Alex has purchased the following assets.

		£
1.10.97	Freehold office premises	32,000
1.10.97	Lorry	8,800
15.6.98	Plant	6,400
30.11.99	Motor car	13,500

On 1 October 1997 Alex introduced his private motor car into the business at its market value of £4,000. This was sold on 30 November 1999 for £2,800, and replaced by the motor car bought on that date. Alex drives 12,000 miles per year, of which 4,800 are for private purposes.

On 10 December 1998 Alex extended the freehold premises using his own materials and labour at a cost of £6,700. The extension would have cost £10,000 if the work had been carried out externally.

(iii)   The estimated market value of the business assets at 31 December 2000 is as follows.

SP. = mv of Assets + Goodwill. *(Fv*

	£
Goodwill	40,000
Freehold premises	75,000
Lorry	4,300
Plant	8,200
Motor car	11,500
Net current assets	21,000
	160,000

∴ Total consideration

(iv)   All of the business assets are to be transferred to Lexon Ltd. The consideration will consist of 1,000 £1 ordinary shares in Lexon Ltd, and a loan account balance of £10,000.

(v)   Alex has capital losses of £12,500 resulting from the sale of investments in 2000/01.

(vi)   Alex is registered for VAT.

Required

(i)   Calculate Alex's Schedule D Case I assessment for 2000/01. You should ignore NIC.   (11 marks)

(ii)   Advise Alex of the capital gains tax implications of incorporating his business on 31 December 2000.   (7 marks)

(iii)   Advise Alex of the VAT implications of incorporating his business on 31 December 2000.   (2 marks)

You should include any tax planning points that you consider relevant.

(b) Alex is in the process of completing his VAT return for the quarter ended 30 November 2000, and wants advice on how to deal with the following.

(i) On 20 May 2000 Alex completed a contract for a customer, and an invoice was raised for £9,400 (inclusive of VAT) on 15 June 2000. The customer paid £2,350 on 30 June 2000, but the balance of the amount owing is now considered to be a bad debt. The full debt was due to be paid within 10 days of the invoice date.

(ii) Alex has mistakenly not been claiming for the input VAT on plant which is leased for £475 (inclusive of VAT) per month. The same amount has been paid since the commencement of business on 1 October 1997.

(iii) A customer was invoiced for £3,400 (excluding VAT) on 30 September 2000. The customer was offered a 5% discount for payment within 30 days, but this was not taken and the customer paid the amount due on 28 November 2000.

Alex does not operate the cash accounting scheme.

Required

Advise Alex in respect of points raised.   (5 marks)

                                                                          (25 marks)

---

26   **SMART AND SHARP (6/96)**   *45 mins*

You are the tax adviser to the partnership of Smart and Sharp, a firm of management consultants. There are currently two partners, Bob and Nick, who share profits equally after paying an annual salary of £180,000 to Bob and £80,000 to Nick. These salaries have not changed since commencement on 1 July 1998. You should assume that today's date is 15 November 2000.

(a) There have been no changes to the constitution of the partnership since commencement, but on 31 December 2000 a new partner, Justin, is to be admitted. From 1 January 2001 profits will be shared equally between the three partners. The tax adjusted Schedule D Case II trading profits have been as follows.

	£
Six months to 31 December 1998	280,000
Year ended 31 December 1999	710,000
Year ended 31 December 2000	640,000

The partners are planning to incorporate the partnership's business on 31 December 2003. Forecast profits to this date are as follows.

	£
Year ended 31 December 2001	750,000
Year ended 31 December 2002	750,000
Year ended 31 December 2003	750,000

Required

Calculate the amount of each partner's Schedule D Case II income where applicable, for the years 1998/99 to 2003/04 inclusive. You should assume that the partnership's business is incorporated on 31 December 2003.   (10 marks)

(b) The partners would like advice as to whether or not it will be beneficial to incorporate the partnership's business. They are concerned that the current level of profits of £750,000 may not be high enough for incorporation to be beneficial.

Upon incorporation, the partnership's business will be transferred to a new company, Smash Ltd. The three partners will all become directors of Smash Ltd, and would each receive directors remuneration of £200,000 pa. Each of the partners has sufficient

Schedule A investment income to utilise their personal allowances and basic rate income tax bands.

Required

Advise the partners as to whether or not it will be beneficial for the partnership's business to be incorporated. Base your answer solely on the current level of profits of £750,000, calculating:

(i)   the annual tax liability of the three partners if the partnership is *not* incorporated; and

(ii) the annual tax liability of Smash Ltd and its directors if the partnership *is* incorporated.

Your answer should take into account the implications of NIC, and should use the tax rates for 2000/01. The figure for profits of £750,000 is *before* the deduction of directors remuneration.   (8 marks)

(c) Explain the alternative ways in which the partners can obtain relief for any overlap profits.   (3 marks)

(d) The partners have asked for your advice regarding the CGT and IHT implications on incorporating the partnership's business. All the partners are aged between 40 and 50.

Required

Draft a reply to the partners.   (4 marks)

(25 marks)

27   **SALLY AND TREVOR ACRE (12/98)**   *45 mins*

Sally and Trevor Acre, a married couple aged 53 and 48 respectively have been in partnership as estate agents since 1 October 1997. Due to Sally's ill health, they are to sell the business on 31 March 2001 to an unrelated third party. You should assume that today's date is 15 March 2001. The following information is available.

(1) Tax adjusted Schedule DII profits/(losses) are as follows:

	£
Period ended 31 March 1998	37,500
Year ended 31 March 1999	74,000
Year ended 31 March 2000	52,000
Year ended 31 March 2001 (estimated)	(68,000)

(2) Profits and losses, whether revenue or capital in nature, have always been shared 70% to Sally and 30% to Trevor.

(3) The market values of the partnership assets at 31 March 2001 are forecast to be as follows:

	£
Goodwill	100,000
Freehold property	230,000
Fixtures and fittings	140,000
Net current assets	80,000
	550,000

The freehold property and fixtures and fittings were purchased on 1 October 1997, and cost £170,000 and £155,000 respectively. Indexation on the property from October 1997 to April 1998 is £6,175. The fixtures and fittings qualify as plant and machinery for capital allowance purposes and no chargeable gain arises on disposal. The partnership assets will all be sold on 31 March 2001 for their market value.

(4)   Sally personally owns a leasehold office building that is used rent-free by the partnership. She paid £85,000 for the grant of a 25-year lease on 1 July 1999. This property is to be sold on 31 March 2001 for £90,000.

(5)   Sally has Schedule A profits of £5,905 p.a. Trevor has Schedule A profits of £2,000 pa. Neither of them plans to reinvest the proceeds from the sale of the business.

(6)   Trevor realised other chargeable gains on the disposal of non business assets in 2000/01. These amounted to £38,000 before deducting taper relief and the annual exemption. The assets were acquired in 1999.

Required:

(a)   Advise Sally and Trevor of the chargeable gains that will be assessed on them for 2000/01. Your answer should include an explanation as to the amount of retirement relief that will be available.   (9 marks)

(b)   (i)   State the possible ways of relieving the partnership's Schedule D Case II trading loss of £68,000 for the year ended 31 March 2001.

       (ii)   Advise Sally and Trevor as to which loss relief claims would be the most beneficial for them.

       (iii)   After taking into account your advice in (ii), calculate Sally and Trevor's taxable income for the tax years 1997/98 to 2000/01, and their net chargeable gains for 2000/01.

You should assume that the tax rates and allowances for 2000/01 apply throughout.

(16 marks)

(25 marks)

DO YOU KNOW - CGT AND BUSINESSES; VALUE ADDED TAX

- *Check that you can fill in the blanks in the statements below before you attempt any questions. If in doubt, you should go back to your BPP Study Text and revise first.*

- Rollover relief …………….. gains on certain assets when the proceeds are reinvested. If proceeds are not completely reinvested the lower of ……………………………….. and the ………………….. is immediately chargeable.

- Retirement relief may permanently exempt a gain on the disposal of a ………………… or of shares in a ……………………………. company. EIS reinvestment relief may …………….. a gain.

TRY QUESTIONS 28 AND 29

- VAT is charged on taxable supplies of goods and services by registered traders.

- Supplies may be taxable at 17½% (the VAT is 7/47 of the gross amount), taxable at 0% or exempt.

- A registered trader deducts VAT suffered on purchases from VAT charged on sales, and pays the net amount to HM Customs & Excise.

  - ○ …………………………… may restrict the recovery of VAT on purchases.

  - ○ Most traders account for VAT …………………….., although monthly and annual accounting are also possible.

  - ○ Returns and VAT are due ……………………………………………………………………..

  - ○ Traders must make monthly payments on account if their VAT liability exceeds …………………… a year.

- Traders must register when their turnover for the previous …………………… exceeds the registration limit.

  - ○ Traders must also register when their anticipated turnover for the next ……………… exceeds the registration limit.

  - ○ Trade within the ……………………………. may also give rise to a requirement to register.

  - ○ Traders may register voluntarily.

- VAT invoices must contain prescribed details, and specified records must be kept.

  - ○ Less detailed invoices may be issued for supplies worth ………………………. including VAT.
  - ○ Registered traders need VAT invoices for purchases in order to reclaim the VAT suffered.

- The …………………… determines in which VAT return a purchase or sale is dealt with.

- The cash accounting scheme allows businesses to account for VAT on the basis of ……………………………………. The scheme can be used by a trader whose taxable turnover, excluding VAT, does not exceed ……………………

- The annual accounting scheme allows traders to make VAT returns ……………………………… The scheme can be used by traders whose taxable turnover, excluding VAT, does not exceed …………………

- Bad debt relief is available if the debt is over ………………………. old measured from ………………………………

- A …………………………. may arise when a VAT return is late.

- A misdeclaration penalty may apply if the VAT which would have been lost as a result of the misdeclaration on a return is at least …………….. or is at least ……% of the ……………………………… …………………………………………….…….. (GAT ie Gross amount of tax).

TRY QUESTIONS 30 AND 31

DID YOU KNOW - CGT AND BUSINESSES; VALUE ADDED TAX

- *Could you fill in the blanks? The answers are in bold. Use this page for revision purposes as you approach the exam.*

- Rollover relief **defers** gains on certain assets when the proceeds are reinvested. If proceeds are not completely reinvested the lower of **proceeds not reinvested** and the **gain** is immediately chargeable.

- Retirement relief may permanently exempt a gain on the disposal of a **business** or of shares in a **personal trading** company. EIS reinvestment relief may **defer** a gain.

TRY QUESTIONS 28 AND 29

- VAT is charged on taxable supplies of goods and services by registered traders.

- Supplies may be taxable at 17½% (the VAT is 7/47 of the gross amount), taxable at 0% or exempt.

- A registered trader deducts VAT suffered on purchases from VAT charged on sales, and pays the net amount to HM Customs & Excise.

  ° **Exempt supplies** may restrict the recovery of VAT on purchases.

  ° Most traders account for VAT **quarterly**, although monthly and annual accounting are also possible.

  ° Returns and VAT are due **one month from the end of the VAT period**.

  ° Traders must make monthly payments on account if their VAT liability exceeds **£2,000,000** a year.

- Traders must register when their turnover for the previous **12 months or less** exceeds the registration limit.

  ° Traders must also register when their anticipated turnover for the next **30 days** exceeds the registration limit.

  ° Trade within the **European Community** may also give rise to a requirement to register.

  ° Traders may register voluntarily.

- VAT invoices must contain prescribed details, and specified records must be kept.

  ° Less detailed invoices may be issued for supplies worth **£100 or less** including VAT.
  ° Registered traders need VAT invoices for purchases in order to reclaim the VAT suffered.

- The **tax point** determines in which VAT return a purchase or sale is dealt with.

- The cash accounting scheme allows businesses to account for VAT on the basis of **cash paid and received**. The scheme can be used by a trader whose taxable turnover, excluding VAT, does not exceed **£350,000.**

- The annual accounting scheme allows traders to make VAT returns **once a year**. The scheme can be used by traders whose taxable turnover, excluding VAT, does not exceed **£300,000.**

- Bad debt relief is available if the debt is over **six months** old measured from **when payment is due.**

- A **default surcharge** may arise when a VAT return is late.

- A misdeclaration penalty may apply if the VAT which would have been lost as a result of the misdeclaration on a return is at least **£1,000,000** or is at least **30%** of the **sum of the true input and the true output tax** (GAT ie Gross amount of tax).

TRY QUESTIONS 30 AND 31

BPP
PUBLISHING

28   TUTORIAL QUESTION: CHOOSING ASSETS TO SELL

Paris Ltd, a company with annual profits of approximately £10,000,000 and no associated companies, makes up accounts annually at 31 March.

(a)   During the year to 31 March 2001 the company was experiencing cash flow difficulties and decided to sell, during February 2001, one of two areas of land it owns, each of which would realise £1,600,000. It is anxious to ensure that it sells that piece of land which will result in the lower taxation liability. Details concerning the two sites are as follows.

Site A

This had been purchased in February 1982 for £700,000 using the full proceeds of a sale, in the same month, of land which had been purchased in 1970 for £100,000. Rollover relief was claimed in respect of the gain arising in February 1982. The value of the land which might now be sold (in February 2001) at 31 March 1982 was £720,000.

Site B

This land was purchased in July 1982 for £900,000 using the full proceeds of a sale, in the same month, of land which had been purchased in 1971 for £150,000. Again, rollover relief was claimed in respect of the gain arising in July 1982.

Required

Compute the corporation tax charge which will arise as a result of each of the above proposed disposals. Assume the retail prices index for February 2001 is 174.0.

(b)   One of the directors of the company, aged 62, intends to sell his holding of 8% of the ordinary shares on 31 March 2001. He acquired these shares and became a full-time director on 1 April 1992.

Draft a brief report to him outlining the rules which determine whether retirement relief will be available and how such relief would be computed.

Guidance notes

1   Site A's cost for capital gains purposes is affected by an earlier rollover claim. Site A was acquired before 31 March 1982. Why should the gain rolled over *not* be halved?

2   With site B, we again have to consider the effect of a rollover claim. Consider whether to halve the gain rolled over, and also consider what indexation allowance, if any, is due on the sale in 1982.

3   In part (b), ensure that your discussion of the rules on retirement relief is related to the particular circumstances of the director.

29   SALLY JONES   *45 mins*

Sally Jones has been a shareholder and the managing director of Zen Ltd since its incorporation on 1 January 1995. Zen Ltd is a UK resident company manufacturing computer equipment. Sally is 58 years old. She has decided to retire as managing director of Zen Ltd on 31 December 2000, and plans to dispose of most of her shareholding on the same date.

Zen Ltd has a share capital of 60,000 £1 ordinary shares of which Sally holds 31,000. The remaining shares are held by the other directors who are not related to Sally. She would like to dispose of 20,000 of her shares but none of the other directors is in a position to purchase them. However, Zen Ltd currently has surplus funds and is prepared to purchase 20,000 of Sally's shares at their market value of £280,000. This will result in a chargeable gain for her, after indexation but before any reliefs, of £170,000.

Sally is paid director's remuneration of £24,000 pa, and she also receives an annual bonus based on Zen Ltd's annual results. For the year ended 31 March 2000 the bonus was £4,200, and for the year ended 31 March 2001 it is expected to be £5,700. The bonuses are agreed by the directors prior to the relevant year end, and then paid on the following 30 April. Sally will be entitled to her full bonus for the year to 31 March 2001 even though she will retire during the year. Zen Ltd is also to give Sally an *ex gratia* lump sum upon her retirement of £80,000, which she is not contractually entitled to. This is to be paid in two equal instalments on 31 March 2001 and 31 March 2002.

Sally has no other income or outgoings apart from a pension of £950 per month (payable at the end of each month) that will commence upon her retirement.

Required

(a) Outline the conditions to be met for the purchase of Sally's shares by Zen Ltd to qualify for the special treatment applying to a company's purchase of its own shares. Your answer should indicate whether or not these conditions are met.   (7 marks)

(b) Assuming that the purchase of Sally's shares qualifies for the special treatment:

  (i)   calculate her income tax for 2000/01; and
  (ii) calculate her capital gains tax liability for 2000/01.

  Your answer should include an explanation of the treatment of Sally's annual bonuses and *ex gratia* payment.   (10 marks)

(c) What deductions will Zen Ltd be entitled to when calculating its corporation tax liability for the year ended 31 March 2001 in respect of the payments and emoluments provided to Sally? Your answer should include a consideration of NIC.

          (8 marks)

          (25 marks)

30   **TUTORIAL QUESTION: REGISTRATION AND ACCOUNTING**

You have recently received a request from the managing director of a newly-created business (which will make no exempt supplies and will have no dealings outside the UK) requesting your help with matters concerning value added tax. The following is an extract from the letter.

(a) We understand that some businesses are registered for VAT whilst others are not registered. We have only recently commenced trading and consider that it will take us about five years to reach full potential sales, which we envisage will rise from £20,000 to £100,000 a year in that period. Could you please advise us of the position regarding registration?

(b) Once we are registered, how should the VAT content of our income and expenditure be reflected in our budgets and final accounts at the year end?

(c) When and how is VAT to be accounted for to HM Customs & Excise, and what is the position if we should pay out more VAT than we charge?

(d) What records must be kept by us in order to satisfy the regulations?

Required

Prepare a letter in response to the above requests.

Guidance notes

1   You are asked for a letter, so you should present your answer in letter format.

2 The company will clearly need to register at some stage. You should explain the rules on registration.

3 For part (b), remember that VAT on some items of expenditure is never recoverable.

4 You should consider the alternatives to quarterly accounting, both monthly and annual accounting. Also, might cash accounting be appropriate?

5 Several records must be kept. Most of these are records which a business would be likely to keep in any case, but you still need to list them because there are penalties for failure to keep the required records.

31 SCHOONER LTD (12/98) *45 mins*

Schooner Ltd is an unquoted company that constructs yachts. The company has recently accepted a large contract to supply yachts to Highseas plc. The new contract will commence on 1 January 2001, and will have the following implications for Schooner Ltd.

(a) Each yacht will take three months to construct, and will be sold for £350,000. Highseas plc will pay a deposit of £50,000 at the beginning of the three-month period, and a further payment on account of £100,000 two months later. An invoice for the total price of £350,000 plus VAT will be raised <u>10 days</u> after completion of each yacht, and the balance due will be paid within 60 days. The three-monthly construction periods will be coterminous with Schooner Ltd's quarterly VAT periods.

(b) Schooner Ltd will acquire <u>new equipment</u> costing £800,000 on 1 January 2001.

(1) The company has sufficient funds to purchase £250,000 of the equipment outright, and all of this is to be imported into the UK. Equipment costing £160,000 will be <u>imported from countries that are members of the European</u> Union, with the remainder imported from countries that are <u>outside the</u> European Union.

(2) Equipment costing £200,000 will be bought on <u>hire purchase</u>, with the company making 16 quarterly payments of £17,250 <u>commencing on 1 January 2001</u>. VAT will be paid with the first quarterly payment.

(3) Equipment costing £350,000 will be <u>leased</u> at a cost of £145,000 pa. The lease will be treated as a finance lease, and the equipment will accordingly be capitalised as a fixed asset by Schooner Ltd.

All figures are <u>exclusive</u> of VAT where appropriate. None of the new equipment is <u>computer equipment</u>.

(c) Schooner Ltd will raise additional finance of £600,000 on 1 January 2001 in order to provide working capital.

(1) The managing director of Schooner Ltd, Alex Barnacle, will borrow £100,000 at an interest rate of 8% using his main residence as security. This amount will be lent interest free to Schooner Ltd. At present, the main residence is not mortgaged. Alex owns 35% of Schooner Ltd's ordinary share capital.

(2) An issue of 10% debentures will raise a loan of £300,000. The debentures will be issued at a 5% discount to their nominal value, and will be redeemable in five years time. Professional fees of £8,000 will be incurred in respect of the issue.

(3) An issue of new ordinary £1.00 shares at £2.00 per share will raise £200,000. Chloe Dhow is to subscribe for 90,000 of the new shares. She presently has no connection with Schooner Ltd, but will be appointed a director following the share issue. Professional fees of £12,500 will be incurred in respect of the issue.

Schooner Ltd makes up its accounts to 31 December. It is a close company, currently has an issued share capital of 1,000,000 £1 ordinary shares, and is a small company as defined by the Companies Acts. The company's sales are all standard rated.

Required:

(a)   Advise Schooner Ltd of the VAT rules relating to the time of supply for goods, and explain the output tax entries that will be made in respect of the new contract on its quarterly VAT returns.   (5 marks)

(b)   (i)   Advise Schooner Ltd of the effect that the acquisition of the new equipment will have on its tax adjusted Schedule D Case I profits for the year ended 31 December 2001.

(ii)   Advise Schooner Ltd of the VAT implications of acquiring the new equipment.
                                                                                                                (9 marks)

(c)   (i)   Advise Schooner Ltd of the effect that raising the additional finance will have on its tax adjusted Schedule D Case I profits for the year ended 31 December 2001.

(ii)   Advise Alex and Chloe of the tax relief that will be available to them in respect of their investment in Schooner Ltd.   (11 marks)

                                                                                                                (25 marks)

47

DO YOU KNOW - CORPORATE TAXATION

- *Check that you can fill in the blanks in the statements below before you attempt any questions. If in doubt, you should go back to your BPP Study Text and revise first.*

- Interest income on .... loan relationships is taxed under Schedule D Case III on an .... basis. Interest income on .... loan relationships is included within Schedule D Case I profits.

- Interest paid on .... loan relationships is a deduction in arriving at Schedule D Case I profits on an .... basis. Interest paid on a .... loan relationship is deducted in arriving at Schedule D Case III income on .... loan relationships.

- A company's profits are computed for *accounting periods*. If a period of account exceeds 12 months, the .... form one accounting period, and the .... forms another.

- Corporation tax is charged on a company's .... These include all of a company's income (except ....) and chargeable gains.

- The rate of corporation tax depends on the level of the company's 'profits'. 'Profits' are .... plus ....

- If 'profits' exceed the .... corporation tax is charged at the .... rate, 30% (FY00). If 'profits' are below the .... corporation tax is charged at .... rate, 20% (FY00). If 'profits' are between the .... corporation tax is charged at the .... rate less marginal relief.

- If 'profits' are below the ...., corporation tax is charged at the ....rate, 10 % (FY00). If 'profits' are between the .... corporation tax is charged at the .... rate less marginal relief.

- The marginal relief formula is ....

- Income tax is accounted for through quarterly returns.

  ° Income tax is deducted from interest at ....%, and from charges at ....%.

- Trading losses and unrelieved trade charges may be carried forward against .... Trading losses may also be set against .... of the period of loss, and may then be carried back against .... of the preceding period(s), later periods first. The carry back period is normally .... but this is extended to .... in the case of a loss arising in the 12 months prior to the cessation of trade.

- A company controlled by .... participators is normally a close company.

  ° Loans to participators give rise to a tax charge equal to ...., which can only be recovered when the loan is repaid.

  ° Benefits in kind, if not taxed under Schedule E, are treated like .... received.

  TRY QUESTION 34

- One company's trading losses may be transferred to another company if they are in a group where there is a ....% effective interest of the holding company in each relevant subsidiary.

  ° Companies in a group should be selected to benefit from group relief depending on their marginal tax rates.

- Companies in a 75% group (with over 50% effective interest) transfer assets between each other at .... Capital losses .... be surrendered.

- Companies that pay tax at the .... rate must pay 72% of their estimated corporation tax liability for the second accounting period ending after 30 June 1999 by .... instalments.

  TRY QUESTIONS 32, 33 AND 35 TO 39

DID YOU KNOW - CORPORATE TAXATION

- *Could you fill in the blanks? The answers are in bold. Use this page for revision purposes as you approach the exam.*

- Interest income on **non-trading** loan relationships is taxed under Schedule D Case III on an **accruals** basis. Interest income on **trading** loan relationships is included within Schedule D Case I profits.

- Interest paid on **trading** loan relationships is a deduction in arriving at Schedule D Case I profits on an **accruals** basis. Interest paid on a **non-trading** loan relationship is deducted in arriving at Schedule D Case III income on **non-trading** loan relationships.

- A company's profits are computed for *accounting periods*. If a period of account exceeds 12 months, the **first 12 months** form one accounting period, and the **balance** forms another.

- Corporation tax is charged on a company's **profits chargeable to corporation tax**. These include all of a company's income (except **UK dividends**) and chargeable gains.

- The rate of corporation tax depends on the level of the company's 'profits'. 'Profits' are **profits chargeable to corporation tax** plus **grossed up dividends received (FII).**

- If 'profits' exceed the **upper limit** corporation tax is charged at the **full** rate, 30% (FY00). If 'profits' are below the **small companies rate lower limit** corporation tax is charged at **small companies** rate, 20% (FY00). If 'profits' are between the **small companies rate upper and lower limits** corporation tax is charged at the **full** rate less marginal relief.

- If 'profits' are below the **starting rate lower limit,** corporation tax is charged at the **starting** rate, 10% (FY00). If 'profits' are between the **starting rate upper and lower limits** corporation tax is charged at the **small companies** rate less marginal relief.,

- The marginal relief formula is $\textbf{(upper limit - 'profits')} \times \dfrac{\textbf{PCTCT}}{\textbf{'profits'}}$ fraction

- Income tax is accounted for through quarterly returns.

  - Income tax is deducted from interest at **20%**, and from charges at **22%**.

- Trading losses and unrelieved trade charges may be carried forward against **future profits from the same trade**. Trading losses may also be set against **total profits** of the period of loss, and may then be carried back against **total profits** of the preceding period(s), later periods first. The carry back period is normally **12 months** but this is extended to **36 months** in the case of a loss arising in the 12 months prior to the cessation of trade.

- A company controlled by **five or fewer** participators is normally a close company.

  - Loans to participators give rise to a tax charge equal to **25% of the loan**, which can only be recovered when the loan is repaid.

  - Benefits in kind, if not taxed under Schedule E, are treated like **dividends** received.

TRY QUESTION 34

- One company's trading losses may be transferred to another company if they are in a group where there is a **75%** effective interest of the holding company in each relevant subsidiary.

  - Companies in a group should be selected to benefit from group relief depending on their marginal tax rates.

- Companies in a 75% group (with over 50% effective interest) transfer assets between each other at **no gain and no loss**. Capital losses **may not** be surrendered.

- Companies that pay tax at the **full** rate must pay 72% of their estimated corporation tax liability for the second accounting period ending after 30 June 1999 by **quarterly** instalments.

TRY QUESTIONS 32, 33 AND 35 TO 39

32   **HIGHRISE LTD (12/95)**   *45 mins*

(a)   Highrise Ltd is an unquoted trading company. Highrise Ltd has always had an accounting date of 30 June, with its most recent accounts being prepared to 30 June 1999. However, the company now plans to change its accounting date to 31 December. Highrise Ltd has forecast that its results for the 18 month period to 31 December 2000 will be as follows.

   (i)   Tax adjusted Schedule D1 trading profits before capital allowances, per six monthly period will be:

	£
Six months to 31.12.99	141,000
Six months to 30.6.00	126,000
Six months to 31.12.00	165,000

   (ii)   The tax written-down value of plant and machinery at 1 July 1999 is £20,000. On 31 May 2000 Highrise Ltd will purchase plant costing £75,000.

   (iii) Highrise Ltd owns two freehold office buildings which have always been rented out unfurnished. These are both to be sold. The first building at Ampton will be sold on 31 December 1999 resulting in a chargeable gain of £42,000, whilst the second building at Bodford will be sold on 31 May 2000 resulting in an allowable capital loss of £38,000.

   (iv)   The building at Ampton is currently let at £48,000 pa rent being due quarterly in advance on 1 January, 1 April etc. The building at Bodford will be let for £1,000 per month until 30 April 2000, but will then be empty. It will be decorated at a cost of £12,000 during May 2000 prior to its disposal. Both lettings are at a full rent and Highrise Ltd is responsible for all repairs.

   (v)   Highrise Ltd has a 20% shareholding in Shortie Ltd, an unquoted trading company. A dividend of £11,250 (net) will be received from Shortie Ltd on 15 June 2000.

Required

Advise Highrise Ltd of whether it would be beneficial to:

(i)   prepare one set of accounts for the 18 month period to 31 December 2000; or

(ii)   prepare separate accounts for the six month period to 31 December 1999 and for the year ended 31 December 2000.

Your answer should include a calculation of Highrise Ltd's total mainstream corporation tax liability for the 18 month period to 31 December 2000 under each alternative.   (17 marks)

(b)   On 1 January 2001, Highrise Ltd is to purchase the 80% of Shortie Ltd's ordinary share capital that it does not already own. Shortie Ltd's results for the year ended 31 March 2001 are forecast to be:

	£
Schedule DI trading loss	155,000
Capital loss of sale of property - 1 September 2000	37,000

Shortie Ltd has a 10% shareholding in Minute Ltd. This investment is currently standing at a substantial capital loss.

Highrise Ltd has a 5% shareholding in Tiny Ltd. This investment is currently standing at a substantial capital gain.

Required

Briefly discuss how Highrise Ltd's acquisition of Shortie Ltd will affect the utilisation of Shortie Ltd's trading loss and capital loss that are forecast to arise in respect of the year ended 31 March 2001, and its unrealised capital loss in respect of its investment in Minute Ltd. You should assume that it is not possible for Shortie Ltd to carry back its trading loss to previous accounting periods. (8 marks)

(25 marks)

33 EASY SPEAK LTD (6/99)   *45 mins*

Easy-Speak Ltd is an unquoted company that manufactures mobile telephones. You should assume that today's date is 15 August 2000.

During 1999 Easy-Speak Ltd purchased a plot of land adjacent to its office building for £224,000, with the intention of having a new factory built on the site. However, the company has now decided to acquire a nearby factory that has recently been built by a building company, and the plot of land is therefore to be sold.

The new factory can be purchased at a cost of £430,000. This includes £80,000 for land, £87,000 for a general office, £44,500 for a drawing office and £28,500 for the heating and ventilation systems. As an alternative to outright purchase, the building company is prepared to grant a 15 year lease on the factory for a period of £280,000, with an annual rent of £27,600 payable in advance.

Easy-Speak Ltd has two alternatives regarding the plot of land acquired during 1999.

(a) The land can be sold in its existing state to a property development company for £320,000 on 25 September 2000. Easy-Speak Ltd will then have sufficient funds with which to acquire the leasehold of the new factory. The premium of £280,000 and the annual rent of £27,600 will be paid on 1 October 2000.

(b) The company can develop the land itself. To finance this development, Easy-Speak Ltd will need to take out a short-term bank loan of £150,000 on 1 September 2000. Interest will be charged on this loan at an annual rate of 12.5%. A building company will then be contracted to construct three industrial units on the site at a cost of £147,500.

   All three industrial units will be sold to a property investment company during December 2000 for £550,000. The short-term loan will be repaid on 31 December 2000. Easy-Speak Ltd will then have sufficient funds with which to purchase the new factory outright for £430,000 on 1 January 2001. This will be brought into trade use immediately.

The managing director of Easy-Speak Ltd understands that if the plot of land is sold in its existing state, then the transaction will be treated as a capital gain. However, if the land is developed, then the transaction is likely to be treated as an adventure in the nature of a trade.

Easy-Speak Ltd's Schedule D Case I profits for the year ended 31 March 2001 are forecast to be £270,000. This is before taking account of any of the above transactions. As at March 2000 Easy-Speak Ltd had unused capital losses of £61,600. The company is a small company as defined by the Companies Acts, and has no associated companies.

Required

(a) Explain the criteria that are used by the courts in deciding whether or not an isolated sale transaction will be treated as an adventure in the nature of trade. Your answer should include an explanation as to why the managing director of Easy-Speak Ltd is probably correct in her understanding of the tax implications arising from the two alternatives regarding the plot of land. You are not expected to quote from decided cases. (9 marks)

(b) Calculate Easy-Speak Ltd's forecast corporation tax liability for the year ended 31 March 2001 if the company:

(i) Sells the plot of land in its existing state and acquired the leasehold of the new factory.

(ii) Develops the plot of land and purchases the new factory outright.

Your answer should include advice as to whether or not it is beneficial for Easy-Speak Ltd to undertake the development of the plot of land. You should assume that the sale of the land in its existing state is treated as a capital gain, whilst the development of the land is treated as an adventure in the nature of trade. The indexation allowance and rollover relief should be ignored. (16 marks)

(25 marks)

34   BARGAINS LTD   *45 mins*

Bargains Ltd is a close company that buys and sells secondhand antiques. The company is under the control of the three Rotter brothers, Rodney, Reggie and Del, who each own one third of its ordinary share capital. However, only Rodney and Reggie are directors of the company, with Del being neither a director nor an employee.

Bargains Ltd was incorporated on 1 August 1999. On 1 January 2000 the company acquired business premises which were in a bad state of repair, and it immediately started to repair and refurbish them. On 1 February 2000 expenditure was incurred on an advertising campaign. The company commenced purchasing antiques for resale on 1 March 2000, but the business premises were not opened until 1 April 2000. On the same day the company registered for VAT and made its first sale. Accounts have been prepared for the period 1 August 1999 to 31 December 2000.

On 1 July 2000 Bargains Ltd bought three new 1,600 cc motor cars costing £10,575 each (including VAT), for the business and private use of Rodney, Reggie and Del. During 2000/01 the brothers' business mileage was Rodney 2,100 miles, Reggie 14,400 miles and Del nil miles. No private fuel is provided.

On 1 October 2000 Bargains Ltd made an interest free loan of £42,000 to Del, which he used to purchase a holiday villa in Spain. The loan has not yet been repaid.

Required

(a) (i) Set out the accounting periods for Bargains Ltd up to, and including, 31 December 2000.

(ii) How will Bargains Ltd's expenditure on its advertising campaign and the refurbishment of its business premises be treated for the purposes of corporation tax and VAT? (9 marks)

(b) What are the tax implications, for both Bargains Ltd and the Rotter brothers, arising from the provision of the three company motor cars? You should ignore the implications of NIC. (8 marks)

(c) Advise both Bargains Ltd and Del of the tax implications arising from the provision of the interest free loan. (4 marks)

(d) Outline the basis on which Bargains Ltd should account for VAT on the purchase and sale of its secondhand antiques. (4 marks)

(25 marks)

35   TARGET LTD (6/97)   *45 mins*

You are the tax adviser to Expansion Ltd, a company involved in the computer business. Expansion Ltd wishes to acquire Target Ltd, and has made an offer to the shareholders of that company which it would like to finalise on 1 July 2000. At present, the ordinary share capital of Target Ltd is owned equally by Arc Ltd, Bend Ltd and Curve Ltd, and it is not known whether one, two or all three of these companies will accept the offer. You should assume that today's date is 15 May 2000. The forecast of results of Expansion Ltd and Target Ltd for the year ended 31 December 2000 are as follows.

	Expansion Ltd	*Target Ltd*
	£	£
Adjusted Schedule D1 profit/(loss)	214,000	(137,700)
Trading losses brought forward	-	(9,200)
Capital gain	-	51,300
Capital losses brought forward	(9,600)	-

Expansion Ltd purchased £120,000 of 8% Company Loan Stock on 1 May 2000 with interest received six monthly in arrears, on 31 October and 30 April. On 31 January 2001 the company is to purchase a new freehold factory for £118,000.

Target Ltd's capital gain is in respect of the proposed sale of a freehold office building for £140,000 on 15 October 2000. One of the building's four floors has never been used for the purposes of Target Ltd's trade.

Expansion Ltd has sufficient internal funds in order to finance the acquisition of either one third or two thirds of Target Ltd's share capital. However, if it acquires all of Target Ltd's share capital it will have to issue £250,000 of 10% debentures on 1 July 2000. The debentures will be issued at a 3% discount to their nominal value, and will be redeemable in five years time. Debenture interest will be paid on 1 July and 1 January, and professional fees of £15,250 will be incurred in respect of the issue. Expansion Ltd's adjusted Schedule DI profit for the year ended 31 December 2000 has been calculated *before* taking into account the issue of debentures. The company's accounting policy is to write off the cost of finance on a straight-line basis over the period of the loan.

Neither Expansion Ltd nor Target Ltd has any subsidiary companies. Arc Ltd, Bend Ltd and Curve Ltd are all profitable companies, and they are not connected to each other or to Expansion Ltd. All the companies are resident in the UK.

Required

Calculate the mainstream corporation tax liability for both Expansion Ltd and Target Ltd for the year ended 31 December 2000 if:

(a)   Expansion Ltd acquires one third of Target Ltd's ordinary share capital from Arc Ltd on 1 July 2000.   (8 marks)

(b)   Expansion Ltd acquires two thirds of Target Ltd's ordinary share capital from Arc Ltd and Bend Ltd on 1 July 2000.   (5 marks)

(c)   Expansion Ltd acquires all of Target Ltd's ordinary share capital from Arc Ltd, Bend Ltd and Curve Ltd on 1 July 2000.   (12 marks)

Your answer should include an explanation of your treatment of Target Ltd's losses, Target Ltd's capital gain, and Expansion Ltd's issue of debentures. You should assume that reliefs are claimed in the most favourable manner.   **(25 marks)**

36   APPLE LTD (12/99)   *45 mins*

You should assume that today's date is 30 November 2001.

Apple Ltd has owned 80% of the ordinary share capital of Bramley Ltd and 85% of the ordinary share capital of Cox Ltd since these two companies were incorporated on 1 April 1999. Cox Ltd acquired 80% of the ordinary share capital of Delicious Ltd on 1 April 2000, the date of its incorporation.

The tax adjusted Schedule D Case I profits/(losses) of each company for the years 31 March 2000, 2001 and 2002 are as follows.

	Year ended 31 March 2000	Year ended 31 March 2001	Year ended 31 March 2002 (forecast)
	£	£	£
Apple Ltd	620,000	250,000	585,000
Bramley Ltd	(64,000)	52,000	70,000
Cox Ltd	83,000	(58,000)	40,000
Delicious Ltd	n/a	90,000	(15,000)

The following information is also available.

(1)   Apple Ltd sold a freehold office building on 10 March 2001 for £380,000, and this resulted in a capital gain of £120,000.

(2)   Apple Ltd sold a freehold warehouse on 5 October 2001 for £365,000, and this resulted in a capital gain of £80,000.

(3)   Cox Ltd purchased a freehold factory on 20 September 2001 for £360,000.

(4)   Delicious Ltd is planning to sell a leasehold factory building on 15 February 2002 for £180,000, and this will result in a capital loss of £44,000.

Because each of the subsidiary companies has minority shareholders, the managing director of Apple Ltd has proposed that:

(1)   Schedule D Case I trading losses should initially be carried back and relieved against profits of the loss making company, with any unrelieved amount then being carried forward.

(2)   Chargeable assets should not be transferred between group companies, and rollover relief should only be claimed where reinvestment is made by the company that incurred the chargeable gain.

Required

(a)   (i)   Explain the group relationship that must exist for Schedule D Case I trading losses to be surrendered between group companies. Distinguish this from the relationship that must exist for chargeable assets to be transferred between two companies in a group without incurring a chargeable gain or an allowable loss.

(4 marks)

       (ii)   Explain the factors that should be taken into account by the Apple Ltd group when deciding which group companies the Schedule D Case I trading losses should be surrendered to.   (3 marks)

       (iii) Explain why it may be beneficial for all of the eligible subsidiary companies to elect that their chargeable assets were transferred to Apple Ltd prior to being disposed of outside the group.   (2 marks)

(b)   (i)   Assuming that the managing director's proposals are followed, calculate the profits chargeable to corporation tax for each of the companies in the Apple Ltd group for the years ended 31 March 2000, 2001 and 2002 respectively.

(5 marks)

(ii)   Advise the Apple Ltd group of the amount of corporation tax that could be saved for the years ended 31 March 2000, 2001 and 2002 if reliefs were instead claimed in the most beneficial manner.   (11 marks)

Assume that Finance Act 2000 rates apply throughout.   **(25 marks)**

37   **ONGOING LTD (12/96)**   *45 mins*

Ongoing Ltd holds 80% of the ordinary share capital of Goodbye Ltd. Goodbye Ltd has faced deteriorating results in recent years, and therefore expects to cease trading on 31 December 2000. The company's expected results up to the date of its cessation are as follows.

	Adjusted D1 profit/ (loss)	Schedule A	Capital gain/ (loss)	Franked investment income	Patent royalty paid (gross)	Gift aid payment to charity (gross)
	£	£	£	£	£	£
12 months to 30.6.96	88,500	6,000	(24,000)	-	(12,000)	-
12 months to 30.6.97	59,000	-	-	-	(12,000)	-
6 months to 31.12.97	62,500	1,500	-	17,500	(6,000)	(1,000)
12 months to 31.12.98	47,000	-	10,800	30,000	(12,000)	(1,000)
12 months to 31.12.99	(68,000)	-	-	-	(15,000)	(1,000)
12 months to 31.12.00	(140,000)	-	72,000	-	(11,250)	(1,000)

The rental income relates to one floor of Goodbye Ltd's office building that was let out until 31 December 1997.

The forecast results of Ongoing Ltd for the year ended 31 March 2001 are as follows.

	£
Adjusted trading profit (before deduction of debenture interest)	93,000
Bank interest accrued	3,500
Debenture interest payable (trade item)	(12,000)

As at 31 March 2000 Ongoing Ltd had unused trading losses of £14,500.

On 1 April 2000 Ongoing Ltd acquired 60% of the ordinary share capital of Forward Ltd. All of the other shareholders in Forward Ltd have holdings of less than 5%.

Required

(a)   Assuming that reliefs for trading losses are claimed in the most favourable manner:

(i)   Calculate Goodbye Ltd's mainstream corporation tax liabilities for all of the accounting periods from 1 July 1995 to 31 December 2000. Ignore group relief.

(10 marks)

(ii)   Calculate the tax refunds that will be due to Goodbye Ltd as a result of the loss relief claims in respect of its trading losses for the years ended 31 December 1999 and 31 December 2000. You should ignore the possibility of any repayment supplement being due.   (4 marks)

(iii)   Calculate Ongoing Ltd's mainstream corporation tax liability for the year to 31 March 2001. You should assume that the maximum amount of group relief is claimed from Goodbye Ltd.   (4 marks)

(b)   Hazell Ltd, an unconnected company, has profits chargeable to corporation tax for the year to 30 June 2001 of £2,000,000. A notice to file its corporation tax return for this accounting period was received on 1 September 2001. The company has always paid corporation tax at the full rate.

    (i)   Calculate the corporation tax liability due on these profits and explain when this will be due for payment. (5 marks)

    (ii)   State the date by which Hazell Ltd's corporation tax return for the year must be filed and explain what rights the Revenue have to enquire into the return. (2 marks)

(25 marks)

38   OCEAN PLC (6/95)   *45 mins*

You are the tax adviser to Ocean plc, the holding company for a group of companies involved in the retail jewellery trade. For some time, Ocean plc has been trying to dispose of three loss making subsidiary companies. These subsidiaries are Tarn Ltd, Loch Ltd and Pool Ltd, all of which are 100% owned. Ocean plc has received an offer from Sea plc, an unconnected company also involved in the retail jewellery trade, who wishes to purchase the following.

(a)   80% of the ordinary share capital of Tarn Ltd
(b)   40% of the ordinary share capital of Loch Ltd
(c)   All of the net assets of Pool Ltd

In each case, the consideration paid by Sea plc will be in the form of cash. Each of these subsidiary companies owns a number of freehold shops whose value is substantially in excess of their original cost. In the case of Tarn Ltd, these shops were acquired from Ocean plc. All three subsidiary companies have unused trading losses. However, it is likely that Sea plc's marketing expertise will result in them becoming profitable within two or three years. All of the above companies are registered for VAT.

Required:

Draft a report covering the tax implications arising from the disposals as they affect:

(a)   Ocean plc;
(b)   Tarn Ltd, Loch Ltd and Pool Ltd;
(c)   Sea plc.

You should include tax planning advice as appropriate.

Your answer should be structured under the following headings as appropriate: 'capital gains', 'group status', 'VAT', 'trading losses' and 'capital allowances'. **(25 marks)**

39   STAR LTD (12/98)   *45 mins*

(a)   Star Ltd has two 100% subsidiaries, Zodiac Ltd and Exotic Ltd. All three companies are involved in the construction industry. The results of each company for the year ended 31 March 2001 are as follows:

	Star Ltd	*Zodiac Ltd*	*Exotic Ltd*
	£	£	£
Tax adjusted Schedule DI profit/(loss)	(125,000)	650,000	130,000
Capital gain	130,000	-	-
Royalty paid (gross)	(10,000)	-	-
Franked investment income	-	-	15,000

Star Ltd's capital gain arose from the sale of a warehouse on 15 April 2000 for £380,000. As at 31 March 2000 Star Ltd had unused trading losses of £7,500.

Required:

Calculate the mainstream corporation tax liability for each of the group companies for the year ended 31 March 2001. You should assume that reliefs are claimed in the most favourable manner. State the amounts that remain to be carried forward at 31.3.01.

(9 marks)

(b) Star Ltd is considering the following alternative ways of reinvesting the proceeds of £380,000 from the sale of its warehouse on 15 April 2000.

(1)   A freehold office building can be purchased for £290,000.

(2)   A leasehold office building on a 45-year lease can be purchased for a premium of £400,000.

(3)   A loan could be made to Zodiac Ltd so that is can purchase a freehold warehouse for £425,000.

Regardless of which alternative is chosen, the reinvestment will take place during February 2002.

Required:

(i)   Advise Star Ltd as to the 'rollover relief' that will be available in respect of each of the three alternative reinvestments.

(ii)   Briefly explain how the claims for rollover relief will affect the way in which Star Ltd's Schedule DI loss for the year ended 31 March 2001 is relieved (as part (a)).

(10 marks)

(c) Star Ltd and its two subsidiaries are registered as a group for VAT purposes, but the inclusion of Exotic Ltd is now being reconsidered. The relevant sales and purchases of the group companies for the year ended 31 March 2001 are as follows.

		Star Ltd £	*Zodiac Ltd* £	*Exotic Ltd* £
Sales:	Standard rated	1,900,000	-	-
	Zero rated	-	1,800,000	-
	Exempt	-	-	950,000
Purchases		(600,000)	(700,000)	(200,000)
Overhead expenditure		(450,000)	-	-
Management fee		100,000	(50,000)	(50,000)

The purchases, overhead expenditure and management fees are all standard rated. Each of the company's purchases relate to its own sales. The overhead expenditure cannot be directly attributed to any of the three companies' sales. All of the above figures are exclusive of VAT where applicable.

Required

Explain why it would have been beneficial to exclude Exotic Ltd from the group VAT registration throughout the year ended 31 March 2001. Your answer should be supported by appropriate calculations.

(6 marks)

(25 marks)

DO YOU KNOW - OVERSEAS ASPECTS AND TAX PLANNING

- *Check that you can fill in the blanks in the statements below before you attempt any questions. If in doubt, you should go back to your BPP Study Text and revise first.*

- The liability of an individual to UK taxation may be affected by their residence, their ordinary residence and their .... In some cases, overseas income is only taxable if it is remitted to the UK.

- Individuals must include the gross amount of overseas income in their income tax computation. Individuals can gross income up for .... tax only.

- Double tax relief for individuals is the lower of:

  o   ....; and

  o   ....

- The UK tax rate is computed by treating the overseas income as the .... of the taxpayer's income.

TRY QUESTIONS 40, 42 AND 43

- The .... amount of a company's foreign income must be included in calculating PCTCT.

- Double tax relief (DTR) is set against the company's corporation tax liability to arrive at its .... DTR on each source of income is the lower of

  ...., and

  ....

- Relief is available for underlying tax relating to a dividend received from a foreign company in which the UK company owns at least ...., either directly or indirectly.

- The formula for calculating underlying tax is:

  ....

TRY QUESTIONS 41 AND 44

- A company may be a controlled foreign company (CFC) if it is resident in a country where tax is payable at less that .... of the rate than it would have been on similar profits in the UK.

TRY QUESTIONS 45, 46 AND 47

- Matters which may affect the choice between trading as a sole trader or through a company include tax rates, tax payment dates, the tax regimes for dividends and salaries, and the taxation of any capital gains on sales of assets.

TRY QUESTIONS 48 TO 51

DID YOU KNOW - OVERSEAS ASPECTS AND TAX PLANNING

- *Could you fill in the blanks? The answers are in bold. Use this page for revision purposes as you approach the exam.*

- The liability of an individual to UK taxation may be affected by their residence, their ordinary residence and their **domicile**. In some cases, overseas income is only taxable if it is remitted to the UK.

- Individuals must include the gross amount of overseas income in their income tax computation. Individuals can gross income up for **withholding** tax only.

- Double tax relief for individuals is the lower of:

  ○ **overseas withholding tax on the overseas income**; and
  ○ **UK tax on the overseas income**.

- The UK tax rate is computed by treating the overseas income as the **top slice** of the taxpayer's income.

TRY QUESTIONS 40, 42 AND 43

- The **gross** amount of a company's foreign income must be included in calculating PCTCT.

- Double tax relief (DTR) is set against the company's corporation tax liability to arrive at its **MCT**.

  DTR on each source of income is the lower of

  UK tax on that income, and

  overseas tax on that income.

- Relief is available for underlying tax relating to a dividend received from a foreign company in which the UK company owns at least **10% of the voting power**, either directly or indirectly.

- The formula for calculating underlying tax is:

$$\textbf{Gross dividend income} \times \frac{\textbf{Foreign tax paid}}{\textbf{After tax accounting profit}}$$

TRY QUESTIONS 41 AND 44

- A company may be a controlled foreign company (CFC) if it is resident in a country where tax is payable at less that **three quarters** of the rate than it would have been on similar profits in the UK.

TRY QUESTIONS 45, 46 AND 47

- Matters which may affect the choice between trading as a sole trader or through a company include tax rates, tax payment dates, the tax regimes for dividends and salaries, and the taxation of any capital gains on sales of assets.

TRY QUESTIONS 48 TO 51

40 TUTORIAL QUESTION: DOUBLE TAXATION RELIEF FOR INDIVIDUALS

(a) Mr Poirot is a Belgian oil engineer who is employed by a Belgian company and who maintains his house in Antwerp. From 1 March 1993 he has worked almost totally in the United Kingdom. His annual salary is paid in the United Kingdom and with benefits in kind totals £45,000. He opened a bank account in London on 7 April 1993: interest credited on 28 February 2001 was £800. Savings income arising in Belgium was £3,500 (when converted into sterling) and was paid into his account in Belgium: no remittance was made to him in the United Kingdom. His wife (who has no income) accompanies him to the United Kingdom: their only previous visits were three short holidays between 1976 and 1987.

Required

Compute Mr Poirot's liability to UK income tax for 2000/01. Ignore non-UK tax.

Outline his residence and domicile status for UK tax purposes.

(b) Mr Wain is a single man whose salary as a sales representative (including benefits in kind) is £31,644 a year. His National Savings Bank investment account interest paid on 31 December 2000 was £1,490. He also has dividends arising outside the United Kingdom of £2,400 a year (sterling equivalent) after the foreign tax withheld of 40%. He remits £2,000 a year to the United Kingdom, the remainder being used to maintain his invalid brother, aged 36, who lives in Spain.

Required

Compute Mr Wain's United Kingdom tax liability for 2000/01.

Guidance notes

1 Before computing Mr Poirot's UK income tax liability, you should consider his domicile. This will affect his liability to UK income tax on some of his income.

2 There is nothing to suggest that Mr Wain is anything other than UK resident, ordinarily resident and domiciled. This determines how much of his overseas income is taxable in the UK.

3 Double taxation relief is given because not all of the gross income from an overseas source is available to the UK taxpayer at the stage immediately before UK tax is imposed: some of the income has already been taken in overseas tax. If credit relief is to be claimed, the gross income must be subject to UK tax.

4 Do check for any restriction on double taxation relief. The UK government does not actually give away money or reduce the UK tax on UK income (as opposed to reducing the UK tax on overseas income) in order to compensate taxpayers for high rates of overseas tax.

41 TUTORIAL QUESTION: DOUBLE TAX RELIEF FOR COMPANIES

Stripe Ltd, is resident in the UK, and had the following results for the year ended 31 March 2001.

	Stripe Ltd £
UK trading profits	800,000
Utopia branch profits (gross)	600,000
UK capital gains	95,000
Dividend income (including withholding tax)	210,000
UK bank interest receivable	Nil
Trade charges paid (gross)	85,000

The Utopian branch profits were subject to overseas taxation at a rate of 37%.

The dividend income represents a dividend on a 20% shareholding in Lesslin Inc, a company resident in Erehwon. Erehwon has a rate of withholding tax of 12%.

The translated accounts of Lesslin Inc for the same period showed:

	£	£
Profit before tax		2,590,000
Less: provision for tax	510,000	
under-provision for previous years	230,000	
		740,000
Profit after tax		1,850,000
Less: dividend paid		1,050,000
Retained profit		800,000

The tax paid for the year was eventually agreed at £305,000.

Required

Calculate the mainstream corporation tax liability of Stripe Ltd for the year ended 31 March 2001.

Guidance notes

1   Start by grossing the dividend income up for underlying tax and then include the gross figure in computing Stripe Ltd's PCTCT.

2   Once you have arrived at PCTCT calculate corporation tax in the normal way and then deduct any double tax relief.

3   Double tax relief on each source of overseas income is the lower of the UK tax on the overseas income and the overseas tax on that income.

42   **OLIVER SEAS (12/99)**   *45 mins*

Oliver Seas, an engineer, commenced employment with Overseas Aid, a charity involved in helping third world countries, on 1 July 2000. Prior to 30 June 2000 he was unemployed. On 1 December 2000 Oliver was sent to the country of Changa for an eighteen-month assignment to help local farmers. Until 30 November 2000 he has always been resident and ordinarily resident in the UK. Oliver has no intention of changing his UK domicile status.

Oliver is paid a salary of £2,600 per month by Overseas Aid, and Changan tax of £140 per month will be payable in respect of this salary while he is working in Changa. Oliver has the following other income for 2000/01.

(1)   Schedule A profits of £825 per month commencing on 1 December 2000 from the rental of his main residence situated in the UK.

(2)   Dividends of £3,600 (net) and £2,340 (net) from a shareholding in Medusa plc, a UK company. The dividends were received on 30 June and 31 December 2000 respectively.

(3)   Schedule D Case V profits of £800 (gross) per month from the rental of a holiday apartment situated in the country of Farland. The profits are subject to Farlandian tax at the rate of 35%.

(4)   Interest of £510 (net) per month from a bank deposit account situated in Farland. The interest is subject to Farlandian withholding tax at the rate of 15%. This account was closed on 5 April 2001, and the capital was reinvested in a bank deposit account situated in the UK.

Oliver originally purchased 10,000 £1 ordinary shares in Medusa plc during 1995. The cost of these shares (indexed to April 1998) was £46,400. During 2000/01 he undertook the following transactions in this company's shares.

| 12 May 2000 | Bought | 4,500 shares for £27,450 |
| 5 October 2000 | Sold | 6,500 shares for £58,500 |

61

| 25 October 2000 | Bought | 2,000 shares for £18,400 |
| 3 April 2001 | Sold | 5,000 shares for £54,000 |

The shares in Medusa plc do not qualify as a business asset for CGT purposes.

There is no double taxation treaty between the UK and Changa. The double taxation treaty between the UK and Farland provides that taxes suffered in Farland are relieved as a tax credit against UK income tax.

All of the above figures are in Pounds sterling.

Required

(a) Explain why Oliver will be treated as not resident or ordinarily resident in the UK during the eighteen-month period working overseas commencing on 1 December 2000.

(3 marks)

(b) (i) Calculate the UK income tax payable by Oliver for 2000/01. Your answer should include an explanation of the double taxation relief that is available to Oliver.

(10 marks)

(ii) Advise Oliver of his UK CGT liability for 2000/01. (6 marks)

(c) Explain why it would have been beneficial for Oliver to have:

(i) Reinvested the capital from the bank deposit account closed on 5 April 2001 in another overseas bank account rather than in an account situated in the UK.

(2 marks)

(ii) Delayed the disposal of the 5,000 shares in Medusa plc on 3 April 2001 until 6 April 2001. (4 marks)

(25 marks)

43 BARNEY HALL (6/98)

45 mins

Barney Hall is employed by Sutol (UK) Ltd as a motor car designer, and he is currently (and has always been) resident, ordinary resident and domiciled in the UK. You should assume that today's date is 15 October 2000. On 1 November 2000 Barney is to be sent to the country of Yalam, where he will work on assignment for the parent company of Sutol (UK) Ltd. The assignment will be for a period of either fifteen months or eighteen months.

The company will pay for his travel expenses to Yalam costing £2,400, and subsistence expenses of £850 per month whilst working in Yalam. Barney's wife will visit him during January 2001, and he will pay for her travel expenses of £700. This amount will be reimbursed by Sutol (UK) Ltd. Barney is paid a salary of £33,600 pa by Sutol (UK) Ltd, and he will continue to be paid at the same rate whilst working overseas. Barney will not be subject to Yalamese tax in respect of his salary. He has the following other income:

(a) Schedule A profits of £2,600 pa from the rental of a property situated in the UK.

(b) Interest of £5,460 (net) pa from a bank deposit account in Yalam. The interest is subject to Yalamese tax at the rate of 30%.

Barney is to dispose of the following assets:

(a) On 15 December 2000 Barney is to sell a plot of land situated in Yalam for 180,000 Yalamese dollars. The exchange rate is currently $8 to £1. The plot of land was acquired as an investment on 1 January 1997 for 84,000 Yalamese dollars, when the exchange rate was $6 to £1. The disposal will not be subject to Yalamese tax.

(b) On 20 December 2001 Barney is to make a gift of 8,000 ordinary shares in ZYX plc to his daughter on her 21st birthday. The shares are currently quoted on the UK Stock Exchange at 210 - 218, and were acquired on 31 January 1997 for £9,450. He has made no previous gifts.

There is no double taxation agreement between the UK and Yalam. All of the above figures are in pounds sterling unless indicated otherwise.

Required

(a) Briefly explain the rules which determine whether a person is resident in the UK during a tax year. Your answer should include details of people leaving the UK and people coming to the UK. (6 marks)

(b) Advise Barney of the income tax and capital gains tax implications for 2000/01 if he works overseas for:
   (i)   a period of fifteen months, returning to the UK on 31 January 2002;
   (ii) a period of eighteen months, returning to the UK on 30 April 2002.

   Your answer should include a calculation of Barney's statutory total income and capital gains for 2000/01 in each case and explain how the gain made on 20 December 2001 will be charged to tax. You are not expected to calculate the tax liabilities. (15 marks)

(c) Comment on the IHT implications of his gift to his daughter in December 2001. Would it have made any difference if he gives her other shares of the same value which are quoted in Yalam instead? (4 marks)

(25 marks)

---

44 **EYETAKI INC (6/97)** *45 mins*

You are the tax adviser to Eyetaki Inc, a company resident in the country of Eyeland. Eyetaki Inc manufactures cameras in Eyeland, and has been selling these in the UK since 1 January 2001. Initially, Eyetaki Inc employed a UK based agent to sell their cameras and rented a warehouse in London in order to maintain a stock of goods. On 1 March 2001 Eyetaki Inc sent an office manager and two sales managers to the UK from their head office in Eyeland and rented an office building and showroom in London.

As the sale of cameras in the UK has been profitable, on 1 July 2001 Eyetaki Inc is to form a 10% subsidiary, Uktaki Ltd, which will be incorporated in the UK. The subsidiary will commence trading on 1 August 2001 and will make up its first accounts for the 18 month period to 31 December 2002. Uktaki Ltd is to initially sell cameras on a wholesale basis, but is to commence retail sales during 2002.

Uktaki Ltd is to purchase a new freehold building. The building will be used to:

(a) assemble cameras from components imported from Eyeland; and
(b) to store components prior to their assembly, and assembled cameras prior to sale.

The building will also contain a showroom and general offices. It is possible that the building will be situated in a designated enterprise zone.

Eyetaki Inc is to export the camera components to the UK at their normal trade selling price plus a markup of 25%. This is because the company wishes to maximise its own profits which are only subject to corporation tax at the rate of 15% in Eyeland.

Eyetaki Inc is to assign a director to the UK for a period of between two and three years in order to manage Uktaki Ltd. The director, who is currently resident and domiciled in Eyeland, will continue to be employed by Eyetaki Inc, and will perform duties both in the UK and Eyeland. The director has income from investments situated in Eyeland.

There is no double taxation treaty between the UK and Eyeland. Eyeland is not currently a member of the European Union, but is expected to become a member in the near future.

Required

(a) (i)   Advise Eyetaki Inc of whether or not it will be liable to UK corporation tax during the period from 1 January 2001 to 31 December 2002, and, if so, how the corporation tax liability will be calculated.

   (ii)   Set out Uktaki Ltd's accounting periods for the period up to, and including, 31 December 2002.   (7 marks)

(b)   Explain as to what extent the new freehold building to be purchased by Uktaki Ltd will qualify for Industrial Buildings Allowance, and state the Industrial Buildings Allowance that will be available.   (6 marks)

(c)   Briefly advise Uktaki Ltd of the basis on which it will have to account for VAT on the components imported from Eyeland. Explain how this basis will alter if Eyeland becomes a member of the European Union.   (4 marks)

(d)   Advise Eyetaki Inc and Uktaki Ltd of the tax implications arising from the invoicing of camera components at their normal trade selling price plus a markup of 25%.

                                                                                (3 marks)

(e)   Briefly state the circumstances in which the director of Eyetaki Inc will be liable to UK income tax in respect of:

   (i)   Emoluments for duties performed in the UK.
   (ii)   Emoluments for duties performed in Eyeland.
   (iii)   Investment income arising in Eyeland.   (5 marks)

                                                                          (25 marks)

45   **MAGEE PLC (PILOT PAPER)**   *45 mins*

(a)   Magee plc, a UK resident company with annual profits of £5,000,000, is planning to form a new 100% subsidiary, Gavin Ltd, that will carry out trading activities through a permanent establishment in Ruritania. There is no double taxation treaty between the UK and Ruritania. Magee plc does not want the company to be regarded as resident in the UK, and is considering three possible structures for Gavin Ltd, as follows.

   (i)   Incorporation in the UK, with directors' meetings being held in Ruritania.
   (ii)   Incorporation in Ruritania, with directors' meetings being held in the UK.
   (iii)   Incorporation in Ruritania, with directors' meetings being held in Ruritania.

   Required

   Advise Magee plc as to which of the above structures will meet its residence requirements for Gavin Ltd. You should give reasons for your conclusions in each case.
                                                                                (4 marks)

(b)   The main reason why Magee plc does not want Gavin Ltd to be regarded as resident in the UK is the low corporation tax rate of 8% that is applicable to companies resident in Ruritania. The forecast results for Gavin Ltd's first year of trading to 31 March 2001 are as follows.

	£
Profits per accounts (before taxation)	400,000
Tax adjusted profits:	
under Ruritanian legislation	450,000
under UK legislation	420,000

There is no withholding tax imposed on dividends paid out of Ruritania.

Required

Assuming that Gavin Ltd is regarded as resident in Ruritania, and is classed as a controlled foreign company:

(i) explain what a controlled foreign company is. You are not expected to explain the various exclusion tests;

(ii) explain why it would be beneficial for Magee plc, if Gavin Ltd were to pay a dividend equivalent to at least 90% of its profits. Your answer should be supported by appropriate calculations. (10 marks)

(c) Magee plc is to send Alex Tower, one of its senior executives, to Ruritania in order to carry out strategic planning duties for Gavin Ltd. Alex will continue to be employed and paid by Magee plc. He will leave the UK on 1 December 2001, and will stay in Ruritania for either 14 or 18 months depending on circumstances. During that period he will return to the UK for holidays at least once every three months, for about two weeks at a time. Alex will not suffer any taxation in Ruritania.

Required

Explain Alex's potential liability to UK taxation whilst he is working in Ruritania.

(7 marks)

(d) Magee plc is to send another senior employee, Tony Smith, to work in Ruritania for a period of nine months. During this period, his wife and two children, aged 15 and 20, plan to visit him twice. Tony will initially pay for all travelling expenses himself, both for himself and his family, but will then be reimbursed by Magee plc.

Required

State whether these reimbursements will be taxable emoluments under Schedule E, and whether he will be able to deduct the travelling expenses under Schedule E.

(4 marks)

(25 marks)

---

46   PADDINGTON LTD (12/97)   *45 mins*

Paddington Ltd, a UK resident company, has two 80% owned subsidiaries, Victoria Ltd and Waterloo Ltd. Victoria Ltd is a UK resident company, but Waterloo Ltd is resident in the country of Westoria. Paddington Ltd manufactures specialised medical equipment, and the equipment is then sold by its two subsidiaries. The forecast results of Paddington Ltd and Victoria Ltd for the year ended 31 March 2001 are as follows.

	Paddington Ltd	*Victoria Ltd*
	£	£
Adjusted Schedule DI profit	79,000	245,000
Capital gain	6,000	-
Patent royalty paid (gross)	(12,000)	-

As at 1 April 2000 Paddington Ltd had unused trading losses of £7,000.

The forecast results of Waterloo Ltd for the year ended 31 March 2001 are as follows.

	£	£
Trading profit		420,000
Taxation:		
Corporation tax	117,600	
Deferred tax	8,400	
		126,000
Distributable profits		294,000
Dividends paid:		
Net	213,400	
withholding tax at 3%	6,600	
		220,000
Retained profit		74,000

Waterloo Ltd's dividends will all be paid during, and are in respect of, the year ended 31 March 2001. The figures are in pound sterling. Waterloo Ltd is controlled from Westoria, and is not classified as a controlled foreign company. The double taxation treaty between the UK and Westoria provides that taxes suffered in Westoria are relieved as a tax credit against UK corporation tax.

In order to encourage inward investment, the country of Westoria is to reduce its rate of corporation tax on 1 April 2001, from the present rate of 30% to 10%.

Required

(a) Calculate Paddington Ltd's mainstream corporation tax liability for the year ended 31 March 2001. (9 marks)

(b) Advise Paddington Ltd as to whether or not the reduction of the corporation tax rate in Westoria will result in Waterloo Ltd being classified as a controlled foreign company. Briefly explain the tax implications of Waterloo Ltd being so classified.

(6 marks)

(c) Open ended investment companies (OEICs) are an investment vehicle designed to replace unit trusts. Briefly compare OEICs with unit trusts and state how a dividend received from an OEIC is taxed. (3 marks)

(d) State who may open an Individual Savings Account, what the maximum investment limit is and what tax reliefs are available on an account. (7 marks)

(25 marks)

47 **GLOBAL PLC (6/99)** *45 mins*

Global plc is a UK resident manufacturing company whose Schedule D case I profits for the year ended 31 March 2001 are forecast to be £2,250,000. The company has asked for your advice regarding transactions taking place during the year ended 31 March 2001. You should assume that today's date is 1 March 2001.

(a) On 1 November 2000 Global plc purchased a 90% shareholding in Nouveau Inc, a manufacturing company resident in and controlled from the country of Northia. Its forecast profits for the year ended 31 March 2001 are £700,000 and these will be subject to corporation tax at the rate of 25% in Northia. On 31 March 2001 Nouveau Inc is planning to pay a dividend of £300,000, and this will be subject to withholding tax at the rate of 5%.

(b) During March 2001 Global plc is planning to sell 10,000 units of a product to Nouveau Inc at a price of £12.75 per unit. This is 25% less than the trade-selling price given to other customers.

(c)   On 1 November 2000 Global plc set up a branch in Eastina. The branch is controlled from Eastina, and its forecast profits for the period to 31 March 2001 are £175,000. These are subject to tax at the rate of 40% in Eastina. 50% of the net of tax profits will be remitted to the UK.

(d)   On 1 December 2000 Global plc set up a 100% subsidiary, Middleman Inc, a company resident in and controlled from the country of Westonia. The subsidiary only sells products manufactured by Global plc, and its forecast profits for the period to 31 March 2001 are £450,000. These will be subject to Estonian corporation tax at the rate of 10%. On 15 April 2001 Middleman Inc will pay a dividend of £85,000.

(e)   On 31 March 2001 Global plc is planning to sell its 80% shareholding in Surplus Ltd, a company resident in the UK, for £1,750,000. The disposal will result in a chargeable gain (after indexation allowance) of £840,000. However, the sale agreement states that the sale proceeds will be reduced by any corporation tax liability that Surplus Ltd has in respect of intra-group capital transactions taking place prior to the date of sales.

Global plc transferred a factory to Surplus Ltd on 20 June 1996, when the factory was valued at £630,000. The factory originally cost Global plc £260,000 on 17 May 1991. It is still owned by Surplus Ltd, and is currently valued at £720,000. The indexation allowance from May 1991 to June 1996 is £48,620, and from May 1991 to March 2001 it is £113,700. Surplus Ltd makes up its accounts to 30 September and pays corporation tax at the full rate.

(f)   On 1 August 2000 Global plc purchased an 85% shareholding in Wanted Ltd, a UK resident company. The company is forecast to make a schedule D case I trading loss of £240,000 for the year ended 31 March 2001. On 20 June 2000 Wanted Ltd sold investments for £425,000 resulting in a capital loss of £170,000.

In all cases, the overseas forecast profits are the same for accounting and taxation purposes. The double taxation treaties between the UK and Northia, Eastina and Westonia provide that overseas taxes are relieved as a tax credit against UK corporation tax.

Required

(a)   Advise Global plc of the corporation tax implications of each of the transactions during the year ended 31 March 2001. Your answer should explain whether or not the overseas subsidiaries will be classified as controlled foreign companies, and should be supported by appropriate calculations.   (21 marks)

(b)   Explain how Global plc will be affected by the requirement to make quarterly instalment payments in respect of its corporation tax liability for the year ended 31 March 2001.   (4 marks)

You are not expected to calculate Global plc's corporation tax liability for the year ended 31 March 2001.

(25 marks)

48   **LUCY LEE (12/96)**   *45 mins*

(a)   'Every man is entitled if he can to order his affairs so that the tax attaching ... is less than it otherwise would be'.   Duke of Westminster v CIR (1935)

Required

Briefly explain the difference between tax avoidance and tax evasion.   (2 marks)

(b) You are the tax adviser to Lucy Lee, who has been a self-employed architect for the previous 20 years. You should assume that today's date is 20 April 2001. Lucy has asked for your advice on the following matters.

(i) From 1 April 2001 Lucy has employed her husband, who was previously unemployed, as a personal assistant at a salary of £28,000 pa. This is more than Lucy's previous personal assistant was paid, but she considers this to be good tax planning. Lucy estimates that her Schedule D Case II profit for the year ended 31 March 2002 will be £180,000. Her husband has no other income.

Lucy wants to know if employing her husband at a salary of £28,000 will result in an overall tax savings and how such an arrangement will be viewed by the Inland Revenue.

(ii) On 1 April 2001 Lucy set up a new business venture in partnership with her brother. The partnership designs building extensions for the general public at a fixed fee of £1,000 (including VAT). The forecast fee income is £35,000 pa. A deposit of £500 is paid upon the commencement of each contract, which takes one month to complete. An invoice is then issued 21 days after the completion of the contract, with the balance of the contract price being due within a further 14 days. The partnership uses the office premises, equipment and employees of Lucy's architectural business.

   (1) Lucy wants to know if the partnership will automatically have to account for VAT on its income as a result of her architectural business being registered for VAT

   (2) Assuming that the new partnership *does* automatically have to account for VAT on its income, Lucy wants advice as to the basis that output VAT will have to be accounted for.

(iii) Lucy's daughter is to get married on 25 May 2001, and Lucy is to make her a wedding gift of £12,500. Lucy's husband does not have any capital of his own, so Lucy is to make a gift of £12,500 to him on 24 May 2001 in order that he can make a similar wedding gift to the daughter. Neither Lucy nor her husband have made any lifetime transfers of value within the previous three years. Lucy wants to know the tax implications of such an arrangement.

Required

Advise Lucy in respect of the matters that she has raised. You should assume that the tax rates and allowances for 2000/01 apply throughout. You should note that marks for this part of the question will be allocated on the basis of:
7 marks to (i)
6 marks to (ii)
4 marks to (iii)   (17 marks)

(c) A company, which is not a member of a group, incurs a schedule D Case I trading loss in its nine month accounting period ended 31.12.01. State the alternative ways in which relief may be given for this loss if

(i)   the company continues trading
(ii) the company ceases trading on 31.12.01   (6 marks)

(25 marks)

49   GEWGAW LTD (6/99)   *45 mins*

Gewgaw Ltd commenced trading as a manufacturer of children's toys on 1 April 2000, and will make up its accounts to 31 March 2001.

VAT return

Gewgaw Ltd is in the process of completing its VAT return for the quarter ended 31 March 2001. The following information is available.

(a) Standard rated sales amounted to £62,500, with £54,200 being received from customers. Gewgaw Ltd offers it customers a 2.5% discount for payment within 30 days, and this is taken by 70% of them.

(b) Standard rated purchases amounted to £21,000, with £19,400 being paid to suppliers.

(c) On 31 March 2001 the company wrote off bad debts of £2,000 and £840 in respect of invoices due for payment on 10 August and 5 November 2000 respectively.

(d) On 1 January 2001 the company purchased a new 2000 cc motor car costing £17,300 for the use of its managing director. This figure includes a sunroof costing £800 that was fitted prior to the delivery of the motor car. Both these figures are inclusive of VAT.

(e) Standard rated expenses amounted to £14,640. This includes £480 for entertaining suppliers, £1,200 for repairs to the managing director's motor car, and the cost of petrol for this motor car of £900. The figure for petrol includes both business and private mileage. The relevant quarterly scale charge is £325 (inclusive of VAT).

Unless stated otherwise all of the above figures are exclusive of VAT.

Gewgaw Ltd does not operate the cash accounting scheme. The company's first three VAT returns were submitted on 20 August 2000, 26 October 2000 and 25 January 2001 respectively. The VAT payable in respect of the second and third returns was not paid until 11 November 2000 and 5 March 2001 respectively

Managing directors' motor car

The managing director drove a total of 11,000 miles during the period 1 January to 31 March 2001 (see (d) and (e) above). His ordinary commuting is a daily total of 85 miles, and this was driven 60 times during the period. In addition, he drove into work on three occasions at the weekend in order to turn off the burglar alarm. For five days the managing director drove directly from home to attend business meetings, with the average daily journey being 120 miles. He also drove 105 miles to attend the annual dinner party of a customer. Private travel amounted to 1,100 during the period, with the balance of the mileage being in respect of journeys made in the performance of the managing director's duties.

Bookkeeping

Gewgaw Ltd's bookkeeping is currently maintained by a bookkeeping agency at a cost of £525 per month net of VAT (this is included within the standard rated expenses of £14,640). An employee of Gewgaw Ltd with the relevant financial experience has offered to do the bookkeeping by working one extra day per week. The employee is currently paid a salary of £15,000 pa, and wants £100 per week, net of all taxes, for the extra day's work. He has no other income.

Required

(a) (i) Calculate the amount of VAT payable by Gewgaw Ltd for the quarter ended 31 March 2001, and explain the implications if this VAT payable is not paid until 20 May 2001. (8 marks)

(ii) State the conditions that Gewgaw Ltd needs to satisfy before it will be permitted to use the cash accounting and annual accounting schemes, and advise the company of whether it will be beneficial for it to use either scheme. (6 marks)

(b) Advise both the managing director and Gewgaw Ltd of the income tax, corporation tax and NIC implications arising from the provision of the company motor car. (8 marks)

(c) Advise Gewgaw Ltd as to whether it would be beneficial to accept the employee's offer to maintain the company's bookkeeping. (3 marks)

(25 marks)

50 DELIA JONES (6/99) *45 mins*

Delia Jones, aged 42, has been running successful restaurant business as a sole trader since 1 September 1996. She has recently accepted an offer from Fastfood Ltd, an unconnected company quoted on the Alternative Investment Market, to purchase her business. Fastfood Ltd would like to complete the purchase on 31 March 2001, but are prepared to delay until 30 April 2001 should this be beneficial for Delia. The purchase consideration will consist of either cash or ordinary shares in Fastfood Ltd. The following information is available.

(a) Delia's Schedule D case I profits are as follows.

	£
Year ended 31 August 1999	65,400
Year ended 31 August 2000	77,200
Period ended 31 March 2001 (forecast)	58,500
April 2001 (forecast)	9,000

The figures for the years ended 31 August 1999 and 2000 are adjusted for capital allowances, whilst those of the period ended 31 March 2001 and for April 2001 are before taking account of capital allowances. Delia has overlap profits brought forward of £24,200.

(b) The forecast market values of Delia's business assets at both 31 March 2001 and 30 April 2001 are as follows.

	£
Goodwill	125,000
Freehold property (1)	462,000
Freehold property (2)	118,000
Fixtures and fittings	240,000
Net current liabilities	(95,000)
	850,000

Freehold property (1) cost £230,000 in 1996 (indexed to April 1998). Freehold property (2) was purchased during June 2000 for £94,000. The goodwill has a nil cost.

(c) The tax written down value of the fixtures and fittings at 31 August 2000 was £114,000. Fixtures and fittings costing £31,000 were purchased on 15 December 2000. All of Delia's fixtures and fittings qualify as plant and machinery for capital allowances purposes, and are being sold for less than original cost.

(d) Delia has unused capital losses of £12,400 brought forward from 1999/00.

(e) Delia currently has no other income or outgoings. Her investment income will exceed £40,000 pa for 2001/02 onwards, regardless of whether the consideration it take as cash or shares.

(f) Delia will not become an employee or director of Fastfood Ltd. If the consideration is in the form of shares in Fastfood Ltd, then Delia's holding will represent 7.5% of the company's share capital. Delia will sell the shares at regular intervals over the next ten years.

(g) Both Delia and Fastfood Ltd are registered for VAT.

Required

(a) Assuming that the business is sold on 31 March 2001 with the consideration being wholly in the form of cash:

    (i) Calculate Delia's Schedule D case I assessment for 2000/01. (5 marks)

    (ii) Calculate Delia's CGT liability for 2000/01 (6 marks)

    (iii) Advise Delia of the VAT implications arising from the sale. (2 marks)

(b) Advise Delia as to the income tax, CGT and NIC implications of:

    (i) Delaying the sale of the business until 30 April 2001. (7 marks)

    (ii) Taking the consideration wholly in the form of ordinary shares in Fastfood Ltd, rather than as cash. (5 marks)

You should assume that the tax rates and allowances for 2000/01 apply throughout.

(25 marks)

---

51 **FRED BARLEY (12/95)** *45 mins*

Fred Barley is a 68 year old farmer who has been in business as a sole trader since 1 June 1997. Due to ill health (you should assume that Fred will not live for more than five years), Fred plans to retire on 31 May 2001 and at that date he will sell the farm to his son, Simon, aged 37. The following information is available.

(a) Due to his ill health, Fred expects to make tax adjusted Schedule D1 trading loss of £36,000 for the five months to 31 May 2001. His tax adjusted profits (before capital allowances) are as follows.

	£
Seven months to 31.12.97	70,000
Year ended 31.12.98	122,000
Year ended 31.12.99	81,000
Year ended 31.12.00	34,000

(b) Simon forecasts that he will make an adjusted trading loss (before capital allowances) of £12,000 for his first year of trading to 31 May 2002, but thereafter expects the business to be profitable.

(c) Apart from the purchase of some items of plant and machinery for a total of £34,000 on 1 October 1997, Fred did not buy or dispose of any plant and machinery. Fred did not claim a first year allowance. Simon does not expect to acquire any plant, other than that taken over from Fred.

(d) The market value of the business at 31 May 2001 is forecast to be £1,000,000, made up as follows.

	£
Farm land and farm buildings	600,000
Investments	250,000
Plant and machinery	35,000
Net current assets	115,000
	1,000,000

The farm land and farm buildings were purchased on 1 June 1997 for £115,000. The agricultural value of the farm land and farm buildings at 31 May 2001 will be £375,000. The investments consist of shares in quoted companies, and were purchased in June 1999 for £35,000. No item of plant and machinery cost in excess of £6,000 or is currently valued in excess of £6,000.

(e) Simon is to take over all of the assets of the business. He will purchase the farm land and farm buildings at their agricultural value of £375,000, but no consideration is to be paid in respect of the other assets.

(f) Fred is a widower, who has no other sources of income, and has not made any lifetime gifts of assets within the previous seven years. The value of his estate (excluding the business and the consideration to be paid by Simon) is £350,000.

Simon is married, and is presently employed by Fred as the farm manager of the business at a salary of £52,500 pa.

Required

(a) Advise Fred and Simon of the income tax implications arising from the sale of the business to Simon on 31 May 2001. You should *ignore* NIC, agricultural buildings allowance, farmers averaging of profits, and the possibility of any repayment supplement being due. (12 marks)

(b) Advise Fred and Simon of the capital gains tax implications arising from the sale of the business to Simon on 31 May 2001. (7 marks)

(c) Advise Fred and Simon of the inheritance tax implications arising from the sale of the business to Simon on 31 May 2001. (6 marks)

Your answer should include any tax planning points that you consider relevant. You should assume that the tax rates and allowances for 2000/01 apply throughout.

(25 marks)

Answer bank

1 TUTORIAL QUESTION: CAR AND TRAVEL

> **Tutor's hint**
>
> (a) **The first £500 of any benefit arising in respect of the private use of computer equipment is exempt.**
>
> (b) Where an employee is absent from the United Kingdom for a **continuous period of 60 days or more the travelling (but not accommodation) expenses of a spouse or child under 18 are allowable** if paid or reimbursed by an employer, in respect of up to two visits by the family in any tax year.
>
> (c) Tax **relief is available for all costs incurred in travelling to a temporary workplace** provided that the employee's attendance there is **necessary** rather than being for his personal convenience.
>
> (d) The loan to Mr Robb is at a low rate of interest. This leads to a taxable benefit.
>
> (e) Foreign pensions and annuities which are **not taxed on the remittance basis** are charged to tax subject to a **deduction of 10%.**

TAXABLE INCOME

	Non-savings £
Salary	20,000
Less superannuation (4%)	(800)
	19,200
Benefits in kind (W)	9,935
Less deductible travel expenses (£1,600 + £800)	(2,400)
Schedule E	26,735
Schedule D Case V foreign pension £750 × 90%	675
STI	27,410
Less personal allowance	(4,385)
Taxable income	23,025

Working: benefits in kind

	£
Car £17,000 × 15%	2,550
Car fuel	3,200
Computer equipment (20% of market value when first provided as a benefit) (20% × £3,300) – £500 (exemption)	160
Reimbursed travel expenses (£1,600 + £800)	2,400
Foreign accommodation	1,000
Loan benefit £25,000 × (10 – 4)% × 5/12	625
Benefits in kind	9,935

2 LANDSCAPE LTD

> **Tutor's hint**. Make sure you make an attempt at each part of the question and do not spend too long on any one part.
>
> **Examiner's comments**. The income tax treatment of shares in part (b) was generally badly answered. Parts (a) and (c) were generally well answered.

(a) *Peter Plain*

The distinction between employment (schedule E) and self employment (schedule D) is a fine one. Employment involves a contract of service, whereas self employment involves a contract for services. Taxpayers tend to prefer self employment because the rules for the deductibility of expenses are more generous but the following factors suggest that the Revenue will regard Peter as an employee rather than self employed:

(i) Peter works five days each week: If Peter cannot work when he chooses it suggests the **company has control** over him and he is an employee.

(ii) Peter **uses the company's equipment.**

(iii) Peter **does not have any other clients.**

(iv) The **computer function (and hence Peter) is an integral part of the company's business.**

Other factors the Revenue may consider are:

- **whether Peter must accept further work;**
- **whether the company must provide further** work;
- **whether Peter hires his own helpers;**
- **what degree of financial risk Peter takes;**
- **what degree of responsibility for investment and management Peter has;**
- **whether Peter can profit from sound management;**
- **the wording used in any agreement between Peter and the company.**

(b) *Richard Rosalind*

Under approved profit sharing schemes **the total of the initial market values of the shares allocated to any participant in a tax year must not exceed £3,000 or, if greater, 10% of an employee's salary, up to a maximum of £8,000.** This means that

Richard Rosalind will have received 2,400 shares $\left(\dfrac{3,600}{1.5} \right)$

As Richard held the shares sold on 31 Janaury 2001 for at least three years after they were allocated to him, no charge to income tax arises in 2000/01.

However, there is a charge to Schedule E income tax on the shares sold on 30 June 2000 on the lower of:

(i) the shares' market value when appropriated to the employee ($\dfrac{3,600}{2} = £1,800$)

(ii) the sale proceeds (£2,800).

That is on £1,800.

(c) *Simon Savanah*

The **statutory redundancy pay of £2,400 is exempt from income tax.** However, **both the holiday pay of £1,500 and the £5,000** in respect of the agreement not to work for a rival company are taxable in 2000/01.

The balance of the lump sum redundancy payment is £46,100 (£55,000 – £2,400 – £1,500 – £5,000). If the payment is a genuine *ex grata* redundancy payment, £27,600 (£30,000 – £2,400) is exempt. £8,500 is taxable in 2000/01. The balance of £10,000 is taxable when received in 2001/02.

(d) *Trevor Tundra*

Landscape Ltd is a close company and Trevor Tundra is a participator. This means that **Trevor will be treated as though he has received dividends equal to the schedule E income that would have arisen in 2000/01 if he had been a director or an employee** of Landscape Ltd:

	£
Car (£14,000 × 35%)	4,900
Loan (£40,000 × 2/12 × 10 %) + (£15,000 × 7/12 × 10%)	1,542
Loan written off	15,000
Amount treated as a net distribution	21,442

(e) *Ursula, Violet and Wilma*

Ursula, Violet and Wilma are all working in Cambridge in the performance of their duties. **Tax relief is available for the cost of travel between home and Cambridge, if Cambridge is a 'temporary' place of work. A place of work is classed as a temporary workplace if the employee does not work there continuously for a period which lasts (or is expected to last) more than 24 months.**

Therefore, the cost of all of Ursula's travel to Cambridge qualifies for tax relief. Under the fixed profit car scheme, the mileage allowance that Ursula receives from the company is tax free and she can make an expense claim as follows:

	£
FPCS:	
4,000 × 45p	1,800
800 × 25p	200
	2,000
Less: mileage allowance received (36p)	(1,728)
Expense claim	272

As Violet was initially expected to work in Cambridge for more than 24 months the train fare initially paid by Landscape Ltd is a taxable benefit in kind. However, from 1 January 2001 no taxable benefit in kind arises in respect of the train fare because Violet's period of secondment to Cambridge is no longer expected to exceed 24 months.

Wilma should be entitled to full tax relief for the cost of her journey's to Cambridge. Under the fixed profit car scheme Wilma will be assessed on a benefit as follows:

	£
Mileage allowance received (18,000 × 36p)	6,480
Less: Fixed profit car scheme	
4,000 × 45p	(1,800)
14,000 × 25p	(3,500)
Taxable benefit in kind	1,180

Marking guide	Marks
Peter Plain	
Contract of service v contract for services	1
Factors 1 mark each max.	5
Conclusion	1
Richard Rosland	
Number of shares	1
Three year time limit	1
Schedule E charge	1
Shares sold on 31 January 2001	1
Simon Savannah	
Statutory redundancy pay	1
Holiday pay/Restrictive covenant	1
Balance of lump sum payment	1
Receipts basis	1
Calculation	1
Trevor Tundra	
Participator	1
Company car	1
Loan	3
Ursula Upland, Violet Veld, and Wilma Wood	
Performance of duties	1
Temporary workplace	1
Ursula	2
Violet	2
Wilma	2
Available	29
Maximum	25

3   CLIFFORD JONES

> **Tutor's hint**. On the facts given, there are several tax effects of marriage and tax planning opportunities. In questions like this one, you should look at each fact in turn to see what effect or opportunity it suggests. This question has been changed to reflect changes to tax reducers. However, there are still many relevant points to note.

(a) In 2000/01 the couple will be entitled to the **married couple's age allowance,** because Clifford was 65 before 6 April 2000. This is a tax reducer, saving tax at 10%. The allowance for 2000/01 is £5,185 maximum, £2,000 minimum. As Clifford's statutory income will be well in excess of the income limit of £17,000 for age allowance purposes, the couple will be entitled to the minimum amount of the MCAA.

The tax reduction will be given to Clifford if no election is made. However, **the couple can jointly elect to transfer all of the minimum amount to Dinah. Alternatively, she can unilaterally elect to have half of the minimum amount transferred to her**. As there is not a full tax month before the marriage there will be no need to pro-rate the amount of allowance available.

Where an income-yielding asset such as the holiday cottage is owned jointly by married couples, the Inland Revenue will **split the income between the spouses equally unless a declaration is made that the interests of the spouses are in fact in**

some other specified proportion. If the 75:25 split is to be maintained, a declaration will have to be made.

(b) On the figures given, Dinah will have some unused basic rate band while Clifford will be a higher rate taxpayer. The main tax planning measure to take is therefore to **transfer income to Dinah, so as to use up her basic rate band.** This can be done by merging the two businesses into a partnership, and by transferring the holiday cottage and the building society account into Dinah's sole name. The 2000/01 tax computations without taking these suggested measures are as follows.

Clifford

	Non-savings	Savings (excl dividend)	Total
	£	£	£
Schedule D Case I	74,000		
Less personal pension contribution (40%)	(29,600)		
	44,400		
Schedule A (75: 25) (assumes declaration made)	3,750		
Building society interest		2,400	
	48,150	2,400	50,550
Less personal allowance	(4,385)		
Taxable income	43,765	2,400	46,165

	£
Income tax on non-savings income	
£1,520 × 10%	152
£26,880 × 22%	5,914
£15,365 × 40%	6,146
Income tax on savings (excl dividend) income	
£2,400 × 40%	960
	13,172
Less MCAA £2,000 × 10%	(200)
Tax liability	12,972
Class 2 NICs £2 × 52	£104
Class 4 NICs 7% × £(27,820 – 4,385)	£1,640

Note

Clifford's income is clearly above the income limit for age allowances and so only the minimum personal allowance and MCAA tax reducer is given.

Dinah

	Non-savings
	£
Schedule D Case I	20,000
Less personal pension contribution (40%)	(8,000)
	12,000
Schedule A (75: 25) (assumes declaration made)	1,250
	13,250
Less personal allowance	(4,385)
Taxable income	8,865

	£
Tax on non-savings income	
£1,520 × 10%	152
£7,345 × 22%	1,616
Tax liability	1,768

Class 2 NICs (£2 × 52)	£104
Class 4 NICs (£20,000 – £4,385) × 7%	£1,093

Capital gains tax

The non-business assets qualify for taper relief only at 5%, so the loss should be allocated against the gains made on these assets:

	£
Gains on non-business assets (£6,500 + £4,200)	10,700
Less loss	(2,400)
Gain benefit taper relief	8,300
Gain on non-business assets after taper relief £8,300 × 95%	7,885
Gain on business asset after taper relief (£9,000 × 75%)	6,750
	14,635
Less annual exemption	(7,200)
Chargeable gain	7,435

Tax at 20% = £1,487.

	Clifford	*Dinah*
Total liabilities (for couple £19,168)	£14,716	£4,452

The income to transfer to Dinah is:

(i)   the £2,400 building society interest: it is assumed that the building society will not insist on crediting the interest to date at the time of transfer into Dinah's sole name;

(ii)   the rental income from the cottage;

(iii) trading income so as to use up the balance of Dinah's basic rate band. The chargeable gain uses up £7,435 of the basic rate band so the amount remaining is:

	£
Basic rate band	26,880
Dinah's non-savings income	(7,345)
Transferred from Clifford (£3,750 + 2,400)	(6,150)
Chargeable gain	(7,435)
	5,950

However, additional trading income will allow additional personal pension contributions, so the unused basic rate band must therefore be grossed up at 40%. £5,950/(1 – 0.4) = £9,917. A partnership agreement should be drawn up to ensure that over the tax year as a whole, Dinah receives the right amount of trading income.

The revised computations are as follows.

Clifford

	Non-savings
	£
Schedule D Case I	64,083
Less personal pension contribution (40%)	(25,633)
	38,450
Less personal allowance	(4,385)
Taxable income	34,065

£

Income tax on non-savings income

	£
£1,520 × 10%	152
£26,880 × 22%	5,914
£5,665 × 40%	2,266
	8,332
Less MCAA £2,000 × 10%	(200)
Tax liability	8,132

Class 2 NICs £2 × 52 £104

Class 4 NICs 7% of profits between £4,385
and £27,820 £1,640

Dinah

	Non savings	Savings (excl dividend)
	£	£
Schedule D Case I	29,917	
Less personal pension contribution (40%)	(11,967)	
	17,950	
Schedule A	5,000	
Total non-savings income	22,950	
Building society interest × 100/80		2,400
Total income	22,950	2,400
Less personal allowance	(4,385)	
Taxable income	18,565	2,400

£

	£
Tax on non-savings income	
£1,520 × 10%	152
£17,045 × 22%	3,750
Tax on savings (excl dividend) income	
£2,400 × 20%	480
Tax liability	4,382

Class 2 NICs (£2 × 52) £104

Class 4 NICs £(27,820 – 4,385) × 7% £1,640

Capital gains tax liability (as before) 1,487

	Clifford	Dinah
Total liabilities (for couple £17,489)	£9,876	£7,613

The total tax saving is £(19,168 – 17,489) = £1,679.

(c) With the wills drafted as they are at present, only partial use will be made of the inheritance tax nil rate band of Clifford should he die first. The transfer to the surviving spouse will be exempt, and when the assets pass to the children on the death of that spouse, they will be subject to inheritance at 40% (possibly with the benefit of business property relief).

To ensure that the nil rate band of the first spouse to die is used in full, the wills should be re-written to leave each spouse's estate to the children, and not to the other spouse. If the spouses do not wish to do this because circumstances might change, the same effect could be achieved following the first death by the use of a deed of variation. Such a deed effectively re-writes the will.

(d) If the assets are put into an interest in possession trust, Dinah will have the use of them and the right to income from them during her lifetime, but will not be able to dispose of them: they will pass to the remainderman (Clifford's son) on Dinah's death.

Income tax

The trust will pay tax on its income at 20% (savings (excl dividend) income) or 22% (non-savings income), and will pay out income to Dinah net of the same tax rates. Dividends will be received by the trust net of a 10% tax credit and no further tax will be payable. Dinah will thus be in the same position as if she had received the income directly, except that there may be trust administration expenses (not tax-deductible) to pay.

CGT

The trust will take over the assets at their market values at Clifford's death, and will pass them on to Clifford's son at their market values at Dinah's death, but there will be no chargeable gains on either death. Gains on disposals by the trustees between the two deaths will be taxable at 34%, subject to an annual exemption of half of an individual's annual exemption.

IHT

The transfer into the trust on Clifford's death will be an exempt inter-spouse transfer because Dinah will have an interest in possession. The trust will not suffer the principal and exit charges, because they only apply to discretionary trusts, but if any property is transferred out of the trust it will be treated as a transfer by Dinah. On Dinah's death, the trust property will be taxed as part of Dinah's estate.

4 CHARLES CHOICE

Tutor's hint. This question has been amended to reflect syllabus changes. Part (c) is now extremely topical.

Examiner's comments. This was a reasonably popular question but not answered as well as would be expected given that the topics covered are examinable at Paper 7.

(a) **Accepting the company motor car**

The annual cost of accepting the company car is:

	£
Car benefit £14,400 × 25%	3,600
Less: contributions 12 × £35 (50 − 15)	(420)
	3,180
Fuel benefit (diesel)	2,170
	5,350

	£
Additional income tax liability at 22%	1,177
Contributions 12 × £50	600
Total annual cost to employee	1,777

Accepting the additional salary

The annual cost of accepting the additional salary is:

	£	£
Salary		2,800
Less: Income tax at 22%	616	
Class 1 NIC (Additional) (below UEL still)		
£2,800 at 10%	280	
		(896)
		1,904
Mileage allowance (£8,000 at 23p)		1,840
Tax relief on expense claim £1,540 × 22% (see below)		339
Additional income		4,083
Running costs	1,650	
Leasing cost (12 × £285)	3,420	
		(5,070)
Total annual cost to employee		987

Based on purely financial criteria, the cash alternative appears to be the most beneficial as it results in a saving of £790 (£1,777 – £987).

Expense claim

Strictly, Charles' mileage allowance is a taxable benefit and Charles can make a claim to deduct the business proportion of his motoring expenses. This results in a net tax deduction as follows:

	£
Taxable mileage allowance (£8,000 × 23p)	1,840
Less: Business proportion of expenses (£5,070 × 8,000/12,000)	(3,380)
Net deduction	(1,540)

Alternatively, Charles can take advantage of the Fixed Profit Car Scheme (FPCS). The mileage allowance of £1,840 is less than the tax free amount laid down under the scheme:

	£
£4,000 × 35p	1,400
£4,000 × 23p	800
Tax free under scheme	2,200

This means the £1,840 Charles receives is tax free and an expense claim can be made by Charles to deduct the excess of £360 (£2,200 – £1,840).

Clearly Charles will obtain a larger net tax deduction under the former alternative.

(b) (i) (1) Charles' contributions to his personal pension scheme for 2000/01 were £5,875 (£23,500 at 25%). Under the company's occupational pension scheme, Charles' contributions for 2001/2002 will be £1,410 (£23,500 at 6%). The saving net of tax is £3,483 (£5,875 – £1,410 = £4,465 less 22%).

(2) With the occupational pension scheme, the Northwest Bank plc will also contribute £1,410 each year on Charles' behalf.

(3) A personal pension scheme is generally more flexible than an occupational pension scheme. This will be an important factor if Charles plans to leave the Northwest Bank plc in the foreseeable future.

(4) The pension payable under a personal pension scheme depends on the performance of the investment fund. The pension payable under an occupational pension scheme is based upon final salary and number of years' service. Thus the final pension received is predictable under the

employer scheme and potentially less at risk than the pension receivable from a personal pension scheme.

(5) The normal earliest retirement age under an occupational pension scheme is 60 but under a personal pension scheme it is 50.

(6) The income tax implications are similar for both schemes.

(ii) The maximum tax deductible contributions that Charles could make into the occupational pension scheme are £3,525 pa (£23,500 at 15%).

Additional voluntary contributions of £2,115 pa (£3,525 – £1,410) could therefore, either be paid into the occupational scheme, or into a separate freestanding scheme. If Charles contributes into the company scheme then tax relief will be given as a deduction against Charles' Schedule E income. If he contributes into a freestanding scheme then tax relief will be given by making the payments net of basic rate tax. Any higher rate tax relief (if due in the future although not due on current salary levels) will be given through the PAYE coding system.

(c) As David Spence is leaving the UK for less than **five complete tax years** the gain on the sale of the holiday cottage will be subject to UK CGT. **Gains made during the year of departure are chargeable in that year**. If the cottage is sold during March 2001 the gain will, therefore, be subject to CGT in 2000/01. **Gains made in subsequent years are chargeable in the year that the individual resumes residence in the UK.** This means that if David delays the sale until September 2001 he will not be assessed on the gain until 2004/2005.

Marking guide		Marks
(a)	*Accepting the company motor car*	
	Car benefit	1
	Contributions	1
	Fuel benefit	1
	Total annual cost	1
	Accepting the cash alternative	
	Income tax liability	1
	Class 1 NIC	1
	Mileage allowance	1
	Running and leasing costs	1
	Expense claim	
	Based on business expenditure	2
	Based on fixed profit car scheme	2
	Conclusion	1
	Maximum/Available	13
(b)	Contributions	2
	Company contributions	1
	Flexibility of personal pension scheme	1
	Pension payable	1
	Retirement age	1
	Income tax implications	1
	Additional voluntary contributions	1
	Schemes available	1
	Tax relief	1
	Available	10
	Maximum	7
(c)	Absent for 5 complete tax years	1
	Year departure	2
	Subsequent years	2
	Maximum/Available	5
		25

5   **WILLIAM WILES**

Tutor's hint. Tax relief is only available for maintenance payments made under a written agreement.

Examiner's comments. Many candidates did not appreciate that furnished holiday lets had to be dealt with separately from other properties.

(a) (i) The houses qualify to be treated as a trade under the furnished holiday letting rules, because they were:

  (1) **let furnished on a commercial basis with a view to the realisation of profits.**

  (2) available for commercial letting to the public **for at least 140 days** during 2000/01 (294 days and 224 days respectively).

  (3) **on average let for at least 70 days.** House 2 satisfies this test since the average for the two houses is 77 days.

  (4) **not occupied by the same person for more than 31 days for at least seven months** during 2000/01.

PUBLISHING

The tax advantages are that:

(1) **Relief for losses is available as if they were trading losses**, including the facility to set losses against other income. The usual Schedule A loss reliefs do not apply.

(2) **Capital allowances are available on furniture.**

(3) **The income qualifies as net relevant earnings for personal pension relief.**

(4) Capital gains tax **rollover relief, retirement relief, relief for gifts of business assets** and **relief for loans to traders are all available.**

(ii) The Schedule A loss on the furnished holiday lets must be calculated separately to the Schedule A loss arising on the other accommodation.

Schedule A loss on furnished holiday lets:

Rental income	£	£
House 1 (14 × £375)		5,250
House 2 (8 × £340)		2,720
		7,970
Expenses		
Business rates (£730 + £590)	1,320	
Insurance (£310 + £330)	640	
Advertising (£545 + £225)	770	
Repairs	6,250	
Capital allowances		
House 1 (£6,500 × 40% (FYA))	2,600	
House 2 (£6,500 × 40% (FYA))	2,600	
Private use (re house 1)		
(£730 + £310 + £2,600) × 10/52	(700)	
		13,480
Schedule A loss		5,510

Schedule A loss on other lettings:

Rental income	£	£
House 3 (£8,600 × 3/12)		2,150
Premium received (W)		448
Furnished room (£4,600 – £4,250)		350
		2,948
Expenses		
Rent	6,200	
Repairs	710	
Wear and tear allowance (£2,150 × 10%)	215	
		7,125
Schedule A loss		4,177

William should claim 'rent a room' relief in respect of the letting of the furnished room in his main residence, since this is more beneficial than the normal basis of assessment (£4,600 – £825 = £3,775).

Working

Premium

	£	£
Premium received		8,000
Less: £8,000 × 2% × (4 − 1)		480
		7,520
Less allowance for premium paid		
Premium paid	85,000	
Less: £85,000 × 2% × (25 − 1)	40,800	
	44,200	
Relief available £44,200 × 4/25		(7,072)
		448

William can claim under s 380 ICTA 1988 to have the Schedule A loss of £5,510 arising in respect of furnished holiday accommodation to be set off against his total income for 2000/01, and/or his total income for 1999/00.

The Schedule A loss of £4,177 will be carried forward and set against the first available Schedule A profits.

(b) (i) **Payments made between 1 July 2000 and 31 December 2000**

No tax relief will be due in respect of voluntary maintenance payments or school fees paid

Payments made under the divorce settlement from 1 January 2001 onwards

The lump sum payment of £25,000 will not attract any tax relief.

The maintenance payments made under written agreement will attract tax relief of £143 (£475 × 3 = £1,425 at 10%) in 2000/01. This is because William was aged 65 before 6 April 2000.

Because the school fees are paid directly to the school (rather than to William's ex-wife) no tax relief is available in respect of them. If they had been channelled through the wife the maximum on which relief is available (£2,000 in 2000/01) means that relief would still have been unavailable for the full amount of maintenance and school fees paid.

(ii) William will be entitled to a personal allowance of £5,790 as he is aged 65 or over. This is reduced by £1 for every £2 of income over £17,000 until the allowance comes down to £4,385. William will also be entitled to a full **married couple's age allowance of for 2000/01**, unless a claim to transfer all or half of the minimum amount to his wife has been made. The maximum MCAA will be £5,185. The MCAA is reduced after the PA. The MCAA qualifies for relief as a tax reducer at 10%.

Marking guide			Marks	
(a)	(i)	*Qualification as furnished holiday letting*		
		Commercial basis	1	
		140 day rule	1	
		70 day rule	1	
		31 day test	1	
		Tax advantages		
		Capital allowances/Net relevant earnings	1	
		Loss relief/CGT reliefs	<u>1</u>	
		Available	<u>6</u>	
		Maximum		5
	(ii)	*Furnished holiday accommodation*		
		Separate identification	1	
		Rental income	1	
		Expenses	2	
		Capital allowances claim	1	
		Private adjustment	2	
		Other lettings		
		Rental income/Premium received - house 3	3	
		Furnished room	1	
		Expenses	2	
		Relief for losses		
		Furnished holiday lettings	1	
		Schedule A loss	<u>1</u>	
		Available	<u>15</u>	
		Maximum		14
(b)	(i)	*Voluntary payments*		
		No tax relief	1	
		Divorce settlement		
		Maintenance payments	2	
		Other payments	<u>1</u>	
		Available/maximum		4
	(ii)	Personal allowance	1	
		Married couple's age allowance	1	
		Income restriction	<u>1</u>	
		Available	3	<u>2</u>
		Maximum		<u><u>25</u></u>

6   DUNCAN MCBYTE

> **Tutor's hints**. It is important to allocate your time carefully when answering written questions.
>
> **Examiner's comments**. Many candidates wasted time by not carefully reading the requirements of the question.

(a) *Income tax*

The salary will be subject to income tax on a receipts basis. The salary assessable to income tax under schedule E in 2000/01 is £48,750 (£65,000 × 9/12). **The contractual entitlement to the termination bonus means that it will also be subject to income tax. However, the termination bonus will only be taxable in the year that it is received.**

The benefit in kind arising in respect of the accommodation will also be subject to income tax under Schedule E. The amount of the benefit in kind taxable in 2000/01 is:

	£
Rateable value (£6,700 × 9/12)	5,025
Additional benefit 10% (£170,000 – £75,000) × 9/12	7,125
Running costs (£6,200 × 9/12)	4,650
Furniture (20% × £21,000 × 9/12)	3,150
	19,950

A mileage allowance of up to the amount laid down by the fixed profit car scheme (FPCS) could be paid to Duncan tax free. If the amount paid by the company exceeds the amount laid down under the FPCS, the excess is taxable but if it is less than the amount laid down under the scheme, Duncan may claim to deduct the shortfall from his schedule E emoluments for the year. The position for 2000/01 is as follows:

FPCS amounts:	£
4,000 × 63p	2,520
5,000 × 36p	1,800
	4,320
Mileage allowance paid by company (9,000 × 40p)	(3,600)
Deductible from schedule E emoluments	720

As an alternative to using the FPCS Duncan could be taxed on the mileage allowance of £3,600 and claim a deduction for his actual business expenditure of £3,975 ((£1,800 × 9/12 + £380 × 9) × 1,000/1,200). Clearly this would be less beneficial for Duncan than using the FPCS.

The benefit in kind arising in respect of the loan is taxable under schedule E. The assessable benefit in kind for 2000/01 is

	£
$\dfrac{£60,000 + 50,000}{2} \times 10\% \times 9/12$	4,125
Less interest paid (£60,000 × 4% × 6/12) + (£50,000 × 4% × 3/12)	(1,700)
	2,425

The alternative method of calculating the interest benefit would give a benefit of £4,250 (£60,000 × 6/12 + £50,000 × 3/12) × 10% so it is assumed that this alternative method would not be used.

There will be no taxable benefit in respect of the subscription to the Institute of Chartered Computer Consultants, the liability insurance or the work related training. However, the £800 paid for the sports club membership will be a taxable benefit in kind in 2000/01. The full amount is taxable as it was all paid during January 2001.

As Duncan was **granted options under an approved company share option scheme there is no income tax on the grant of the options or on the profit arising from the exercise of the options** on 30 June 2003.

National insurance contributions

Employee Class 1 National insurance contributions (NIC) will be due in respect of both the salary and the termination bonus. The salary alone exceeds the Class 1 upper limit so the maximum amount of employee NICs will be due. **Employer NICs will also be due on the salary and the termination bonus.** Class 1A NICs will also be payable by the employer on the benefits in kind which are taxable under income tax.

(b) **If the options had not been granted under an approved company share option scheme a schedule E charge would arise on the exercise of the options** on 30 June 2003. If the market value of the shares on 30 June 2003 is £5 per share, the amount assessable under schedule E will be £48,750 (15,000 × £(5-1.75)). **If the share option**

scheme was approved there would be no tax charge until the shares were disposed of and the amount subject to capital gains tax is likely to be lower than the amount that would have been taxable had the option been unapproved.

(c) **As the residence is expected to be**

(i) **available for letting for at least 140 days in the tax year, and**
(ii) **actually let for at least 70 days of the year.**

the letting can be treated as a furnished holiday let. This means that capital allowances can be claimed and the amount assessable under Schedule A will be:

	£
Rental income	21,000
Letting Agency (22.5%)	4,725
Running costs	900
First year allowances (£24,000 × 40%)	9,600
Interest (£5,400 × 9/12)	4,050
	1,725

Marking guide

		Marks	
(a)	*Schedule E*		
	Salary	1	
	Termination bonus	1	
	Living accommodation:		
	Basic benefit	1	
	Additional benefit	2	
	Furniture/running costs	1	
	Mileage allowance		
	Fixed profit car scheme	2	
	Expense claim based on business expenditure	2	
	Beneficial loan		
	Benefit in kind	3	
	Alternative method	1	
	Other payments		
	Sports club membership	1	
	Other payments	1	
	Share options	2	
	National insurance contributions	2	
	Available	20	
	Maximum		17
(b)	No Schedule E charge on exercise	2	
	Lower capital gains tax charge	1	
	Maximum/Available		3
(c)	Qualification as furnished holiday letting	2	
	Interest	1	
	Rental income/Letting agency	1	
	Running costs	1	
	Capital allowances	1	
	Available	6	
	Maximum		5
	Maximum		25

7   **HAROLD AND WILMA CHAN**

> **Tutor's hints.** It was important to ensure that your answer to part (b) was accurate and contained sufficient detail to score high marks.
>
> **Examiner's comments.** Very few candidates appreciated that interest from national savings certificates is exempt from tax.

(a) (i)   *Harold*

	Non-savings £	Total £
Pension	16,000	
Schedule D Case V	1,150	
	17,150	17,150
Less: Personal allowance (W1)	(5,715)	
	11,435	11,435

	£
Income tax on non-savings income	
£1,520 × 10%	152
£9,915 × 22%	2,181
	2,333
Less: MCAA (£5,185 × 10%)	(519)
	1,814
Less: double tax relief	
Lower of (i) UK tax £269 (W2)	
(ii) overseas tax £403	(269)
Income tax liability	1,545

Wilma

	Non-savings £	Savings (excl dividend) £	Total £
Salary	45,000		
Pension (6%)	(2,700)		
	42,300		
Building society interest		4,500	
UK government stocks		2,400	
Schedule D Case V	1,150		
Schedule A	4,800		
	48,250	6,900	55,150
Less: Personal allowance	(4,385)		
	43,865	6,900	50,765

	£
Income tax on non-savings income	
£1,520 × 10%	152
£26,880 × 22%	5,914
£15,465 × 40%	6,186
Income tax on savings (excl dividend) income	
£6,900 × 40%	2,760
	15,012
Less: double tax relief	
Lower of (i) UK tax, £460	
(ii) Overseas tax, £403	(403)
Income tax liability	14,609

Tutorial note. Interest on national savings certificates is exempt from tax.

(ii)   Wilma's salary of £45,000 means that she will be a 40% taxpayer whether or not she receives any investment income. Harold, on the other hand, is a basic rate taxpayer. This means that all of the property, the building society account and the government stock should be transferred to Harold. The resulting tax computations for 2000/01 would have been:

Harold

	Non-savings £	Savings (excl dividend) £	Total £
Pension	16,000		
Schedule D Case V	2,300		
Schedule A	4,800		
Building society interest		4,500	
Interest on government stock		2,400	
	23,100	6,900	30,000
Less: Personal allowance	(4,385)		
	18,715	6,900	25,615

	£
Tax on non-savings income	
£1,520 × 10%	152
£17,195 × 22%	3,783
Tax on savings (excl dividend) income	
£6,900 × 20%	1,380
	5,315
Less: MCAA (£2,000 × 10%)	(200)
DTR lower of:	
(i) Overseas tax £805	
(ii) UK tax (£2,300 × 22%)	(506)
Income tax liability	4,609

Wilma

	Non-savings £	Total £
Salary	45,000	
Pension (6%)	(2,700)	
	42,300	42,300
Less: Personal allowance	(4,385)	
	37,915	37,915

	£
Income tax on non-savings income	
£1,520 × 10%	152
£26,880 × 22%	5,914
£9,515 × 40%	3,806
Income tax liability	9,872

Wilma's income tax liability has decreased by £4,737 (£14,609 – £9,872) whilst Harold's income tax liability has increased by £3,064 (£4,607 – £1,545). There would therefore have been an overall tax saving despite the fact that some double tax relief is lost and the rise in STI means that Harold would have lost his entitlement to both the age allowance and the full amount of MCAA.

(b) (i)   **ISAs are tax efficient savings accounts which can be made up of three components.**

- **Cash**
- **Life insurance**
- **Stocks and shares**

There are three distinct types of ISA:

(1) **Maxi-accounts** which must contain a stocks and shares component and may contain the other two components (either one or both):

(2) **Mini-accounts** which comprise a single component only; and

(3) **TESSA only** accounts, which consist of a cash component and can only accept subscriptions by way of transfers from matured tax exempt special savings accounts (TESSAs) (See below)

A 'maxi-account', must contain a stocks and shares component with or without other components. Subscribing to a maxi-account in one year precludes an investor from also subscribing to a mini-account of any type in that year. Investment in a TESSA only account in the same year is not, however, prohibited. **There is an annual subscription limit for maxi-accounts of £7,000 of which a maximum of £3,000 can be in cash and £1,000 in life insurance.** Harold and Wilma each have their own limits.

A **mini-account** comprises a single component only. Once a mini-account, for any component, has been subscribed to for a particular tax year the only other ISAs that may be subscribed to for that year are other mini-accounts comprising different components and a TESSA only account. **The annual subscription limits for mini-accounts are:**

(1) cash component accounts; £3,000
(2) insurance component accounts; £1,000
(3) stocks and shares component accounts; £3,000

A **TESSA only** ISA can accept subscriptions by way of transfers from matured TESSAs only and from no other source. Harold and Wilma's TESSAs will continue to operate and earn tax free interest until they mature at the end of their five year life. A transfer can then be made to a TESSA only ISA or to a cash ISA already opened as a mini-ISA or as part of a maxi-ISA.

The maximum investment in a TESSA only ISA is equal to the capital deposited in the matured TESSA. This means that it could be any amount up to £9,000; the maximum permitted investment in a TESSA over its 5 year life. The subscription limit of a TESSA only ISA is free-standing, it does not interact with the limits for maxi- or mini-accounts. The transfer from a TESSA to a TESSA only ISA account must be made within six months of the TESSA maturing.

(ii) **Investments within an ISA are exempt from both income and capital gains tax. In addition, up to and including 2003/04, the 10% tax credit is repayable on dividends from UK shares.**

There is no statutory minimum period for which an ISA must be held. A full or partial withdrawal may be made at any time without loss of the tax exemption.

Workings

1   *Personal allowance*

	£
Personal age allowance	5,790
Less: reduction	
½ (17,150 – 17,000)	(75)
	5,715

2   *UK tax on overseas income*

UK tax without overseas income:

	Non-savings £	*Total* £
Pension	16,000	
Less: personal allowance	(5,790)	
	10,210	10,210

	£
Income tax on non-savings income	
£1,520 × 10%	152
£8,690 × 22%	1,912
	2,064
Less MCAA	(519)
	1,545
UK tax with foreign income	(1,814)
Tax on foreign income	269

Marking guide

			Marks
(a)	**Income tax liability**		
	Pension/Schedule E	1	
	Pension contribution	1	
	BSI/Gilt interest	1	
	Schedule A/Schedule D Case V	1	
	Personal allowances	1	
	Income tax	1	
	MCAA	1	
	Double taxation relief	1	
		Maximum/Available	8
	Income tax saving		
	Utilisation of basic rate band	1	
	BSI/Gilt interest/UK property	2	
	Overseas property	1	
	Age related allowances	1	
	Overall decrease in tax liability	1	
	Calculation: Interest/Schedule A	1	
	Calculation: Schedule D Case V	1	
	Calculation: Personal allowance/MCAA	1	
		Available	9
		Maximum	8
(b)	Maxi-ISAs	2	
	Mini ISAs	2	
	TESSA only ISAs	2	
		Available	6
	Withdrawals any time	1	
	No income tax	1	
	No capital gains tax	1	
	Tax credit on dividends	1	
		Available	4
		Maximum	3
		Maximum	25

8 TUTORIAL QUESTION: A CHATTEL, LAND AND SHARES

(a) (i) **The vase**

	£
Proceeds	10,900
Less cost	(8,400)
Unindexed gain	2,500
Less indexation allowance	
$\dfrac{162.6 - 79.4}{79.4} = 1.048 \times £8,400 = £8,803$, but limited to £2,500	(2,500)
Chargeable gain	0

(ii) **The land**

	Cost £	31.3.82 value £
Proceeds	54,000	54,000
Less incidental costs of sale	(985)	(985)
Net sale proceeds	53,015	53,015
Less: cost	(2,000)	
value on 31.3.82		(15,000)
enhancement expenditure 1.6.84	(3,000)	(3,000)
Unindexed gain	48,015	35,015
Less indexation allowance:		
on 31.3.82 value		
$\dfrac{162.6 - 79.4}{79.4} = 1.048 \times £15,000$	(15,720)	(15,720)
on 1.6.84 expenditure		
$\dfrac{162.6 - 89.2}{89.2} = 0.823 \times £3,000$	(2,469)	(2,469)
	29,826	16,826

The chargeable gain is £16,826.
Gain after taper relief (6 April 2000 = 2 years plus additional year = 3 years)
95% × £16,826   £15,985

(iii) **The Index plc shares**

The May 1999 shares	£
Proceeds 2,000/12,000 × £42,000	7,000
Less cost	(5,314)
Chargeable gain	1,686

Tutorial note. There is no indexation after April 1998. No taper relief available on this non-business asset owned for one year only.

The 1982 holding	*No of shares*	*Cost* £	*31.3.82 value* £
Acquisition 1.5.81	10,000	9,000	
Acquisition 1.3.82	2,000	2,000	
	12,000	11,000	16,800

	£
Proceeds 10,000/12,000 × £42,000	35,000
Less 31 March 1982 value (gives a lower gain than cost)	
10,000/12,000 × £16,800	(14,000)
Unindexed gain	21,000
Less indexation allowance	
$\frac{162.6 - 79.4}{79.4} = 1.048 \times £14,000 =$	(14,672)
Chargeable gain	6,328
Gain after taper relief (3 years) 95% × £6,328	£6,012

(iv) **The property**

	£
Proceeds	60,000
Less cost	(25,000)
Unindexed gain	35,000
Less indexation allowance	
$\frac{162.6 - 87.2}{87.2} = 0.865 \times £25,000$	(21,625)
Chargeable gain	13,375

This is a business asset so taper relief is available for 6.4.98 – 5.4.00 = 2 years

Gain after taper relief (£13,375 × 75%)	£10,031

(v) **Tax liabilities**

Income tax position

	Non-savings £	*Dividends* £	*Total* £
Salary	6,000		
Dividends £16,875 × 100/90		18,750	
STI	6,000	18,750	24,750
Less personal allowance	(4,385)		
Taxable income	1,615	18,750	20,365

Income tax on non-savings income	£
£1,520 × 10%	152
£95 × 22%	21
Income tax on dividend income	
£18,750 × 10%	1,875
Income tax liability	2,048
Less tax credits on dividends £18,750 × 10%	(1,875)
Tax payable (subject to tax paid under PAYE)	173

Capital gains tax position

	£
Gain on vase	0
Gain on land	15,985
Gain on shares: May 1999 acquisition	1,686
the 1982 holding	6,012
Gain on tenanted property	10,031
	33,714
Less annual exemption	(7,200)
Taxable gains	26,514

Capital gains tax	£
£8,035 (£28,400 – £20,365) × 20%	1,607
£18,479 × 40%	7,392
Tax payable	8,999

(b) Capital gains tax for 2000/01 is due on 31 January 2002.

9   **ARTHUR RICH**

> **Tutor's hint.** Keep CGT and IHT aspects of a question separate, whenever possible.
>
> **Examiner's comments.** The answers of some candidates to part (a) were badly presented making it difficult to know which part of the question was being answered.

(a) **CGT implications of gifts**

(i)   *20.5.00*

	£
Deemed consideration (£3.40 × 100,000)	340,000
Less: indexed cost (£189,200 × $\frac{100,000}{200,000}$)	(94,600)
Gain eligible for retirement relief	245,400
Retirement relief	
100% × (£150,000 × 60%)	(90,000)
50% × (£245,400 – £90,000)	(77,700)
Gain after retirement relief	77,700

Arthur is entitled to retirement relief because he is over 50 years old, is a full time working director of Legacy Ltd, a trading company, and he owns not less than 5% of the ordinary share capital. As Arthur was only a shareholder for six years the upper and lower limits for retirement relief purposes are multiplied by 60%.

As Legacy Ltd is an unquoted trading company, Arthur and his son can jointly elect for gift relief to defer the gain remaining after retirement relief. If gift relief is claimed the base cost of the son's share will be reduced by £77,700 and no gain will remain chargeable on Arthur. However, this will result in a loss of taper relief of 25% of the gain. His son will start a new period of ownership for taper relief at the date of the gift.

(ii)   *30.6.00*

	£
Deemed proceeds	275,000
Less: cost	(47,600)
	227,400

Less: indexation to April 1998

$$£47,600 \times \left(\frac{162.6 - 81.9}{81.9}\right) = 0.985$$ (46,886)

Gain	180,514

Less: PPR exemption

$$£180,514 \times \frac{138}{216}$$ (115,328)

	65,186

Less: letting relief
Lower of:
(i)   £40,000
(ii)   £115,328
(iii)   £65,186   (40,000)

	25,186

The proportion of the gain arising during the period when Arthur occupied the house as his main residence and during the last 36 months of ownership is covered by the principal private residence exemption and is therefore, exempt. Letting relief, to a maximum of £40,000, is available to relieve the gain arising whilst the property was let.

As to the gift to the discretionary trust is a CLT for inheritance tax purposes, Arthur can make a gift relief claim to have the remaining gain of £25,186 held over. The gain of £25,186 is then deducted from the base cost of the property given to the trust and no gain remains chargeable on Arthur in 2000/01. Again there is a loss of taper relief, but only 5%.

(iii)   *28.11.00*

The disposal is initially matched with the acquisition in the next 30 days.

	£
Deemed proceeds (2,000 × £3.07 (W1))	6,140
Less: cost (16.12.00)	(6,500)
Allowable loss	(360)

Next match the disposal with the acquisitions since 6.4.98 on a LIFO basis.

	£
Deemed proceeds (10,000 × 3.07) (W1)	30,700
Less: cost	(23,700)
Gain before taper relief	7,000

Taper relief not due.

Finally match the disposal with shares in the FA 1985 pool.

	£
Deemed proceeds (12,000 × £3.07) (W1)	36,840
Less: indexed cost ($27,600 \times \frac{12,000}{15,000}$)	(22,080)
Gain before taper relief	14,760

No gift relief is available for quoted shares not in a personal company gifted to an individual. The loss should be set off against the shares with no taper relief ie,

	No taper £	*Taper* £
Shares acquired 30.6.00	7,000	
Shares in FA 1985 pool		14,760
Less: loss on shares acquired 16.12.00	(360)	
	6,640	14,760

Gains after taper relief	£
£6,640 × 100%	6,640
£14,760 × 95%	14,022
Total gains £(6,640 + 14,022)	20,662

(iv) *Motor car*

Motor cars are exempt assets for CGT purposes so there no CGT consequences arise as a result of the gift of the car.

IHT implications of gifts

(i) *PET*

	£
Value of Legacy Ltd shares before gift (200,000 × £5.50) (W2)	1,100,000
Less: value of Legacy Ltd shares after gift (100,000 × £3.75) (W2)	(375,000)
Diminution in Arthur's estate	725,000

This PET of £725,000 will become chargeable only if Arthur dies before 20 May 2007. Provided Arthur's son still holds his shares 100% business property relief will be available to reduce the value of the PET to £nil.

(ii) *Chargeable lifetime transfer*

CLT	£275,000

	£
IHT at lifetime rates	
£234,000 × 0%	NIL
£41,000 × 20/80	10,250
IHT payable by Arthur by 30.4.01	10,250

As Arthur will pay the IHT, the gift must be grossed up, giving a gross chargeable transfer of £285,250.

(iii) *PET to granddaughter*

	£
Gift (24,000 × £3.07) (W1)	73,680
Less: marriage exemption	(2,500)
	71,180

Arthur made a PET of £71,180 on 28.11.00 which will only become chargeable should he die before 28.11.07.

(iv) **As Arthur may drive the car whenever he pleases, the gift to his son is a gift with reservation of benefit.** As a result if Arthur dies IHT must be calculated by:

(1) treating the gift as a PET made on 8.12.00; and

(2) including the gift in Arthur's death estate at its market value on the date of death.

The higher of the IHT charges under (1) and (2) above then applies.

The gifts with reservation of benefit rules would be avoided if Arthur paid his son the full market value of his use of the car.

(b) Maximum IHT payable by trustees of rust as a result of Arthur's death.

  (i) **PET becomes chargeable**.

   Any IHT on the PET made to Arthur's son will be payable by his son rather than by the trustees of the discretionary trust. However, if his son disposes of the shares before the PET becomes chargeable, BPR will not be available and the PET will use up all of the £nil band.

  (ii) **Gross gift to trust** (part (a))   £285,250

   Assume nil band already used in previous seven years.

   IHT due by trustees:

	£
£285,250 × 40%	114,100
Less: lifetime tax	(10,250)
Maximum IHT	103,850

   ∴The maximum amount of insurance that the trustees should purchase is £103,850.

(c) **The discretionary trust will also be subject to the following IHT charges.**

  (i) **An exit charge on the value of any property removed from the trust.**

  (ii) **A principal charge on the capital value of the trust on every tenth anniversary following its creation.**

Workings

1   *Grant plc*

   The value of the shares is the lower of:

  (i) $\frac{1}{4}$ up principle
    $304p + \frac{1}{4}(320 - 304) = 308p$

  (ii) Average of highest/lowest marked bargains

    $\frac{288 + 326}{2} = 307p$

    ie 307p

2   *Legacy Ltd shares*

   For IHT purposes Arthur's wife's shares are related property. This means that he is initially treated as having part of a 60% holding. After the gift Arthur is treated as having part of a 40% holding.

Marking guide

		Marks	
(a)	**Ordinary shares in Legacy Ltd – CGT implications**		
	Entitlement to retirement relief	1	
	Gift relief	1	
	Capital gain	1	
	Retirement relief	1	
	Loss of taper relief	1	
	Gift to discretionary trust – CGT implications		
	Capital gain	1	
	Exemption	2	
	Letting relief	1	
	Gift relief	1	
	Ordinary shares in Grant plc – CGT implications		
	Value per share	1	
	Acquisition on 16 December 2000	1	
	Acquisition on 30 June 2000	1	
	1985 pool	1	
	CGT liability	1	
	Motor car		
	CGT exemption	1	
	Ordinary shares in Legacy Ltd – IHT implications		
	Potentially exempt transfer	1	
	Value transferred	2	
	Business property relief	1	
	Gift to discretionary trust – IHT implications		
	Chargeable lifetime transfer	1	
	IHT liability	1	
	Ordinary shares in Grant plc – IHT implications		
	Wedding exemption/potentially exempt transfer	1	
	Motor car		
	Gift with reservation	1	
	Potentially exempt transfer	1	
	Included in estate/relief for double charge	1	
	Available	26	
	Maximum		20
(b)	Additional IHT liability	1	
	Business property relief not available	1	
	Conclusion	1	
	Principal charge	1	
	Exit charges	1	
	Maximum/Available		5
	Maximum		25

10   ABC LTD

Tutor's hint. For individuals indexation is only available until April 1998.

(a) Agnes' CGT liability

Agnes is entitled to retirement relief because:

(i)   she is at least 50 years old;
(ii)   she is a full time working director of ABC Ltd;
(iii)   she owns at least 5% of the ordinary share capital;
(iv)   ABC Ltd in a trading company.

The relief will be restricted as follows.

(i)   **The gain eligible for relief is restricted by the ratio of the market value of ABC Ltd's chargeable business assets to its chargeable assets;**

$$\frac{500,000+1,050,000+400,000}{500,000+1,050,000+400,000+700,000} = \frac{1,950,000}{2,650,000}$$

(ii) The limits for retirement relief are restricted by $7/2/10$ since Agnes has only been both a shareholder and full time working director for seven years and six months.

As the freehold office building is sold at the same time as her shareholding and it has been let rent free to ABC Ltd it is treated as an associated disposal. Retirement relief is therefore available on the disposal, the qualifying period being also seven years and six months.

Capital gains tax liability

	£	£	£
Capital gain on shares in ABC Ltd (W1)			576,571
Gain eligible for relief			

$£576,571 \times \dfrac{£1,950,000}{£2,650,000} = \underline{£424,269}$

	£	£	£
Retirement relief			
£150,000 × $7^{1}/_{2}/10$		112,500	
50% (£424,269 – £112,500)		155,885	
			(268,385)
			308,186
Capital gain on freehold office building (W2)		110,066	
Retirement relief			
£600,000 × $7^{1}/_{2}/10$	450,000		
Less: used	(424,269)		
	25,731	(12,865)	
			97,201
			405,387

The assets disposed of are business assets that have been owned for two years.

Gain remaining after taper relief:

	£
(£405,387 × 75%)	304,040
Less annual exemption	(7,200)
	296,840
Capital gains tax at 40%	£118,736

Workings

1   **Shareholding in ABC Ltd**

	£
Deemed proceeds (£20,000 × £30)	600,000
(MV as Agnes, Betty and Chloe are connected persons)	
less: cost	(20,000)
	580,000
Indexation allowance to April 1998 £20,000 × $\dfrac{162.6-138.8}{138.8}$	(3,429)
Gain	576,571

2   **Freehold office building**

	£
Sale proceeds	200,000
Less: cost	(78,000)
	122,000
Indexation allowance £78,000 × $\dfrac{162.6-141.0}{141.0}$ (0.153)	(11,934)
Gain	110,066

(b) **IHT Liabilities**

31.12.00 PET

	£
Value transferred (£600,000 – £400,000)	200,000
BPR £200,000 × 100% × $\dfrac{(3,500,000-700,000)}{3,500,000}$	(160,000)
	40,000
Annual exemption 2000/01	(3,000)
1999/00	(3,000)
Value of PET	34,000
Chargeable transfers in previous 7 years	Nil
Nil band remaining	234,000
IHT liability £34,000 × Nil%	Nil

30 June 2003 Death estate

	£	£
Death estate (prior to transfers)		400,000
Cash proceeds (£400,000 + £200,000)	600,000	
Less CGT liability (see part (a))	(118,736)	
		481,264
Chargeable estate		881,264
Chargeable transfers in previous 7 years		34,000
Nil band remaining (£234,000 – £34,000)		200,000
IHT liability		
£200,000 at Nil%		Nil
£681,264 at 40%		272,506
		272,506

(c) **Interest free loan of £200,000**

As Chloe is a participator the following tax implications apply:

(i)   ABC Ltd must pay an amount of tax of £50,000 (£200,000 × 25%).

(ii)   This is due on 1 July 2002 (9 months after the end of the accounting period in which the loan is made).

(iii)   If part of the loan is repaid before 1.7.02, the tax charge is not due on the part repaid.

(iv)   The tax will be refunded when the loan is repaid (repayment is made 9 months after the end of the accounting period in which the loan is repaid).

(v)   There are no tax implications in respect of the above for Chloe unless the loan, or part of it, is written off.

(vi)   However, since Chloe is not a director or employee of the company the 'benefit' of an *interest free loan* will not be caught under Schedule E. Thus Chloe will be treated as though she had received a dividend from the company equal to the amount that would have been chargeable under Schedule E had she been an employee.

(d) **Purchase of shares by ABC Ltd**

(i)   Agnes will be taxed on £422,222 (£380,000 × 100/90) in 2000/01

Additional income tax liability

	£
£422,222 × 32.5%	137,222
Less: tax credit (422,222 × 10%)	(42,222)
	95,000

(ii) Since ABC Ltd is a close company and the purchase of own shares is an alteration in that company's unquoted share capital (purchased shares are cancelled) there has been a disposition by the participators of the company for IHT purposes. A transfer of value by the close company is apportioned amongst the participators according to their respective interests in the company immediately prior to the transfer (ie a 20% interest for Agnes). Such transfers are not PETs but rather are chargeable lifetime transfers.

	Marking guide	**Marks**	
(a)	*Retirement relief*		
	Qualifying conditions	1	
	Restriction to 75%	1	
	Restriction to chargeable business assets	1	
	Associated disposal	2	
	Calculation of CGT liability		
	Capital gain	1	
	Proportion relating to chargeable business assets	1	
	Retirement relief	1	
	Gain on freehold office building	1	
	Retirement relief on associated disposal	1	
	Annual exemption/CGT	1	
	Maximum/Available		11
(b)	*Potentially exempt transfer*		
	Value transferred	1	
	Business property relief	2	
	Annual exemptions/IHT liability	1	
	Estate at death		
	Capital gains tax deduction	1	
	Calculation of IHT liability	2	
	Maximum/Available		7
(c)	Payment of tax	1	
	Repayment of loan	1	
	Tax position of participator	2	
	Maximum/Available		4
(d)	Assessment on shareholder	2	
	IHT	2	
	Available	4	
	Maximum		3
	Maximum		25

11 BLUETONE LTD

> **Tutor's hint.** It is important to be aware of the different share valuation rules for inheritance tax and capital gains tax.
>
> **Examiner's comments.** In part (c) some candidates wasted time by explaining the conditions to be met for the purchase to be treated as a capital gain when this was clearly not a requirement of the question.

(a) *Melody's IHT liability*

The lifetime gifts made by her father will affect Melody's IHT liability as they will use up part of the available nil rate band. The amount of the lifetime gifts are:

		£
PET		30,000
Less:	Marriage exemption	(5,000)
	Annual exemption (96/97)	(3,000)
	Annual exemption (95/96)	(3,000)
		19,000

		£
Chargeable lifetime transfer		
Gift		164,000
Less:	Annual exemption (97/98)	(3,000)
		161,000

The available nil band on death is therefore £(234,000 – 19,000 – 161,000) = £54,000:

Death estate	£	£
Personalty		
Bluetone Ltd Shares (Note 1)		
£11 × 50,000		550,000
Expanse plc shares		
Lower of		
$\frac{1}{4}$ up $\frac{320-312}{4}+312=314$		
and		
mid-bargain $\frac{324+282}{2}=303$		
ie 303p x 42,000		127,260
World-Growth units (80p × 26,000)		20,800
Building society deposits (Note 2)		32,000
Life policy (proceeds)		61,000
		791,060
Less: income tax	6,600	
Gambling debts (Note 3)	Nil	
Funeral expenses	3,460	(10,060)
		781,000
Realty		
House	125,000	
Less: secured debt	(42,000)	83,000
Chargeable estate		864,000

Notes:

1 No BPR is available as Melody's father did not own the Bluetone shares for at least two years prior to his death.

2 No IHT relief is given to an ISA: only IT and CGT reliefs.

3 Gambling debts are not deductible.

IHT on estate

£(864,000 − 54,000) = £810,000 × 40% = £324,000

Melody's IHT

$$\frac{550,000}{864,000} \times £324,000 = \underline{\underline{£206,250}}$$

£206,250 is all due for payment on 31 August 2001 (or the delivery of the IHT account, if earlier).

Melody can elect to pay the tax in 10 equal annual interest-free instalments of £20,625. The first instalment is due on 31 August 2001.

(b) *CGT on Liam's gift*

	£
Deemed proceeds (£9 × 30,000)	270,000
Less: cost	(30,000)
Unindexed gain	240,000
Less: IA to April 1998	
$\dfrac{162.6 - 135.1}{135.1} \times £30,000$	(6,107)
Indexed gain	233,893

Gain immediately chargeable to CGT (excess proceeds):

£(75,000 − 30,000) = £45,000

	£
Gain after taper relief (75% × £45,000)	33,750
Less: Annual exemption	(7,200)
Taxable gain	26,550
Tax @ 40%	10,620

Gift relief £(233,893 − 45,000) = £188,893

No taper relief is available to reduce the gain deferred. Liam's son's qualifying period for taper relief will run from 20 March 2001. Thus the remainder of Liam's taper relief will be lost.

IHT on Liam's gift

The value of the lifetime transfer will be:

		£
Before:	50,000 × £15 (part of 50% holding with Opal)	750,000
After:	20,000 × £12.50 (part of 35% holding with Opal)	(250,000)
		500,000
Less:	Proceeds paid	(75,000)
Gift		425,000

BPR will be available at 100% as these are unquoted trading company shares. However, the relief will be withdrawn if Liam dies within seven years and his son does not own the shares as business property at the date of Liam's death (unless the shares have been sold and replaced with other business property).

(c) *Noel*

If repurchase treated as distribution:

£(550,000 − 50,000) = £500,000 net

	£
Grossed up $100/90 \times £500,000 =$	555,556
Tax @ 32.5%	180,556
Less: credit	(55,556)
Tax to pay	125,000

If treated as CGT disposal:

	£
Proceeds	550,000
Less: cost	(50,000)
Unindexed gain	500,000
Less: IA to April 1998	
$\dfrac{162.6 - 135.1}{135.1} \times £50,000$	(10,178)
Indexed gain	489,822
Less: retirement relief (9½ years)	
95% × £150,000 in full	
(Upper limit 95% × £600,000 = £570,000)	(142,500)
£(489,822 – 142,500) × 50%	(173,661)
Gain after retirement relief	173,661
Gain after taper relief (75% × £173,661)	130,246
Less Annual exemption	(7,200)
Taxable gain	123,046
Tax @ 40%	£49,218

Therefore it is better to use the CGT route (which is mandatory if the relevant conditions are satisfied in any case). Neither option has any effect for Bluetone Ltd.

Marking guide

			Marks
(a)	Wedding gift		1
	Chargeable lifetime transfer		1
	Shares in Expanse plc		1
	Shares in Bluetone Ltd/units in Word-Growth		1
	BPR not available		1
	Building society deposits/life policy		1
	Income tax/funeral expenses		1
	House		1
	IHT liability/IHT due by Melody		2
	Due date/instalments		1
		Available	11
		Maximum	10
(b)	CGT:		
	Gift relief		2
	Deemed consideration		1
	Cost/Indexation		1
	Taper relief		1
	Annual exemption/CGT		1
	IHT Value transferred		2
	BPR		1
		Available/Maximum	9
(c)	Retirement relief		2
	Capital gain		1
	Taper relief		1
	Additional income tax liability on distribution		1
	Conclusion		1
		Available/Maximum	6
		Maximum	25

12   MONTY NOBLE

Tutor's hint. It was necessary to consider the IHT position with and without the plan.
Examiner's comments. This was a popular question but the majority of candidates answered it quite badly.

(a) (i)   **IHT position prior to the implementation of the plan**

No IHT liability will arise at the date of Monty's death since his entire estate is left to his wife.

Upon Olive's death on 31 December 2003, the IHT liability will be as follows.

	£	£
Personalty		
Building society deposits		285,000
Ordinary shares in Congo Ltd 20,000 at £3.50 (note 1)	70,000	
Business property relief £70,000 × $\frac{80(100-20)}{100}$ × 100%	(56,000)	
		14,000
Agricultural land and buildings	225,000	
Agricultural property relief (note 2)	(180,000)	
		45,000
		344,000
Realty		
Main residence		330,000
Holiday cottages (£47,500 + £58,100 + £54,400)		160,000
Chargeable estate		834,000

IHT liability	£234,000 at nil %	nil
	£600,000 at 40%	240,000
	£834,000	240,000

IHT of £240,000 will be payable by the executors of Olive's estate by 30 June 2004 (or delivery of account if earlier).

Notes

1   BPR is only given in respect of assets used wholly or mainly for the purposes of the business. Property being let out is not being used for the business so BPR will not be due on that proportion of the asset.

2   APR is available since the property is let out for the purposes of agriculture, and has been owned for at least seven years. Olive is deemed to own the property for the period that Monty owned it. APR of 100% is thus available against the agricultural value of the asset.

IHT position following the implementation of the plan:
Monty's estate

	£	£
Personalty		
Building society deposits		285,000
Ordinary shares in Congo Ltd (W1)		70,000
Agricultural land and buildings	225,000	
Agricultural property relief	(180,000)	
		45,000
		400,000
Realty		
Main residence		255,000
Holiday cottages (3 × £55,000)	165,000	
Relief for reduction in value (W2)	(3,300)	
		161,700
		816,700
Exempt legacy - Olive (£255,000 + £270,000)		525,000
Chargeable estate		291,700
IHT liability £234,000 at nil %		nil
£57,700 at 40%		23,080
£291,700		23,080

£23,080 will be payable by the executors of the estate by 31 January 2001 (or delivery of account, if earlier).

Gift of main residence

The gift of the main residence by Olive to Peter will be a PET. It is unlikely to be treated as a gift with reservation since Olive is paying a commercial rent for the use of the two rooms. As a result of Olive's death within seven years, the PET will become chargeable as follows.

		£	£
Main residence			255,000
Annual exemptions	2000/01	3,000	
	1999/00	3,000	
			(6,000)
			249,000

		£
IHT liability	£234,000 at nil%	nil
	£15,000 at 40%	6,000
		6,000

IHT after taper relief £6,000 × 80% = £4,800

£4,800 must be paid by Peter by 30 June 2004.

Olive's estate

IHT on Olive's estate will be as follows.

	£
Cash	270,000
IHT liability £270,000 at 40%	108,000

£108,000 will be payable by the executors of Olive's estate by 30 June 2004.

IHT payable

	£
No plan	240,000
With plan (£23,080 + £4,800 + £108,000)	135,880
IHT saving	104,120

Workings

1 **BPR**. BPR is not available to offset against the value of the Congo Ltd shares since Monty has not owned the shares for at least two years.

2 Land and buildings sold within four years after death

A claim can be made to reduce the value of the holiday cottages to the **gross sale proceeds**. The relief is restricted because of the reinvestment in farm land.

	£
Cottage 1 (£55,000 – £47,500)	7,500
Cottage 2 (£55,000 – £58,100)	(3,100)
	4,400
Restriction £4,400 × $\dfrac{£27,000-£600}{£47,500+£58,100}$	(1,100)
	3,300

The loss on cottage 3 of £600 (£55,000 – £54,400) is ignored as it is less than £1,000.

(ii) A deed of variation must be made within **two years** of Monty's death. The deed must be **in writing**, and must be **signed by the beneficiaries under the original will** (in this case only Olive) **and the new beneficiaries under the revised terms of the will. A written election must then be made to the Inland Revenue within six months,** so that the will is treated as rewritten for IHT purposes.

(iii) The shares in Congo Ltd should be left to Olive. By the time of Olive's death the joint ownership period will be sufficient to ensure that 100% BPR will be available, resulting in an IHT saving of £22,400 (£56,000 at 40%). The shares will be included in Olive's death estate computation so the IHT of £5,600 (£14,000 at 40%) will be postponed until Olive's death.

Under the plan the full fall in value of cottage 1 is not taken into account due to the profit made on cottage number 2 and the reinvestment in land by the estate. The full £7,500 fall in value of cottage 1 would be available if cottage 2 is left to Peter or Penny (who could subsequently sell it), and the trust purchased the field itself by being left additional cash. This would save IHT of £1,680 (£7,500 – £3,300 = £4,200 at 40%).

(b) An **accumulation and maintenance trust** is one where the beneficiary or beneficiaries become **entitled to the trust assets or to interests in possession therein on or before attaining the age of 25.**

The proposed trust will not qualify as an accumulation and maintenance trust because the elder two children will be over the age of 25 when the youngest reaches 18.

The advantages of being treated as an accumulation and maintenance trust rather than a discretionary trust are:

(i) there is **no exit charge** when assets leave the trust;

(ii) there is **no principal charge** on every 10th anniversary of the trust's creation.

13   MING WONG

> **Tutor's hints**. In part (b) it was important to include an explanation of why assets were or were not subject to IHT. If you merely calculated the increase in the IHT liability, you would have lost many easy marks.
>
> **Examiner's comments**. The majority of candidates answered this question very well and there were a number of near perfect answers.

(a)   (i)   **Ming will be treated as domiciled in the UK if she has been resident in the UK for at least 17 out of the 20 tax years ending with the year in which any chargeable transfer is made.**

As Ming has been resident in the UK since 1986/87, she will become domiciled here for IHT purposes in respect of any chargeable transfers made in 2002/03 and later years.

(ii)   **Ming could acquire a domicile of choice in the UK under general law by severing all her ties with Yanga and settling in the UK with the clear intention of making her permanent home here.**

(b)   If Ming is non-UK domiciled only her UK assets are subject to UK IHT. However, once she becomes UK domiciled all of Ming's assets will be subject to IHT. The following rules apply in deciding which of Ming's assets are UK assets.

(i)   **Property is situated where it is physically located.** This means the residence is a UK asset but the house in Yanga is not.

(ii)   **The shares are not UK assets because they are not registered or normally dealt with in the ordinary course of business in the UK.**

(iii)   **The antiques are a UK asset because they are physically located in the UK.**

(iv)   **Bank deposits are situated at the branch that maintains the account** so the £30,000 at the London branch is a UK asset but the other £20,000 is not.

(v)   **A debt is situated where the debtor resides** so the loan is not a UK asset.

(vi)   **Government stocks are situated at the place of registration** so the UK government stocks are a UK asset. This makes the trust a UK asset.

Ming's IHT liability if she is domiciled and she is non-UK domiciled is, therefore, as follows:

	UK Domiciled £	Non-UK domiciled £
Residence	245,000	245,000
House in Yanga	60,000	-
Ganyan Inc shares	124,000	-
Antiques	35,000	35,000
Bank deposits	50,000	30,000
Loan	15,000	-
Trust	18,500	18,500
	547,500	328,500

IHT:	£	£
£234,000 × 0%	-	-
£313,500/£94,500 × 40%	125,400	37,800

Less: DTR

Lower of (i) £48,000

(ii) £125,400 × $\dfrac{184,000}{547,500}$ (42,144)

IHT liability	83,256	37,800

The potential increase in Ming's IHT liability if she were to become UK domiciled is £45,456.

(c) (i) Whilst non-UK domiciled Ming is not liable to UK income tax on income arising in Yanga unless it is remitted to the UK. This means her income tax liability for 2000/01 is

	Non-savings income £	Savings (excl dividend) income £	Total £
Schedule E	29,000		
Bank deposit interest		2,100	
	29,000	2,100	31,100
Less: personal allowance	(4,385)		
Taxable income	24,615	2,100	26,715

Non-savings income

	£
£1,520 × 10%	152
£23,095 × 22%	5,081
Savings (excl dividend) income	
£2,100 × 20%	420
	5,653
Less: tax suffered on bank interest	(420)
Income tax payable (subject to tax under PAYE)	5,233

(ii)   If Ming had been UK domiciled her UK income tax position would have been:

	Non-savings £	Savings (excl dividend) £	Dividend £	Total £
Schedule E	29,000			
Schedule D Case V:				
Rents	7,500			
Dividends (× 100/85)			7,000	
Bank interest (× 100/85)		1,800		
UK bank interest (× 100/80)		2,100		
	36,500	3,900	7,000	47,400
Less: personal allowance	(4,385)			
Taxable income	32,115	3,900	7,000	43,015

	£
Tax on non-savings income:	
£1,520 × 10%	152
£26,880 × 22%	5,914
£3,715 × 40%	1,486
Tax on savings (excl. dividend) income:	
£3,900 × 40%	1,560
Tax on dividend income:	
£7,000 × 32.5%	2,275
	11,387
Less: Double tax relief (W)	
Rental income	(2,625)
Dividends (£7,000 × 15%)	(1,050)
Bank interest (£1,800 × 15%)	(270)
	7,442
Less: tax suffered on bank interest	(420)
Income tax payable (subject to tax under PAYE)	7,022

Ming's additional income tax payable if she had been UK domiciled during 2000/01 would have been £1,789 (£7,022 – £5,233).

Working

1   **Double tax relief**

As the rents are taxed most highly overseas, they are treated as the top slice of income: taxable non savings income excluding the rents is, therefore, £24,615 and the UK tax liability is:

	£
On non-savings income	
£1,520 × 10%	152
£23,095 × 22%	5,081
On savings (excl dividend) income:	
£3,785 × 20%	757
£115 × 40%	46
On dividend income	
£7,000 × 32.5%	2,275
	8,311

The UK tax on the overseas rental income is therefore £3,076 (£11,387 – £8,311) and DTR is the lower of:

(i)   UK tax   £3,076
(ii) Overseas tax   £2,625

ie £2,625

Marking guide

			Marks
(a)	17 out of last 20 years		1
	Application to Ming		1
	Domicile of choice		1
	Procedure involved		1
		Maximum/Available	4
(b)	*Location of assets*		
	Land and buildings		1
	Registered shares and securities		1
	Bank accounts		1
	Chattels/Debtor		1
	Property held in trust		1
	Chargeable estate - Not domiciled in UK		2
	- Domiciled in UK		2
	IHT liability		1
	Double taxation relief		2
	Endowment mortgage (not deducted)		1
	Additional IHT liability		1
		Available	14
		Maximum	12
(c)	*Income tax liability – Not domiciled in the UK*		
	Taxable income		1
	Income tax		1
	Remittance basis		1
	Income tax liability - Domiciled in the UK		
	Taxable income		2
	Income tax		2
	Double taxation relief		3
	Additional income tax liability		1
		Available	11
		Maximum	9
		Maximum	25

---

14   JANE MACBETH

> **Tutor's hint**. Remember to start with lifetime transfers and then move on to the death estate.
>
> **Examiner's comments**. This question was very well answered and a number of candidates achieved maximum marks.

(a) (i)   *IHT payable on lifetime gifts*

       CLT - 28.11.92

		£
Gift		76,000
Less:	Annual exemption (92/93)	(3,000)
	Annual exemption (91/92)	(3,000)
		70,000

The gift fell within the £nil band. This means that no lifetime IHT was paid by Jane and the value of the gross chargeable transfer was £70,000.

No IHT arises on this gift as a result of Jane's death because the gift was made more than seven years before her death.

PET - 15.4.96

	£
Gift of shares	155,000
Less: Business property relief (80%)	(124,000)
	31,000
Less: Marriage exemption	(5,000)
Less: Annual exemption (96/97)	(3,000)
Annual exemption (95/96)	(3,000)
	20,000

The PET becomes chargeable on death £164,000 (£234,000 – £70,000) of the £nil band remains so IHT due is:

£20,000 × 0% = £Nil

CLT - 10.3.97

Gross gift (W1)	£259,000

In the previous seven years £90,000 of the £nil band has been used in calculating death tax so, £144,000 (£234,000 – £90,000) remains:

	£
£144,000 × 0%	Nil
£115,000 × 40%	46,000
	46,000

	£
Tax due after taper relief (80%)	36,800
Less: Lifetime tax paid (W1)	(19,000)
IHT due as a result of Jane's death	17,800

Death estate on 20.11.00

	£	£
Main residence	235,000	
Less: mortgage	(40,000)	
		195,000
Building society deposits		87,000
Banquo plc		
Lower of:		
$\frac{1}{4}$ up 945 + $\frac{1}{4}$ (957 – 945) = 948p		
Average marked bargain		
$\frac{1}{2}$ (937 + 961) = 949p		
ie 10,000 × £9.48		94,800
Life assurance policy		104,000
Agricultural land	168,000	
Less: APR	(110,000)	
		58,000
Chargeable estate		538,800

In the seven years prior to death, the £nil band was fully utilised by the CLT made on 10.3.97 and the PET made on 15.4.96.

	£
∴ IHT due	
£538,800 × 40%	215,520
Less: Quick succession relief	
$\dfrac{54,000}{360,000} \times 68,000 \times 60\%$	(6,120)
IHT payable	209,400

Tutorial note: APR is available as the agricultural property is let for agricultural purposes and has been owned for seven years.

(ii)   £17,800 due in respect of the CLT made on 10.3.97 must be paid by the trustees of the discretionary trust by 31 May 2001.

£209,400 due in respect of the death estate must be paid by Jane's personal representatives on the earlier of when probate is obtained and when they deliver their account. The time limit for delivery of the account is 30.11.01.

IHT on land of $\dfrac{58,000 + 195,000}{538,800} \times 209,400$

= £98,326 could be paid in 10 equal annual instalments commencing on 31.5.01.

Inheritance

Jane's children will inherit £339,400 (£538,800 + £110,000 − £100,000 − £209,400) since specific gifts of UK property do not bear their own tax.

(b) (i)   **The beneficiaries of the will must execute a deed of variation in writing within two years of death and the Revenue must receive a written election that the deeds are to be effective for IHT purposes within six months of the date of the deed.**

(ii)   The result of the revised plan is that the IHT of £209,400 previously due on the death estate will no longer be payable because the transfer to Duncan will be exempt. The gifts to the children and Jane's brother will be PETs made by Duncan against which Duncan will be able to set any amount of unused annual exemptions of £3,000 per annum.

The value of the remaining PETs will be completely exempt if Duncan survives for seven years after making the gifts. If Duncan dies within 3 and 7 years of making the gifts the PETs will be chargeable but taper relief will be available to reduce the amount of IHT due.

Workings

1   *Lifetime tax*

CLT - 10.3.97 - £240,000

In the seven years prior to this CLT, £70,000 of the £nil band had been used, leaving £164,000. ∴ Lifetime tax:

	£
£164,000 × 0%	Nil
£76,000 × $^{20}/_{80}$	19,000
£240,000	19,000

£19,000 lifetime tax was paid by Jane and the value of the gross chargeable transfer was £259,000 (£240,000 + £19,000)

Tutorial note. The PET made on 15.4.96 was not chargeable during Jane's lifetime so it did not use any of the £nil band for the purpose of calculating lifetime tax on the later CLT. However, the 1996/97 and 1995/96 annual exemptions are allocated to the PET before it becomes chargeable and so are not available to set against the CLT.

Marking guide		Marks	
(a)	*Lifetime transfers of value*		
	Chargeable transfer on 28 November 1992	1	
	PET on 15 April 1996 - BPR	1	
	Marriage exemption	1	
	Annual exemptions	1	
	Chargeable transfer on 10 March 1997	2	
	Revised cumulative total	1	
	Additional IHT	2	
	Estate at death		
	Cumulative total	1	
	Building society deposit/Life assurance policy	1	
	Ordinary shares in Banquo plc	1	
	Main residence	1	
	Agricultural land	1	
	IHT liability	1	
	Quick succession relief	1	
	Payment of IHT liability		
	Additional IHT	1	
	Estate	1	
	Instalment option	2	
	Inheritance		
	Calculation of inheritance	<u>1</u>	
	Available	<u>21</u>	
	Maximum		19
(b)	*Variation of the terms of Jane's will*		
	Conditions	1	
	Written election to Revenue	1	
	Proposed plan		
	Exempt transfer	1	
	PETs/Completely exempt after seven years	1	
	Tapering relief/Annual exemptions	1	
	IHT liability	1	
	Due date	<u>1</u>	
	Available	<u>7</u>	
	Maximum		<u>6</u>
	Maximum		<u>25</u>

15 MICHAEL EARL

Tutor's hint. As Michael Earl died on 30.6.00, IHT at death rates is due on all gifts made after 30.6.93 and on the value of his chargeable estate at death. Before calculating the tax due on death, you should calculate any lifetime tax which was paid on the gifts Michael made after 30.6.93.

Examiner's comments. In part (a) the calculation of the related property valuation of the unquoted shares caused problems, and business property relief was often overlooked.

(a)   (i)   **Lifetime tax**

10 July 1999 - Gift to daughter

This was a PET so no IHT was due when the gift was made.

19 August 1999 - Transfer to discretionary trust

This transfer was a CLT in August 1999. As Michael paid the tax, the gift made was a net gift and the IHT payable was (£310,000 (W1) – £234,000) × 1/4 = £19,000. The gross gift was £329,000.

IHT arising as a result of Michael's death on 30.6.00

PET on 10.7.99

The value of Michael's shareholdings must take into account Naomi's shares as Naomi's shares are related property.

	£
Value of Michael's holding before the gift 100,000 × £10	1,000,000
Value of Michael's holding after gift 50,000 × £7	(350,000)
PET	650,000

Business property relief is not available as the shares had not been owned for two years.

None of the £nil band had been used in the seven years prior to this PET. So IHT due is:

£		£
234,000 × 0%		Nil
416,000 × 40%		166,400
650,000		166,400

IHT of £166,400 must be paid by Michael's daughter, Jade, by 31.12.00.

CLT on 19.8.99

These shares have fallen in value by 30.6.00 (W2) so the IHT payable by the trustees by 31.12.00 is calculated as:

	£
CLT on 19.8.99	329,000
Less: Fall in value (W2)	(30,000)
	299,000

All of the £nil band had been used in the seven years prior to 19.8.99 so IHT due is:

	£
£299,000 × 40%	119,600
Less: Lifetime tax already paid	(19,000)
Additional tax payable by trustees by 31.12.00	100,600

Chargeable estate on 30.6.00

	£
Compact Ltd shares (W3) 50,000 × £8.40	420,000
Diverse Inc shares	
Lower of (i) 1/4 up principle (281p)	
(ii) average of highest/lowest marked bargains (280p)	140,000
Other assets	850,000
	1,410,000
Less: Exempt legacy to non domiciled spouse	(55,000)
Chargeable estate	1,355,000

The IHT on the chargeable estate at death is calculated ignoring the fall in value of the Diverse Inc shares.

In the seven years before death, the £nil band had been fully utilised, so IHT on death estate is £1,355,000 × 40% = £542,000.

The IHT payable by the executor's of Michael's estate on the earlier of 31.12.00 and the date of delivery of their account is:

	£
IHT due	542,000
Less: DTR	
Lower of UK tax (£140,000 × 40% = £56,000)	
Overseas tax (£35,000)	(35,000)
	507,000

(ii) **Relief for related property**

The valuation of the Compact Ltd shares in Michael's death estate took into account Naomi's share as these were related property. However, as Michael's shares were sold within three years of his death for less than their related property valuation, the executor's of Michael's estate can claim relief based on the unrelated valuation of the shares.

	£
Original valuation	420,000
Less: unrelated valuation 50,000 × £6.00	(300,000)
	120,000

Reduction in IHT liability £120,000 × 40% = £48,000. Clearly such a claim is beneficial.

Relief on sale of quoted investments within twelve months of death

As the quoted shares in Diverse Inc were sold within 12 months of death for less than their probate value the executor's can claim relief for the loss.

	£
Probate value	140,000
Sale proceeds	(120,000)
Loss	20,000

Reduction in IHT liability = £20,000 × 40% = £8,000. Clearly such a claim is beneficial.

(b) (i) **Jade - CGT liability**

	£
Sale proceeds	285,000
Deemed cost	(250,000)
Gain before taper relief	35,000

Unquoted shares are a business asset for CGT taper relief purposes.

The gain after taper relief is £30,625 (£35,000 × 87.5%).

Capital gains tax £30,625 × 40%	£12,250

(ii) If Jade and the executors of Michael's estate make a claim for <u>holdover relief</u> in respect of the gift on 10 July 1999, then Jade will be able to <u>deduct the IHT</u> payable as a result of the PET becoming chargeable, when calculating her chargeable gain. Her CGT liability would be as follows.

	£	£
Sale proceeds 10/12/00		285,000
Deemed cost	250,000	
Gain held over (W4)	(50,000)	
		(200,000)
		85,000
Less: IHT liability £167,600 restricted to		(85,000)
		Nil

	£
Capital gains tax	Nil

The 1999/00 CGT liability of £20,000 (£50,000 at 40%) due out of Michael's estate will no longer be payable. This will increase Michael's estate by £20,000, and additional IHT of £8,000 (£20,000 at 40%) will be due. Claiming holdover relief would therefore result in an overall tax decrease.

	No claim	Holdover relief claim
	£	£
CGT liability - Jade	12,250	0
- Michael's estate	20,000	0
Additional IHT liability	0	8,000
	32,250	8,000

Workings

1 **CLT August 1999**

The transfer is valued at the lower of,

(a) ¼ up principle (308p + ¼ (316p– 308p) = 310p ✓
(b) average of highest and lowest marked bargains ½ (296 + 328) = 312p.

That is 100,000 × 310p = £310,000

2 **Diverse Inc**

The value of the shares on 30.6.00 was the lower of:

(a) 279 + 1/4 (287 – 279) = 281p
(b) 1/2 (275 + 285) = 280p

The shares have fallen in value since the date of the CLT and the trustees can make a claim for the fall in value of £30,000 (£310,000 – £280,000) to be taken into account in calculating the additional IHT due. However, the cumulative total of gifts is not reduced by this fall in value.

3 **Shares in Compact Ltd**

These shares must be valued taking into account the shares held by Naomi as Naomi's shares are related property. There is no BPR as the shares have not been owned for two years

4 **Gain on gift 10.7.99**

	£
Deemed proceeds	250,000
Less: cost	(200,000)
Gain	50,000

No indexation or taper relief due.

16   MING LEE

> **Tutor's hint**. You were given taxable profits for tax years so you did not need to apply basis period rules.
>
> **Examiner's comment**. In part (a), many candidates forgot about the earnings cap.

(a)   PERSONAL PENSION PREMIUM

The maximum percentages of net relevant earnings for all years are as follows.

Year	Earnings	Percentage	Amount
	£	%	£
1993/94	26,000	20	5,200
1994/95	34,500	20	6,900
1995/96	47,000	25	11,750
1996/97	53,000	25	13,250
1997/98	63,500	25	15,875
1998/99	70,000	25	17,500
1999/00	90,000 90600.	25	22,500
2000/01	91,800 (cap)	30	27,540

The 1997/98 premium will have used up the 1997/98 relief and £(20,000 − 15,875) = £4,125 of the 1993/94 relief.

The maximum 2000/01 premium is as follows.

	£
To relate back to 1999/00 to use the 1999/00 relief	22,500
To relate back to 1999/00 and use the remaining 1993/94 relief of £(5,200 − 4,125)	1,075
	23,575
To relate back to 1999/00 and/or claim in 2000/01: £(6,900 + 11,750 + 13,250 + 17,500)	49,400
To claim in 2000/01	27,540
	100,515

Ming should pay this maximum amount, but should divide it between 2000/01 and 1999/00 so as to get tax relief at 40% on the whole amount. A split such as £32,425 claimed in 2000/01 and £68,090 related back to 1999/00 would achieve this.

This is likely to be a suitable investment, because of the tax relief and because on retirement 25% of the fund's value can be taken as a tax-free lump sum. However, the pension obtained may not be high because the fund may only be invested for a few years.

Nevertheless the tax deductibility of premiums paid and the tax exempt status of most income makes a pension fund attractive.

(b)   OTHER INVESTMENTS

(i)   **Repayment of the mortgage**

Ming currently obtains no tax relief on her mortgage so the cost to her is £12,000 pa. If she were to pay off her mortgage using some of her building society deposit, she would therefore save considerably more interest than she would lose (£8,700 × 120/140 × 100/80 × 60% = £5,593). There would also be no investment risk, although there would be some loss of flexibility because Ming would no longer be able to invest her savings to take advantage of any good opportunities which might arise.

(ii) **National Savings Certificates**

These offer a modest return, but it is guaranteed and is also tax-free. This last point is particularly valuable to a higher rate taxpayer such as Ming: a 6% tax-free return is as good as a 10% taxable return. This investment may well be suitable for Ming. The two main disadvantages are the need to invest for five years in order to obtain the best rate of return, and the limit on the investment, usually £10,000 per issue of certificates.

(iii) **Enterprise zone trusts**

In an enterprise zone trust, investors pool their funds to buy commercial buildings in enterprise zones. Each investor gets an appropriate share of the 100% initial allowance, and in Ming's case this would save her tax at 40% (though her marginal rate will be less than this beyond the point where her taxable income is reduced below the top of the basic rate band). The tax saving may well make this investment suitable for Ming, but she should consider the following disadvantages.

(1) The sale proceeds of buildings will be taxable income up to the original cost, and may give rise to chargeable gains if they exceed this amount.

(2) There is a considerable risk: the value of property, and the rental income from it, can fall.

(c) INCORPORATION

Ming should consider the following factors when deciding whether or not to incorporate her business.

(i) **Adjustments to basis periods**

On the cessation of a sole trade (which includes incorporation) the basis period for the final tax year runs from the end of the previous basis period to the date of cessation. Relief will be available for any unrelieved overlap profits. The long basis period may lead to higher taxable profits than had been anticipated. The extent of the problem will depend on the time of incorporation.

(ii) **Capital gains**

A capital gain will arise on incorporation in respect of the goodwill, but if the consideration is shares this gain will be rolled over against the cost of the shares.

Taper relief already built up on the unincorporated business will be lost, however.

Incorporation will not affect Ming's entitlement to retirement relief, because the pre-incorporation and post-incorporation periods of trading can be aggregated. However, the eligible gain would be less than the full gain if the company were to acquire any chargeable non-business assets.

Retirement relief is to be abolished on 6 April 2003 so it may be worth Ming crystallising a gain on incorporation in order to take advantage of the relief while it is still available. Ming will need to weigh up the benefits of the retirement relief that is available now with the decreased rates of taper relief that are available on an early sale.

(iii) **The taxation of profits**

At present, Ming's profits are subject to income tax, with a marginal rate of 40%. If her business were incorporated, profits would only be taxed at rates of up to 20% and Ming could limit her total income (salary, dividends and sources from outside the business) so as to avoid higher rate tax. The retention of profits in the company would increase Ming's gain on its eventual disposal, but until 2002/03 retirement relief should limit the effect of this.

For a small company, corporation tax is due nine months after the end of the accounting period. Income tax on an unincorporated business's profits is due on 31 January following the tax year, but with payments on account 12 months and six months earlier.

(iv) **National Insurance contributions**

The combined burden of NICs on a company and on Ming as a director will be much higher than the burden on Ming as a sole trader, unless Ming draws a very low salary. She could also draw dividends (which do not attract NICs).

(v) **Pension contributions**

Ming could continue to make personal pension contributions following incorporation, but based only on her remuneration, not on dividends.

If the business is incorporated, the company could alternatively set up an approved occupational scheme for her. She could contribute up to 15% of her remuneration, and the company's contributions would not be subject to any percentage limit. However, benefits would be limited, based on Ming's (fairly short) period of service, and the effective limit on contributions would be the rule that such schemes must not be over-funded. On balance, Ming could probably obtain a better pension by putting 30% of her earnings into her personal pension fund.

(vi) **Value added tax**

The transfer of Ming's business to a company as a going concern will be outside the scope of VAT, so there will be no VAT consequences of incorporation.

17 MURIEL GRAND

> **Tutor's hint**. Many topics in this question were new when the question was set. This demonstrates how important the examiner considers current developments to be.
>
> **Examiner's comment**. A considerable number of candidates were unaware of the new schedule A rules, despite this topic being included in the examiner's newsletter article on the most recent Finance Act.

(a) MURIEL'S CAPITAL GAINS TAX LIABILITY

	£
Deemed proceeds	320,000
Less: cost (W1)	(45,000)
Unindexed gain	275,000
Less: Indexation to April 1998 $£45,000 \times \dfrac{162.6 - 94.8}{94.8}$ (0.715)	(32,175)
	242,825
Less: PPR exemption (W2) $£242,825 \times \left(\dfrac{138}{189}\right)$	(177,301)
	65,524

Gain after taper relief (6 April 1998 – 5 April 2000 = 2 years plus additional year = 3 years) 95% × £65,524 = £62,248

CGT liability £24,899 (£62,248 × 40%)

(b) **EIS: Capital gains tax relief**

It may be possible for Muriel to defer the gain on the house if she invests in newly issued EIS shares. The company issuing the shares must be unquoted. It could be on the AIM. An amount equal to at least the full amount of the gain of £65,524 must be invested if Muriel wishes to defer the full gain. Any amount of the gain not invested will be chargeable immediately.

The deferred gain becomes chargeable on the disposal of the new shares or on a breach of any of the various conditions within a three year period.

Reinvestment in qualifying EIS shares must be made in the period from 1 January 2000 to 31 December 2003.

EIS: Income tax relief

In addition to rollover relief Muriel will be entitled to 20% income tax relief in respect of any amount (up to £150,000) invested in EIS shares. This income tax relief is withdrawn if the shares are disposed of within three years.

Venture capital trusts (VCT): Capital gains tax

Alternatively, Muriel will be entitled to rollover relief and 20% income tax relief in respect of any amount (up to £100,000) invested in VCT shares.

Investment in a VCT must be made in the period from 1 January 2000 to 31 December 2001. The VCT is itself quoted but 70% of its investments must be in unquoted trading companies. 30% of the investments must be in new ordinary shares.

VCT: Income tax relief

The income tax relief is again withdrawn if the shares are disposed of within three years. Any gain on the disposal of VCT shares is exempt. Any loss will not be allowable in any circumstances. Dividend income from a VCT is exempt from income tax.

Investment in a VCT is less risky than investment under the EIS as a spread of unquoted shares are invested in.

(c) The rental income from Bertie's letting business will be taxed on an **accruals basis under Schedule A** whether the house is let unfurnished or as furnished holiday accommodation. In either case **revenue expenses will be deductible if they are incurred wholly and exclusively for the letting business.**

The cost of repairing the roof will not be deductible in calculating Schedule A profits in either case. **The repairs must be done before the house can be let and so, following the decision in *Law Shipping Co Ltd v CIR (1923)*, the repairs are capital rather than revenue expenses**. The capital expenditure will, however, be deductible in calculating any gain or loss arising on the disposal of the house.

The other tax implications depend on whether the house is let unfurnished or as furnished holiday accommodation.

Unfurnished letting

Decorating costs will normally be deductible revenue expenses. Revenue expenses incurred before the letting business begins will be treated as a deductible expense on the day the business begins. However, if the house was in a bad state of repair when it was acquired some of the £3,500 may be classified as capital rather than revenue expenditure.

Any capital gain arising on the disposal of the property will be subject to capital gains tax.

Furnished letting

It is likely that the £42,000 spent on converting the house into two separate units will be capital expenditure which can be deducted from any chargeable gain arising on the disposal of the property. Any items of revenue expenditure that are included in the £42,000 will be deductible in calculating schedule A profits.

The £9,000 spent on furniture will be a capital expense. However, Bertie will either be able to claim a wear and tear allowance or he will be able to claim for capital expenditure on furniture to be deductible on a renewals basis. **The wear and tear allowance will equal 10% of, rent less any water rates or council tax** paid by Bertie.

Bertie will also be able to deduct the following expenses from his annual gross rents of £45,000:

(i)   Loan interest of £6,000 (£50,000 × 12%)
(ii)   Letting agency fees of £10,125 (£45,000 × 22.5%)
(iii)   Other running costs of £3,500

The amount of the deductible expenses will be restricted if Bertie occupies the house for his own use.

If, in any tax year, the house is available for **commercial letting to the public for at least 140 days, is actually let for at least 70 of those days, and is not normally in the same occupation for more than 31 days for at least seven months (including the 70 days), the special rules applicable to furnished holiday lettings will apply.** This means

(i)   **Capital allowances will be available for expenditure on plant and machinery** such as the furniture. This will almost certainly be more beneficial than the wear and tear allowance or the renewals basis.

(ii)   The **Schedule A profits will be net relevant earnings** for personal pension purposes.

(iii)   **Relief for any losses will be available as if they were trading losses**, including the facility to set losses against other income. The schedule A loss rules will not apply.

(iv)   **CGT rollover relief, gift relief and relief on loans to traders will also be available.** The property will be treated as a business asset for taper relief purposes.

(v)   **VAT registration will be required if rental income in any twelve month period exceeds the VAT registration threshold**. The letting of holiday accommodation is standard rated.

Conclusion

Letting the house as a furnished holiday letting will produce annual income of approximately £25,375 (£45,000 − £6,000 − £10,125 − £3,500), compared to £28,000 if the house is let unfurnished. It will also be necessary to incur additional expenditure of £47,500 (£42,000 + £9,000 − £3,500). This must be compared the benefits available if the house is let as furnished holiday accommodation.

(d) **Independent financial advice**

Independent advice could be obtained from accountants, solicitors and stockbrokers. In addition some banks and building societies (if they are not tied advisers) may provide independent advice.

Workings

1   **Cost relating to land disposed of in 1986**

$$£60,000 \times \frac{24,000}{24,000 + 72,000} = £15,000$$

∴ cost relating to land given to brother £45,000 (£60,000 – £15,000)

2   **PPR exemption**

	Actual or deemed occupation	*Other*
1.4.85-30.9.93	102	
1.10.93-31.12.97		51
1.1.98-31.12.00 (last 36 months)	36	
	138	51

18   MARY MOLE

Tutor's hint. It is important to ensure you practice answering written questions like this concisely.

Prizewinners point. It is generally not possible to avoid income tax by buying stocks 'ex-interest' and selling them 'cum interest'. This is because there is an anti-avoidance scheme called the accrued income scheme. The interest included in the buying and selling prices will be taxed in the same way as if the interest was actually received.

Examiner's comments. There was a lack of depth in many answers with many candidates showing poor exam technique by repeating the same point several times.

(a)   *Investments*

Option 1

The maximum amount that Mary could invest in a maxi-ISA for 2000/01 is £7,000. This must comprise a stocks and shares element (up to £7,000). It can also include a cash element (maximum £3,000) and a life assurance element (maximum £1,000), in which case the stocks and shares element limit is reduced appropriately. In view of the possibility of the investment being needed in about 3 years time, a shares only investment or a shares and cash investment would seem appropriate, as the life assurance element can only be on the life of the investor.

The stocks and shares that can comprise this element include gilt edged stocks (at least 5 years from redemption), shares listed on a recognised stock exchange, securities (not short dated) issued by a company listed on a recognised stock exchange and shares and securities in certain investment trusts, companies and funds. **In general, therefore, the stocks and shares investments would not be considered high risk.**

Investments in an ISA are exempt from both income and capital gains tax. In addition, up to and including 2003/04, the 10% tax credit is repayable on dividends from UK companies. **There is no statutory minimum period for holding the ISA, so the investments could easily be liquidated in three years time if needed, without any adverse tax consequences.** However, the investment would not reduce Mary's tax liability in 2000/01.

Mary should look at a wide range of ISAs, not just those being offered by the bank and should in particular look at the charges levied.

The balance of the inheritance £(25,000 – 7,000) = £18,000 invested in a unit trust will not gain any tax relief. **Income received from a unit trust is usually taxed as if it were dividend income** (ie. with a 10% non-repayable tax credit). **Capital gains tax will be**

chargeable on any gains made when units are sold, in the same way as shares. Again, unit trusts are not considered a high risk investment.

Option 2

Mary's maximum personal pension premium deductible in 2000/01 is £27,050:

	Age at start of tax year	%	Net relevant earnings £	Maximum premium £
1994/95	32	17.5	46,200	8,085
1995/96	33	17.5	12,600	2,205
1998/99	36	20	8,100	1,620
1999/00	37	20	18,300	3,660
2000/01	38	20	57,400	11,480
				27,050

Mary could therefore invest all of her inheritance in a personal pension and obtain tax relief in 2000/01. This would save Mary tax at her marginal rate of 40% in 2000/01 and therefore meet her first investment criteria.

Benefits under a personal pension can be taken when Mary reaches 50 and at that date she can withdraw 25% of the accumulated income as a tax-free lump sum. The pension itself will be taxable as non-savings income under Schedule E.

This option should provide reasonable capital growth and is not considered high risk. However, the capital will not be available in three years time.

Option 3

A VCT allows an investor to invest indirectly in unquoted companies, thus spreading the risk of investment. The VCT itself is a quoted company. However, although there may be capital growth, a VCT investment is still relatively high risk.

An investor in a VCT obtains a tax reduction of 20% of the amount invested in the year that the investment is made ie. if Mary invests £25,000 (maximum investment per tax year is £100,000) she will be entitled to a tax reducer of £5,000. If Mary disposes of the shares within three years, the relief will be subject to a claw-back.

Dividends from a VCT are generally tax-free income. Capital gains are also exempt from CGT, but, again, the shares must be retained for three years to qualify for this relief. It is also possible to claim a 'reinvestment relief' if Mary has a gain within 12 months before and 12 months after the investment. Again, a claw-back charge will arise on the disposal of the VCT shares.

As disposal within three years will result in the withdrawal of tax relief, this investment may not be suitable for Mary.

Option 4

Interest on government stocks is normally paid gross but Mary will be liable to income tax at 40% on the interest received. Any chargeable gains arising on government stocks are exempt. Losses are not allowable.

It is generally not possible to avoid income tax by buying stocks 'ex-interest' and selling stocks 'cum interest'. This is because there is an anti-avoidance scheme called the accrued income scheme. The interest included in the buying and selling prices will be taxed in the same way as if the interest was actually received.

This option would not reduce Mary's income tax liability for 2000/01. Mary could buy short dated stocks for redemption in three years time. This would ensure that her capital is intact and government stocks are not high risk. However, she would not obtain capital growth.

(b) (i) **Tied advisers only recommend the investment products of the financial institution to which they are tied. An independent adviser is able to give recommendations about investment products from any source.**

(ii) The statements of principle are that an authorised person should:

(1) Act with high standards of integrity and market conduct.

(2) Act with due skill, care and diligence.

(3) Obtain relevant information about, and provide appropriate information to, clients.

(4) Avoid conflicts of interest.

(5) Safeguard assets held on behalf of clients.

(6) Maintain adequate financial resources and internal organisation.

(7) Deal with the regulator (ACCA in this case) in an open and co-operative manner.

Marking guide		Marks
(a) *Option 1*		
Maxi-ISA CGT/IT exemptions		2
Limits on investment		2
Risks		1
Liquidity		1
Suitability for Mary		1
Unit trusts		1
Other providers		1
Option 2		
Tax deductible amount in 2000/01		2
Benefits on retirement		1
Suitability given Mary's investment criteria		2
Option 3		
Tax relief/3 year period		1
Dividends/disposal		1
Re-investment relief		1
Suitability for Mary		1
Option 4		
Paid gross		1
Income tax		1
Chargeable gains exempt/losses not allowable		1
Accrued income scheme		1
Suitability for Mary		2
	Available	24
	Maximum	21
(b) (i) Tied advisers/independent advisers		1
(ii) *Statements of principle*		
Integrity/skill etc		1
Information		1
Conflicts of interest/safeguard assets		1
Financial resources/regulator		1
	Available	5
	Maximum	4
	Maximum	25

19 MR ROWE

> **Tutor's hint**. You might well have found part (b) of this question the most straightforward. In such cases, and provided you are satisfied that the answer to an easy part does not depend on the answer to earlier parts, there is no harm in answering the easy part first, so as to start earning marks and at the same time improve your grasp of the question as a whole. However, you must make it absolutely clear to the examiner which part of your answer relates to which part of the question.
>
> **Examiner's comment**. This question was well done. However, many candidates did not appreciate the interaction between chargeability to inheritance tax and the availability of CGT gift relief.

(a) (i) **An accumulation and maintenance trust**

Such a trust may only be set up if **all the beneficiaries will become beneficially entitled to the trust assets, or to interests in possession therein, on reaching specified ages which are not greater than 25.**

George's transfer of property into such a trust would be a potentially exempt transfer. It would be exempt if he were to survive for seven years after the transfer. If he did not, inheritance tax would be payable as follows (assuming that the rates applicable to transfers on or after 6 April 2000 continue to apply).

		£
Transfer of value		248,000
Less annual exemptions: 2000/01		(3,000)
1999/00		(3,000)
Chargeable transfer		242,000
Less nil rate band		(234,000)
Taxable at 40%		8,000
IHT at 40%		£3,200

In addition, if George were to die more than three years after the transfer, the tax would be reduced by tapering relief of between 20% (for death up to four years after the transfer) and 80% (for death over six years after the transfer).

Additional capital gains tax of £35,000 × 40% = £14,000 would arise. The transfer would not be immediately chargeable to inheritance tax, so gift relief would be unavailable.

(ii) **A discretionary trust**

There would be an **immediate liability to inheritance tax,** based on half scale rates and applying grossing-up (because George is to bear the tax). This liability would be £8,000 × 1/4 = £2,000, giving a gross chargeable transfer of £242,000 + £2,000 = £244,000.

If George were to die within seven years, tax at the full rates would be computed on this gross chargeable transfer. The tax would be reduced by tapering relief as above, and by the tax of £2,000 already paid, and only the balance of tax would be payable. However, none of the £2,000 tax already paid could be refunded.

A capital gains tax liability of £14,000 would normally arise. However, because the transfer would be immediately chargeable to inheritance tax George could elect for gift relief. The trustees would then have a deemed acquisition cost equal to George's acquisition cost plus indexation allowance up to April 1998.

(b) INCOME TAX COMPUTATION

	Non-savings £	Dividend £	Total £
Salary	63,000		
Dividends £28,800 × 100/90		32,000	
Statutory total income	63,000	32,000	95,000
Less personal allowance	(4,385)		
Taxable income	58,615	32,000	90,615

	£	£
Income tax on non-savings income		
£1,520 × 10%		152
£26,880 × 22%		5,914
£30,215 × 40%		12,086
Income tax on dividend income		
£32,000 × 32.5%		10,400
Tax liability		28,552
Less: tax credits on dividends	3,200	
PAYE tax deducted	18,150	
		(21,350)
Tax payable		7,202

(c) If George were to live in the house at any time in the period between the end of his period of employment elsewhere in the UK and the date of sale, up to four years of that period of employment elsewhere in the UK would, like his previous absence, be treated as a period of occupation. The consequence would be that the principal private residence exemption would increase, and George's allowable loss would be smaller. He should, therefore, not re-occupy the house. The allowable loss which will arise if he follows this advice is as follows.

	£
Proceeds	200,000
Less cost (31 March 1982 value identical)	280,000
Loss (indexation allowance cannot increase a loss)	80,000
Less exemption (W) £80,000 × $\frac{210}{225}$	(74,667)
Allowable loss	5,333

This loss would be set against the chargeable gains of £90,000 which have already been realised.

Working: PPR exemption

	Exempt Months	Chargeable Months
1. 4.82 - 30. 6.82 (occupation)	3	
1. 7.82 - 31.12.83 (overseas duties)	18	
1. 1.84 - 30. 9.96 (occupied)	153	
1.10.96 - 31.12.97		15
1. 1.98 - 31.12.00 (last 36 months)	36	
	210	15

The last 36 months of ownership must be treated as exempt. Periods of ownership before 31 March 1982 are ignored.

20   TONY TORT

> **Tutor's hints**. It was important to realise in part (a) that you needed to calculate the 2000/01 income tax and Class 4 NIC liability in order to work out the amount by which payments on account were underpaid.
>
> **Examiner's comments**. This question was answered badly which was disappointing given that self assessment had been covered in my newsletter articles.

(a) (i)   Payments due during 2001:

	Amount due £	Due date	Date paid	Days late	Interest at 10% £
1999/00 balancing payment	19,033	31.1.01	10.5.01	99	516.24
2000/01 First payment on account	2,500	31.1.01	15.6.01	135	92.47
	2,604 (W)	31.1.01	31.1.02	365	260.40
	5,104				
2000/01 Second payment on account	2,500	31.7.01	31.7.01	0	-
	2,604 (W)	31.7.01	31.1.02	184	131.27
	5,104				

(ii)   *Surcharge*

A surcharge of 5% may be levied on the late payment of the 1999/00 balancing payment because it was not paid within 28 days of the due date. Tony may, therefore, be liable to a surcharge of £951.65 (£19,033 × 5%). However, the Revenue may mitigate this if there is reasonable excuse for the late payment. Surcharges are not levied in respect of payments on account.

Penalties

Unless he has a reasonable excuse, **Tony will be subject to a £100 penalty for the late filing of his tax return.** In addition a daily penalty of £60 could have been imposed if leave to do so was given by the Commissioners.

A penalty could also be charged if Tony made the claim to reduce his payments on account fraudulently or negligently. Since Tony made his claim for cash flow reasons it was negligently made and the Revenue could impose a penalty of £5,208 (£2,604 × 2).

(b) (i)   **The Revenue may have randomly selected Tony's tax return for an enquiry or they may have made the enquiry because of a suspected tax risk.**

(ii)   **Tony has 30 days from the end of the enquiry to amend his self assessment in accordance with the Revenue's conclusions. Tony can appeal at the end of the enquiry if he does not accept the Revenue's conclusions.**

(iii) Tony's additional income tax liability as a result of the enquiry is £1,800 (£4,500 × 40%). Interest will run on this amount from 31.1.01. There will be no surcharge unless the tax is paid later than 28 days after the due date (which is 30 days from the date of the amendment to the assessment). A penalty of up to £1,800 could be imposed if Tony's tax return was fraudulently or negligently submitted.

However, the Revenue can at their discretion mitigate this penalty.

(c) The maximum tax deductible pension premium in 2000/01 is 20% of:

	£
2000/01 net relevant earnings (W1)	39,040
1999/00 net relevant earnings b/f to 2000/01	
(£61,535 + 4,500)	66,035
	105,075

20% × £105,075 = £21,015

Therefore relate the whole of the £20,000 contribution back to 2000/01 to reduce his income tax liability by:

£		£
6,255 (W1) (£34,655 - £28,400) × 40%		2,502
13,745 × 22%		3,024
20,000		5,526

The income tax reduction will not affect the payments on account that were due for 2000/01 or the interest on them. The tax reduction will either be set against Tony's 2001/02 tax liability or will be given by way of a refund in respect of 2000/01.

Working

1   2000/01 income tax liability

	£
Profits	52,100
Less: capital allowances	
Computer (FYA @ 100%)	(5,200)
Photocopier (FYA @ 40%)	(1,760)
Plant and machinery (WDA @ 25%)	(3,400)
Private use car (£3,000 × 90%)	(2,700)
Schedule D Case II	39,040
Less: personal allowance	(4,385)
Taxable income	34,655

	£
Tax on non-savings income	
£1,520 × 10%	152
£26,880 × 22%	5,914
£6,255 × 40%	2,502
Income tax liability	8,568
Class 4 NICs: (£27,820 – 4,385) × 7%	1,640
Total tax M A Y	10,208

Payments on account should therefore have been reduced to £5,104 rather than £2,500. Interest will run on the underpaid £2,604 (£5,104 – £2,500) from the due dates for the payments on account.

Marking guide

			Marks	
(a)	(i)	Calculation of taxable income	2	
		Income tax	1	
		Class 4 NIC	1	
		Underpayment of payments on account	1	
		Calculation of interest on payments	2	
	(ii)	*Tax return for 1999/00:*		
		Fixed penalty	1	
		Daily penalty	1	
		Surcharge	2	
		Penalty for fraudulent or negligent reduction	1	
		of payments on account	2	
		Available	14	
		Maximum		12
(b)		*Reasons for enquiry*		
		Inland Revenue suspicions	1	
		Random enquiry	1	
		Completion of the enquiry		
		Amendment of self assessment	1	
		Right of appeal	1	
		Interest, surcharges and penalties		
		Interest	1	
		Surcharge	1	
		Penalty	1	
		Available/Maximum		7
(c)		Calculation of maximum tax deductible premium	2	
		Conclusion	1	
		Income tax reduction	2	
		Set off in 2001/2002/claim for refund	1	
		Interest/Payments on account	1	
		Available	7	
		Maximum		6
		Maximum		25

22 CECILE GRAND

> **Tutor's hint.** This was a straightforward question if you had learnt the rules.
>
> **Examiner's comments.** The failure to give due dates lost several easy marks.

(a) (i) **Cecile's payments on account for 2001/02 will be based on her income tax and class 4 NIC liability for 2000/01 as follows.**

	Non-savings £	Dividends £	Total £
Schedule D Case I	38,400		
Pension contribution	3,500		
	34,900		
Schedule A	800		
Dividends (£4,860 × 100/90)		5,400	
	35,700	5,400	41,100
Personal allowance	(4,385)		
Taxable income	31,315	5,400	36,715

	£
Income tax on non-savings income	
£1,520 at 10%	152
£26,880 at 22%	5,914
£2,915 at 40%	1,166
Income tax on dividend income	
£5,400 × 32.5%	1,755
	8,987
Tax credit - dividends (£5,400 at 10%)	(540)
	8,447
Class 4 NIC (£27,820 – £4,385) × 7%	1,640
	10,087
Payment on account due 31.1.02 – 50%	£5,043.50
Payment on account due 31.7.02 – 50%	£5,043.50

Cecile's forecast actual tax liability for 2001/02 is as follows.

	Non-savings £	Dividends £	£
Schedule D Case I	21,750		
Dividends (£4,320 × 100/90)	-	4,800	
	21,750	4,800	26,550
Personal allowance	(4,385)	-	
Taxable income	17,365	4,800	22,165

Income tax on non-savings income		£
£1,520 at 10%		152
£15,845 at 22%		3,486
Income tax on dividend income		
£4,800 at 10%		480
		4,118
Tax credit on dividends (£4,800 at 10%)		(480)
		3,638
Class 4 NIC (£21,750 − £4,385) × 7%		1,216
	£	4,854
Capital gain	14,300	
Annual exemption	(7,200)	
Chargeable gain	7,100	
Capital gains tax		
£6,235 (28,400 − 22,165) at 20%	1,247	
£865 at 40%	346	
		1,593
		6,447
Paid on account		(10,087)
Balancing refund		(3,640)

Cecile is due a tax refund of £3,640 since the payments on account made by her exceed the actual tax payable for 2001/02.

(ii) The forecast actual income tax and Class 4 NIC payable (not CGT) for 2001/02 is £4,854. Cecile could reduce her payments on account to this amount resulting in the following payment schedule.

31.1.2002	£2,427	(£4,854/2)
31.7.2002	£2,427	(£4,854/2)
31.1.2003	CGT only due of £1,593	

(b) (i) **If Cecile's payments on account are too low, then she will be charged interest. This will run from the due dates for each payment on account of 31 January 2002 and 31 July 2002 respectively, until the date of payment,** which will presumably be 31 January 2003. A penalty will also be charged if a claim to reduce payments on account is made fraudulently or negligently.

(ii) **The Inland Revenue can enquire into Cecile's tax return, provided they give written notice.** The time limit for giving notice of an enquiry is 31 January 2004 assuming that the return was filed on time (later enquiry notification dates apply to returns filed late). If the return was filed on time and the Inland Revenue do not give notification of an enquiry by 31 January 2004 then an enquiry after that date can normally only be made where the taxpayer has been fraudulent or negligent.

(iii) Following the completion of an enquiry, the Inland Revenue will inform Cecile of their findings. Cecile would then normally amend her tax return to take account of the Inland Revenue's conclusions. A new self-assessment of tax would be calculated by Cecile and **the additional tax liability will be due 30 days from the date of the notice of amendment. Interest will be charged on the additional tax liability from 31 January 2003 (the due date for the tax return). No surcharge will be due provided that the additional tax liability is paid by the due date.** A penalty will only be charged where a tax return is filed incorrectly due to fraud or negligence.

(c) (i) For Cecile's change of accounting date to be valid:

  • The change must be notified to the Inland Revenue by 31 January 2004; and

135

- There must have been no previous change of accounting date in the last five tax years. This condition will not apply if the present change is to be made for genuine commercial reasons.

(ii) Following Cecile's change of accounting date, the basis period for 2002/03 will be the twelve months to 30 September 2002. The profits of this period will be:

	£
Year ended 31.3.02 (£21,750 × 6/12)	10,875
Period ended 30.9.02	18,000
	28,875

The profits of £10,875 for the period 1 October 2001 to 31 March 2002 are overlap profits, having already been assessed in 2001/02. These overlap profits may be relieved when Cecile ceases trading.

(iii) **Advantages**

The main advantage of Cecile changing her accounting date to 30 September is that she should have actual Schedule D Case I profits available before the first payment on account for a tax year is due on 31 January in the tax year. Also, the time between earning profits and paying the related tax liability will be six months later than it was with a 31 March year end.

Disadvantages

The disadvantages are that the final assessment upon cessation may be for a longer period with a 30 September year end. Also the change of accounting date creates overlap profits which will not be relieved until the business ceases.

22   FIONA FUNG

> **Tutor's hint**. In part (c)(ii) look at the effect of loss relief in relation to the rate of tax and the use of personal allowance.
>
> **Examiner's comments**. This was a reasonably popular question and, with the exception of the loss relief claim, was generally answered quite well.

(a)

	£
Disposal proceeds	650,000
Less: cost	(100,000)
Unindexed gain	550,000
Less: Indexation to April 1998	
$\dfrac{162.6 - 111.0}{111.0} \times £100,000$	(46,486)
	503,514

Gain eligible for retirement relief

$£503,514 \times \dfrac{1,400,000}{1,680,000}$

= £419,595

100% × (£150,000 × 90%)	(135,000)
50% × (£419,595 − 135,000)	(142,298)
Chargeable gain before taper relief	226,216

(b) **Tax avoidance involves the reduction of tax liabilities by the use of lawful means. By contrast, tax evasion involves the reduction of tax liabilities by illegal means.** Fiona's actions during the week ending 5 April 2001 appear to be within the ambit of tax avoidance, since they involve the careful timing of transactions in order to reduce her tax liability. However, if the reality of the situation has been misrepresented (for example, the sale of goods actually took place on 5 April 2001, but the sales invoice was dated 6 April 2001), then this comes within the scope of tax evasion.

(c) (i)

	£
Trading profit	25,400
Less: Bonuses	(20,000)
Capital allowances (W1)	(70,200)
Industrial buildings allowance (W2)	(5,400)
Write down stock	(9,800)
Schedule D Case I loss	80,000

(ii) *Loss relief claim*

Claiming relief under s 380 ICTA 1988 against total income for 2000/01, and then under s 72 FA 1991 against the chargeable gain of the same year, means that Fiona's loss of £80,000 is fully relieved in 2000/01. Although, the claim wastes her personal allowance for 2000/01 it does save a significant amount of CGT at 40%. The alternative ways of relieving the loss are:

1   The loss could be carried forward under s 385 ICTA 1988 against future trading profits, but relief would be delayed and might not be at the rate of 40%.

2   The loss is incurred in the first four years of trading, so relief could be claimed under s 381 ICTA 1988 against total income for 1997/98 to 1999/00. Relief would only partly be at the rate of 40%, and personal allowances for two years will be wasted.

3   A claim could be made under s 380 ICTA 1988 against total income for 1999/00, but the same comments as per (2) apply.

(iii) *Income tax and CGT liabilities for 2000/01*

Fiona will have a nil income tax liability for 2000/01 as her Schedule E income of £17,500 is fully relieved by the claim under s 380 ICTA 1988. Fiona's CGT liability for 2000/01 is as follows:

	£
Chargeable gain before taper relief (part (a))	226,216
Loss claim s 72 FA 1991 £(80,000 – 17,500)	(62,500)
	163,716

	£
Gain after taper relief (75%)	122,787
Annual exemption	(7,200)
	115,587

	£
£1,520 × 10%	152
£26,880 × 20%	5,376
£87,187 at 40%	34,875
	40,403

The shares qualify as a business asset. The taper relief period is 6 April 1998 to 5 April 2000, which is 2 years.

Workings

1   *Capital allowances*

	£	Pool £	Private use asset £	Allowances £
Additions			22,000	
WDA (restricted)			(1,500) ×80%	1,200
Additions	172,500		20,500	
FYA @ 40%	(69,000)			69,000
		103,500		70,200
		103,500	20,500	

2   *Industrial buildings allowance*

Reside after sale of factory - £189,000

Remaining tax life = 17½ years

$$\text{Industrial buildings allowances} = \frac{£189,000}{17.5} = £10,800 \text{ per annum}$$

$$\text{IBAs period to } 5.4.01 = £10,800 \times \frac{6}{12} = £5,400$$

Marking guide		**Marks**	
(a) Proceeds/cost		1	
Indexation		1	
Retirement relief - Factor of 90%		1	
Chargeable business assets		1	
Calculation		1	
	Maximum /Available		5
(b) Tax avoidance		1	
Tax evasion		1	
Fiona's actions		2	
	Available	4	
	Maximum		3
(c) *Schedule D1 trading loss for 2000/01*			
Bonus		1	
Stock write-down		1	
Industrial buildings allowance		2	
First year allowance		1	
Motor car		1	
Postponed contract		1	
Loss relief claim			
S 380 ICTA 1988 and s 72 FA 1991		2	
S 385 ICTA 1988		1	
S 381 ICTA 1988		2	
S 380 ICTA 1988 for 1999/00		1	
Income tax and CGT liabilities for 2000/01			
Nil income tax liability		1	
Loss claim		1	
Taper claim		2	
Annual exemption		1	
Capital gains tax		1	
	Available	19	
	Maximum		17
	Maximum		25

23   **BASIL NADIR**

> **Tutor's hint**. It is important to carefully plan your answer to a written question like this in order to ensure you answer all parts of the question in the allotted time.
>
> **Examiner's comments**. In part (a) a number of candidates wasted time by repeating the same point several times.

(a)   The distinction between employment and self-employment is a fine one. It has been held that **employment involves a contract of service, whereas self employment involves a contract for services**. There is no single test that is conclusive in deciding whether a person is employed or self-employed and each case must be decided on its own facts. The criteria that will be used in deciding whether Basil will be classified as employed or self employed in respect of his contract with Ace Computers Ltd include:

(i)   the degree of control exercised over him;

(ii)   whether he must accept further work;

(iii)   whether Ace Computers Ltd must provide further work;

(iv)   whether he provides his own equipment;

(v)   whether he hires his own helpers;

(vi)   what degree of financial risk he takes;

(vii)   what degree of responsibility for investment and management he has;

(viii) whether he can profit from sound management;

(ix)   whether he can work when he chooses;

(x)   the wording of the contract between Basil and Ace Computers Ltd.

The fact that Basil does a large amount of work for Ace Computers Ltd and the fact that he was previously employed by the company are likely to have led the Revenue to have queried Basil's self employed status.

The following factors could be put forward to justify Basil's self employed status.

(i)   He has bought his own equipment.

(ii)   He has his own office at home.

(iii)   He has five other clients.

(iv)   The change in his rights since being an employee. For instance he may no longer be entitled to holiday pay or sick pay.

In addition it may be possible to use the terms of the twelve month contract with Ace Computers Ltd to help justify Basil's status. For instance, if the contract is to be done for a fixed fee, self employment rather than employment is indicated. If, however, the contract requires Basil to work two specific days a week, then it is likely that Basil is an employee.

(b)   If Basil is classified as self-employed, all of his income will be taxed under Schedule D Case II. The costs of running an office from home and the costs of travelling between home and the offices of Ace Computers Ltd should be deductible. Basil's income tax and NIC liabilities for 2000/01 will therefore be as follows.

	£	£
Income		60,600
Expenses		
Use of office (£1,800 × 2/8)	450	
Telephone (£150 × 4)	600	
Motor expenses (£3,500 × 20,000/25,000)	2,800	
Capital allowances		
Computer equipment (£7,375 × 100% (FYA))	7,375	
Motor car (£10,000 × 25% × 20,000/25,000)	2,000	
		(13,225)
Schedule D case II		47,375
Personal allowance		(4,385)
Taxable income		42,990

	£
Income tax: £1,520 at 10%	152
£26,880 at 22%	5,914
£14,590 at 40%	5,836
	11,902

	£
Class 2 NIC (52 × £2)	104
Class 4 NIC (£27,820 – £4,385) × 7%	1,640
	1,744

The total income tax and NIC liability is £13,646 (£11,902 + £1,744)

If Basil is classified as employed in respect of his contract with Ace Computers Ltd, then his tax liabilities will increase as a result of the following.

(i) Basil's travelling costs between home and the offices of Ace Computers Ltd of £1,400 (£3,500 × 10,000/25,000) will not be deductible. The capital allowances in respect of Basil's motor car will be reduced by £1,000 (£10,000 × 25% × 10,000/25,000). As a result Basil's income tax liability will increase by £960 (£2,400 × 40%).

(ii) Basil will be liable to the maximum employee's class 1 NIC in respect of his £30,300 Schedule E earnings from Ace Computers Ltd. These will be £22,568 (£27,820 – £3,952) × 10% = £2,387.

Thus the increase in national insurance contributions will be £643 (£2,387 – £1,744).

(c) **Basil will become liable to register for VAT if at the end of any period of up to twelve consecutive calendar months, the value of his taxable supplies (excluding VAT) exceeds the registration limit.** The registration limit is £52,000.

The registration limit will be exceeded on 28 February 2001 as the value of Basil's taxable supplies in the eleven months to 28 February 2001 will be £55,550 (£60,600 × 11/12). Basil will have to notify HM Customs and Excise that he is required to be registered within 30 days, that is by 30 March 2001. He will be registered from 1 April 2001.

Implications of VAT registration

From the date of registration, Basil will have to account for output tax on his income. Since Ace Computers Ltd and his other clients are presumably VAT registered, Basil will be able to charge VAT on top of his fees charged. His output tax will amount to £10,605 pa (£60,600 × 17.5%). **Basil will be able to recover the input tax on the business use of light and heat of £25 pa (£100 × 2/8), the business use of his telephone of £89 pa (£150 × 7/47 × 4), and motor expenses of £400. He will have**

to account for output tax based on the fuel scale charge, since fuel is being provided for private use. This can be avoided by not reclaiming any input tax in respect of fuel, although due to Basil's high business mileage this is unlikely to be beneficial.

Voluntary registration

Upon registering for VAT, **Basil will also be able to recover pre-registration input tax of £1,098 (£7,375 × 7/47) in respect of his computer equipment, provided that it is still owned at the date of VAT registration. He will only be able to recover input tax on the business use of light and heat, the business use of his telephone, and motor expenses, incurred within the six months prior to VAT registration.** Basil would therefore be advised to voluntarily register for VAT on or before 5 October 2000, in order to maximise the recovery of input tax.

---

24   BASIL PERFECT

> **Tutor's hint.** Basil will be treated as changing his accounting date for Schedule D Case I purposes on the merger.
>
> **Examiner's comments.** Part (b) was generally badly answered with far too many candidates not being able to calculate the VAT partial exemption aspects of the question.

(a)   (i)   **Basil's Schedule D Case I profit**

	£	£
1998/99 (1.7.98 – 5.4.99)		
9/12 × £38,640		28,980
1999/00 (y/e 30.6.99)		38,640
2000/01 (1.7.99 – 31.3.01)		
12 m/e 30.6.00	49,920	
9 m/e 31.3.01	47,700	
21 months	97,620	
Less: Overlap relief	(28,980)	68,640
2001/02 (y/e 31.3.02)		
£80,000 × 75%		60,000

Tutorial note. Basil is treated as changing his accounting date in 2000/01. This means that overlap relief is available to reduce the number of months worth of profit assessed in the year to 12.

Sybil's Schedule D Case I profits

	£
2000/01 (1.6.00 – 31.3.01)	11,100
2001/02 (y/e 31.3.02)	
25% × £80,000	20,000

(ii)   Disadvantages and advantages of having an accounting date of 31 March as compared with 30 June are:

- Profits of each nine month period to 31 March are taxed in an earlier tax year leading to earlier due dates for the payment of tax on these profits.

- As all profits of a period to 31 March are taxed in the year in which they arise there is less time available for preparing accounts or for planning for the payment of tax deductible amounts such as pension premiums.

- No overlap profits arise with an accounting date of 31 March so the calculation of assessable amounts is straightforward.

(b) (i) **VAT payable by Basil as sole trader:**

	£
Output tax	
Standard rated supplies (£170,000 × 17.5%)	29,750
Exempt supplies	-
Less: input tax	
25% × £160,000 × 17.5%	(7,000)
Non-attributable (W1)	(7,560)
VAT payable by Basil	15,190

	£
VAT payable by partnership	
Output VAT	
£155,000 × 17.5%	27,125
£47,000 × 7/47	7,000
Less: input VAT (W2)	
25% × £160,000 × 17.5%	(7,000)
Non attributable (W2)	(7,938)
Sybil (£11,000 × 7/40)	(1,925)
Output VAT payable by partnership	17,262

If a partnership is formed, additional VAT of £2,072 will be due.

(ii) **HM Customs and Excise will make a direction under the disagregation rules if they consider there are significant financial, economic or organisation links between Basil and Sybil's businesses.**

(iii) If profits are shared 75%/25%

	Basil	Sybil
	£	£
Profits (£80,000)	60,000	20,000
Less: Pension (30%)	(18,000)	-
	42,000	20,000
Less: Personal allowance	(4,385)	(4,385)
Taxable income	37,615	15,615

Basil will pay maximum Class 4 NICs of £1,640 whilst Sybil will pay £1,093 (£20,000 – £4,385) × 7%.

If profits are shared 60%/40%:

	Basil	Sybil
	£	£
Profits (£80,000)	48,000	32,000
Less: Pension (30%)	(14,400)	
	33,600	32,000
	(4,385)	(4,385)
	29,215	27,615

The amount of personal pension premium that Basil can pay is reduced by £3,600 in these circumstances. However, Sybil is now making better use of her basic rate tax band which she did not do with a 75%/25% split. This will save the couple income tax of £720 (£8,400 × 40% – £12,000 × 22%).

Maximum Class 4 NICs of £1,640 will be payable by both Basil and Sybil.

Workings

1 *Non-attributable input tax*

Non attributable amount

£160,000 × 45% × 17.5%   £12,600

$$\frac{\text{Taxable supplies}}{\text{Total supplies}} = \frac{170,000}{285,000} = 59.6\%$$

= 60% (rounded up to nearest whole %)

Deductible amount: £12,600 × 60% =   £7,560
Exempt amount: £12,600 × 40% =   £5,040

2   *Non-attributable input VAT for partnership*

Non-attributable amount = £12,600

$$\frac{\text{Taxable supplies}}{\text{Total supplies}} = \frac{170,000 - 15,000 + 40,000}{170,000 - 15,000 + 40,000 + 115,000}$$

$$= \frac{195,000}{310,000} = 62.9\%$$

$$= 63\% \text{ (rounded up to nearest whole \%)}$$

Deductible: $63\% \times £12,600 = £7,938$

Exempt: $37\% \times £12,600 = £4,662$

Marking guide			Marks	
(a)	Schedule D1 assessments		1	
	Change of accounting date		2	
	Basil – 2000/01		1	
	Sybil – 2000/01		1	
	Accounting date			
	Calculation of assessable profits straightforward/No overlap		2	
	Tax liability due earlier		1	
	Tax return/Personal pension contributions		1	
		Available	9	
		Maximum		8
(b)	*Additional VAT*			
	Supply to Sybil		1	
	Output VAT		2	
	Input VAT		1	
	Partial exemption		1	
	Percentage recovered		2	
	Additional recovery		1	
	Additional VAT payable		1	
	Direction under the disaggregation rules			
	Extension of Basil's business		1	
	Financial links/Economic links		1	
	Organisation links		1	
		Available	12	
		Maximum		11
(c)	*Income tax*			
	Personal pension contributions		1	
	Tax relief at 40%		1	
	Reduced tax relief		1	
	Sybil's basic rate tax band		1	
	Tax saving		1	
	Class 4 NIC			
	Maximum Class 4 NIC		1	
	Additional cost		1	
	Conclusion		1	
		Available	8	
		Maximum		6
		Maximum		25

BPP
PUBLISHING

25 ALEX ZONG

> **Tutor's hints**. Take care with taper relief. It is deducted after current and brought forward capital losses.
>
> **Examiner's comments**. Poorly laid out answers and a failure to show workings (such as the private use adjustment) lead to a loss of marks.

(a) (i) **Schedule DI assessments**

The Schedule D Case I profits for each accounting period are:

		£
P/E 30.6.98	£28,000 – £8,050 (W)=	19,950
Y/E 30.6.99	£44,000 – £2,388 (W)=	41,612
Y/E 30.6.00	£53,000 – £3,007 (W)=	49,993
P/E 31.12.00	£29,000	29,000

Overlap profits on commencement were.

	£
1.10.97 to 5.4.98 (£19,950 × 6/9)	13,300
1.7.98 to 30.9.98 (£41,612 × 3/12)	10,403
	23,703

Alex's Schedule D Case I assessment for 2000/01 will be as follows.

	£
Y/E 30.6.00	49,993
P/E 31.12.00	29,000
	78,993
Relief for overlap profits	(23,703)
	55,290

Working

Capital allowances

	FYA £	Pool £	Private use £		Allowances £
Period ended 30.6.98					
Additions	15,200		4,000		
FYA @ 50% /WDA (25% × 9/12)	(7,600)		(750)	× 60%	8,050
TWDV c/f		7,600	3,250		
Year ended 30.6.99					
WDA - 25%		(1,900)	(813)	× 60%	2,388
WDV c/f		5,700	2,437		
Year ended 30.6.00					
Disposal			(2,800)		
Balancing charge			363	× 60%	(218)
Addition			13,500		
WDA 25%/(restricted)		(1,425)	(3,000)	× 60%	3,225
TWDV c/f		4,275	10,500		3,007

Note 1

Alex should elect to transfer plant to Lexon Ltd at its written-down value. This avoids the balancing charges that would otherwise arise in the final period. The market values of the lorry and plant (£4,300 + £8,200 = £12,500) and the motor car (£11,500) both exceed their respective written-down values.

(ii) **Capital gains tax**

The assets will be deemed to be disposed of at their market values:

	£	£
Goodwill		
Proceeds		40,000
Cost		nil
Capital gain		40,000
Freehold premises		
Proceeds		75,000
Cost	32,000	
Enhancement expenditure	6,700	
		(38,700)
Indexation allowance to April 1998		36,300

$$£32,000 \times \frac{162.6 - 159.6}{159.6} = 0.019 \qquad (608)$$

Indexed gain	35,692

Total gains (before taper relief) total £75,692 (40,000 + 35,692).

Alex qualifies for incorporation relief since the business is transferred as a going concern, and all of the business assets are being transferred. However since Alex is receiving some shares and some cash (loan account) not all of the gain can be rolled over in this way. Alex will have a chargeable gain before taper relief of £4,731 (£75,692 × 10,000/160,000) which will be completely extinguished by the capital losses made in the year.

However, to avoid wasting taper relief and the annual exemption. Alex should consider increasing the amount of the loan account to £46,716:

	£
$£75,692 \times \dfrac{46,716}{160,000} =$	22,100
Less capital loss	(12,500)
Net gain for year	9,600

	£
Gain remaining after taper relief (£9,600 × 75%)	7,200
Less: Annual exemption	(7,200)
	nil

(iii) **Value added tax**

The incorporation of a business is outside the scope of VAT. This means there will be no VAT charged on any assets transferred to Lexon Ltd.

Lexon Ltd will be able to take over Alex's VAT registration number if it wishes. However, if this is done then the company assumes Alexs' VAT liabilities.

(b) (i) **Bad debt**

Bad debts relief is given six months after the time that payment was due, provided that the debt has been written off. Since an invoice was not raised until 15 June 2000, bad debt relief can not be claimed in the VAT return for the quarter ended 30 November 2000. The amount of the relief to be claimed in the following VAT return will be £1,050.

(ii) **Refund of VAT**

A claim must be made for the repayment of the VAT underclaimed. The amount due cannot just be put through on the next VAT return, since the error exceeds £2,000. Claims for the refund of VAT are subject to a three year

time limit, and so the claim will cover the period 1 December 1997 to 30 November 2000. The repayment will be for £2,547 (£475 × 36 × 17.5/117.5).

(iii) **Discount**

Where a discount is offered for prompt payment, VAT is due on the net amount even if the discount is not taken. The output VAT due is therefore £565 (£3,400 × 95% × 17.5%).

26 SMART AND SHARP

> **Tutor's hint.** Always start a partnership question by dividing partnership income between the partners before allocating the income to tax years.
>
> **Examiner's comment.** The NIC implications in part (b) caused problems for some candidates, and there is little excuse for not knowing the correct NIC calculations when the rates are given on the examination paper.

(a) The profits of each period of account must first be divided between the partners.

Period	Total £	Bob £	Nick £	Justin
Six months to 31.12.98				
Salaries (6/12)	130,000	90,000	40,000	
Balance	150,000	75,000	75,000	
	280,000	165,000	115,000	
Year to 31.12.99	£	£	£	
Salaries	260,000	180,000	80,000	
Balance	450,000	225,000	225,000	
	710,000	405,000	305,000	
Year to 31.12.00	£	£	£	
Salaries	260,000	180,000	80,000	
Balance	380,000	190,000	190,000	
	640,000	370,000	270,000	
	£	£	£	£
Year to 31.12.01 (1:1:1)	750,000	250,000	250,000	250,000
Year to 31.12.02 (1:1:1)	750,000	250,000	250,000	250,000
Year to 31.12.03 (1:1:1)	750,000	250,000	250,000	250,000

Next the amount of each partner's Schedule D Case II income in each tax year can be calculated.

Bob

Year	Basis period	£	£
1998/99	1.7.98-5.4.99 (£165,000 + $^3/_{12}$ × £405,000)		266,250
1999/00	Year to 31.12.99		405,000
2000/01	Year to 31.12.00		370,000
2001/02	Year to 31.12.01		250,000
2002/03	Year to 31.12.02		250,000
2003/04	Year to 31.12.03	250,000	
	Less: overlap relief	(101,250)	
			148,750

Nick

Year	Basis period	£	£
1998/99	1.7.98-5.4.99 (£115,000 + $^3/_{12}$ × £305,000)		191,250
1999/00	Year to 31.12.99		305,000
2000/01	Year to 31.12.00		270,000
2001/02	Year to 31.12.01		250,000
2002/03	Year to 31.12.02		250,000
2003/04	Year to 31.12.03	250,000	
	Less: overlap relief	(76,250)	
			173,750

Justin

Year	Basis period	£	£
2000/01	1.1.01-5.4.01 ($^3/_{12}$ × £250,000)		62,500
2001/02	Year to 31.12.01		250,000
2002/03	Year to 31.12.02		250,000
2003/04	Year to 31.12.03	250,000	
	Less: overlap relief	(62,500)	
			187,500

As the partnership is incorporated on 31 December 2003, 2003/04 is the year of cessation for all partners and overlap relief is available for the overlap profits that arose on commencement.

(b) **Partnership not incorporated**

If the partnership is not incorporated the partners will each have Schedule D Case I income of £250,000. Their additional income tax and NIC liabilities will be:

	£
Income tax (£250,000 × 40%)	100,000
Class 2 (£2 × 52)	104
Class 4 (£27,820 – £4,385) × 7%	1,640
	101,744

The total NIC and income tax liabilities of the three partners will be:

3 × £101,744 = £305,232

Partnership incorporated

The annual tax liability of Smash Ltd will be:

	£
Trading profit	750,000
Less: director's remuneration (3 × £200,000)	(600,000)
Employer's Class 1 NIC (£200,000 – 4,385) × 3 × 12.2%	(71,595)
PCTCT	78,405

	£
Corporation tax at 20%	15,681
Employer's Class 1 NIC	71,595
	87,276

Tax liability of directors

The annual tax liability of each director will be as follows.

	£
Taxable income - Schedule E	200,000
Income tax at 40%	80,000
Employees Class 1 NIC	
(£27,820 – £3,952) × 10%	2,387
	82,387

The total annual tax liability of Smash Ltd and the three directors will be £334,437 (£87,276 + (£82,387 × 3)). This is an increase of £29,205 (£334,437 − £305,232) compared to the total annual tax liability of the three partners.

Conclusion

Since incorporating the partnership's business will result in an increase in the overall annual tax liability, incorporation does not appear to be beneficial.

(c) **Each partner will be entitled to overlap relief for his overlap profits when he ceases to be a member of the partnership.** This could be on incorporation of the business or on some other event when the partner leaves the partnership business. Relief is given by **deducting overlap profits in the final tax year the business is carried on.**

Relief for overlap profits may also be available if the partnership changes its accounting date. If a change of accounting date results in more than twelve months worth of profits being taxed in a tax year, **overlap relief is given to reduce the number of months worth of profit taxed in that year to twelve.**

(d) **CGT implications**

The incorporation of the partnership's business will be a disposal for CGT purposes. Provided that the disposal is in return for shares in Smash Ltd, any gains arising from the disposal of chargeable business assets can be held over against the base cost of the shares received. For this relief to apply the partnership's business must be transferred as a going concern, and all the assets of the partnership's business (excluding cash) must be transferred.

IHT implications

There are **not normally any IHT implications of an incorporation** itself as there is not normally a transfer of wealth. At present, were they to die, the existing partners would be entitled to BPR at the rate of 100% in respect of their partnership share. The new partner will not be entitled to BPR until he has been a partner for two years.

Following the incorporation of the partnership's business, BPR will only be available at 100% if the company remains unquoted and continues to carry on a qualifying trade. The partners will be able to carry their unincorporated business ownership period forward in relation to the shares.

27 SALLY AND TREVOR ACRE

> **Tutor's hints.** In part (b) it was important to provide adequate justification for your choice of loss relief.
>
> **Examiner's comments.** Candidates are advised to read the question carefully since a significant number confused the ages of the two partners.

(a) **Partnership assets**

	£
Freehold property - market value	230,000
Less: cost	(170,000)
Unindexed gain	60,000
Less: indexation to April 1998	(6,175)
Gain on property	53,825
Gain on goodwill	100,000
Gains on partnership assets before taper relief	153,825

These gains are split between Trevor and Sally in their profit sharing ratio:

Trevor (30%) = £46,147

Sally (70%) = £107,678

Trevor is not old enough to qualify for retirement relief so his chargeable gain after taper relief is £34,610 (£46,147 × 75%).

Sally qualifies for retirement relief on her gain of £107,678 and on the gain made on the disposal of the leasehold premises as the disposal is an associated disposal:

Leasehold property

	£
Proceeds	90,000
Less: cost	
$£85,000 \times \dfrac{78.055 + (79.622 - 78.055) \times 3/12}{81.100}$	(82,219)
Gain before taper relief	7,781

Sally's gains eligible for retirement relief:

	£
Partnership assets	107,678
Leasehold property	7,781
	115,459

The partnership business was carried on for three years and six months so the lower and upper limits for retirement relief are multiplied by 3½/10.

Lower limit £150,000 × 3 ½ /10	=	£52,500
Upper limit £600,000 × 3 ½ /10	=	£210,000

The relief should be set against the gain on the leasehold office first as this only attracts one year's taper relief.

	Partnership	*Office*
	£	*£*
Gains before retirement relief	107,678	7,781
Less: relief @ 100% on office		(7,781)
relief @ 100% on partnership £(52,500 – 7,781)	(44,719)	
relief @ 50% on partnership £(107,678 – 44,719)	(31,480)	
Gain left in charge	31,479	nil
Gain after taper relief (75%)	£23,609	

(b) Each partner can claim for their share of the loss.

(i)   Under s380 ICTA 1998 a partner can set their loss against their statutory total income in the year of the loss (2000/01) and/or in the preceding year (1999/00). A s380 ICTA claim in any tax year can be extended to set any remaining loss against net chargeable gains of that year.

(ii) Under s388 ICTA 1988 the loss could be carried back to set against Schedule D Case II income of the three preceding years, latest year first.

(iii) Under s381 ICTA 1988 the loss could be set against the statutory total income of the three preceding years, earliest year first.

Sally's share of the loss is £47,600.

S388 ICTA 1988 relief would be:

	1998/99	*1999/00*
	£	*£*
Schedule D Case II	51,800	36,400
Less: s388 ICTA 1988 relief	(11,200)	(36,400)
	40,600	-

Schedule A profits remain in 1999/00 to use the personal allowance and 10% rate band, so the tax relief is at 22% and 40%. Relief in 1998/99 is at 40%. This means all of the loss is saving tax at the marginal rates of 22% or 40%.

Under s380 ICTA 1988 in 1999/00, £36,400 of the loss would be relieved as above. In addition £5,905 of the loss would be relieved against Schedule A income wasting the benefit of the personal allowance and 10% rate band, so this claim cannot be as beneficial as the above claim.

Similarly in 2000/01 a s380 claim would waste the personal allowance and starting rate band. If Sally made a claim in order to then set her loss against her chargeable gains she would save capital gains tax at 10% and 20% but this claim is less beneficial than the s388 ICTA 1988 claim, discussed above.

Relief under s381 ICTA 1988 will be:

	1997/98	1998/99
	£	£
Schedule D Case II	26,250	51,800
Schedule A	5,905	5,905
	32,155	57,705
S 381 relief	(32,155)	(15,445)
	-	42,260

In 1997/98 relief wastes the personal allowance and the starting rate band. Some of the loss is relieved at 22%. In 1998/99 relief is at 40%. This relief is not as beneficial as the s388 ICTA 1988 claim where all the loss saves tax at 22% or 40%.

The most beneficial claim for Sally is the s388 ICTA 1988 claim. Her taxable income each year if this claim is made is:

	1997/98	1998/99	1999/00	2000/01
	£	£	£	£
Schedule D Case II	26,250	51,800	36,400	-
Less: s388 relief	-	(11,200)	(36,400)	
Schedule A	5,905	5,905	5,905	5,905
	32,155	46,505	5,905	5,905
Less: personal allowance	(4,385)	(4,385)	(4,385)	(4,385)
Taxable income	27,770	42,120	1,520	1,520

Sally's chargeable gain in 2000/01 is:

	£
Gain after taper relief (part a)	23,609
Less: annual exemption	(7,200)
	16,409

Trevor

Trevor's share of the loss is £20,400.

S388 ICTA 1988 relief would be:

	1998/99	1999/00
	£	£
Schedule D Case II	22,200	15,600
Less: s388 ICTA 1988	(4,800)	(15,600)
	17,400	-
Schedule A	2,000	2,000
	19,400	2,000
Personal allowance	(4,385)	(2,000)
Taxable income	15,015	-

In 1999/00 £2,385 of the personal allowance and the £1,520 starting rate band, are wasted. The rest of the loss, £16,495, saves tax at 22% in either 1998/99 or 1999/00.

A s 380 claim in 1999/00 would relive £15,600 as above but it would also waste £2,000 of the personal allowance. This means this relief is not as beneficial as the s 388 claim discussed above.

A s 380 claim in 2000/01 would also waste £2,000 of personal allowances but it would also allow Trevor to set the remaining loss of £18,400 against chargeable gains 2000/01. Trevor would choose to set the £18,400 against gains on his non-business assets as these do not qualify for taper relief:

	£
Gains on non business assets	38,000
Less: loss relief	(18,400)
	19,600
Gains on partnership assets (part (a))	34,610
	54,210
Less: annual exemption	(7,200)
Chargeable gains	47,010

The £18,400 has saved CGT at 40% - £7,360.

This claim is clearly more beneficial than a s388 ICTA 1988 claim.

S381 ICTA 1988 relief would be:

	1997/98	1998/99
	£	£
Schedule D Case II	11,250	22,200
Schedule A	2,000	2,000
	13,250	24,200
Less: loss relief	(13,250)	(7,150)
	0	17,050
Less: personal allowance	-	(4,385)
Taxable income	-	12,665

The personal allowance and the lower rate band are wasted in 1997/98. The rest of the loss, £14,495, saves tax at 22% in either 1997/98 or 1998/99.

The most beneficial claim for Trevor is the s380 and s72 claim in 2000/01. His resulting income is:

	1997/98	1998/99	1999/00	2000/01
	£	£	£	£
Schedule D Case II	11,250	22,200	15,600	-
Schedule A	2,000	2,000	2,000	2,000
	13,250	24,200	17,600	2,000
Less: s380				(2,000)
Less: PA	(4,385)	(4,385)	(4,385)	
Taxable income	8,865	19,815	13,215	-

Trevor's chargeable gains in 2000/01 are, as calculated above, £47,010.

Marking guide

		Marks	
(a)	*Capital gains*		
	Goodwill	1	
	Freehold property	1	
	Leasehold property	2	
	Trevor Acre		
	Share of chargeable gains	1	
	Retirement relief not available	1	
	Sally Acre		
	Share of chargeable gains	1	
	Calculation of retirement relief	4	
	Gain after taper relief	1	
	Available	12	
	Maximum		9
(b)	S 380 ICTA 1988 (against STI)	1	
	S 72 FA 1991 (against gains)	1	
	S 388 ICTA 1988 (terminal loss relief)	1	
	S381 ICTA 1988 (relief for early year loss)	1	
	Division of loss between partners	1	
	Sally Acre		
	Alternative claim under s 380 ICTA 1988	1	
	Claim under s 388 ICTA 1988	2	
	Claim under s 381 ICTA 1988	1	
	Taxable income and chargeable gains	2	
	Trevor Acre		
	Claim under s 388 ICTA 1988	1	
	Claim under s 380 ICTA 1988	1	
	Claim under s 72 FA 1991	2	
	Claim under s 381 ICTA 1988	1	
	Taxable income and chargeable gains	2	
	Available	18	
	Maximum		16
	Maximum		25

---

28 TUTORIAL QUESTION: CHOOSING ASSETS TO SELL

(a) **Site A**

The gain would be based on the value at 31 March 1982 as follows.

	£
Proceeds	1,600,000
Less value on 31 March 1982	(720,000)
	880,000
Less indexation allowance: $\dfrac{174.0-79.4}{79.4} = 1.191 \times £720,000$	(857,520)
Chargeable gain	22,480
Corporation tax at 30%	£6,744

The gain using cost less the rolled over gain ie (base cost = £700,000 – £600,000 = £100,000) would clearly have been higher.

Site B

Since the asset was not held on 31 March 1982 but the old land was sold before 6 April 1988, the base cost less the rolled over gain must be reduced by one half of the gain originally rolled over. This compensates for the non-availability of rebasing to 31 March 1982 on either the old or the new asset.

		£
Proceeds of 1982 sale		900,000
Less cost		(150,000)
		750,000
		(4,650)
Less indexation allowance: $\dfrac{81.9-79.4}{79.4} = 0.031 \times £150,000$		
Gain rolled over		745,350

	£	£
Proceeds		1,600,000
Less cost	900,000	
Less half of rolled over gain (£745,350 × 50%)	(372,675)	
		(527,325)
		1,072,675
Less indexation allowance: $\dfrac{174.0-81.9}{81.9} = 1.125 \times £527,325$		(593,241)
		479,434
Corporation tax at 30%		£143,830

Selling site A would lead to a much lower corporation tax liability.

(b) To: A Director
    From: A N Accountant
    Date: 20 February 2001
    Subject: Retirement relief on the proposed disposal of your shareholding

The following conditions, which appear to be met in your case, apply to retirement relief on a disposal of shares and securities.

(i)   The **vendor must be aged at least 50**, or retiring through ill health.

(ii)   The company must be the vendor's personal company. This is so if the **vendor holds at least 5% of the voting rights**.

(iii) At least 5% of the voting rights must have been held for a **qualifying period of at least one year during which the vendor was a full-time working officer or employee**.

The maximum relief is all gains up to the lower limit, plus 50% of gains above the lower limit up to the upper limit. The limits in 2000/01 are £150,000 and £600,000 when the qualifying period is at least ten years, and are scaled down when it is shorter than this. In your case the limits will therefore be 9/10 of these figures, that is £135,000 and £540,000. The limits will decrease further after 2000/01 as retirement relief is gradually being phased out by 2003/04.

The gain eligible for relief is the total gain, multiplied by the ratio of the market value of the company's chargeable business assets to the market value of its chargeable assets. The latter excludes assets on which no chargeable gain would arise on disposal, such as debtors and stock; the former also excludes assets not used in the business, such as investments.

Any gain remaining chargeable after deducting retirement relief is eligible for taper relief. The shares are a business asset so in 2000/01 only 75% of the gain will remain chargeable after taper relief. If you actually retire after 31 March 2001, the amount of taper relief will increase but, from a tax planning point of view this has to be weighed against the reduction in the retirement relief limits.

29   **SALLY JONES**

> **Tutor's hint.** You might reasonably have been uncertain about the treatment of the ex gratia payment. The £30,000 exemption is only available if the payment is not treated as a lump sum payment under an unapproved retirement benefit scheme. How a payment is treated will depend on all the circumstances, particularly the age of the recipient and whether or not the recipient goes on to other employment.
>
> **Examiner's comment.** In part (b), many candidates had difficulty with the retirement relief calculation.

(a) **If a company buys its own shares for more than the amount originally subscribed, general tax rules state that there is a distribution of the excess.**

However, a capital gains tax disposal occurs rather than a distribution, when an unquoted trading company (or the unquoted parent of a trading group) other than a company whose trade consists of dealing in shares, securities, land or futures, **buys back its own shares in order to benefit its trade. No relief is given if a main objective is tax avoidance.** On the other hand, **if the conditions for the relief are satisfied the relief is compulsory.**

The conditions to be satisfied by the vendor shareholder are as follows.

(i)   The vendor must be **resident and ordinarily resident in the UK** when the purchase is made.

(ii)   **The shares must have been owned by the vendor or her spouse throughout the five years preceding the purchase.** (Sally has owned her shares for six years.) This is reduced to three years if the vendor is the personal representative or the heir of a deceased member, and previous ownership by the deceased will count towards the qualifying period.

(iii) **The vendor and her associates must as a result of the purchase have their interest in the company's share capital reduced to 75% or less of their interest before the disposal.** Associates include spouses, minor children, controlled companies, trustees and beneficiaries. Sally's holding falls from 51.67% to 11/40 = 27.5%, a 47% reduction.

(iv)   **The vendor must not after the transaction be connected with the company or any company in the same 51% group.** A person is connected with a company if he can control more than 30% of the ordinary share capital, the issued share capital and loan capital or the voting rights in the company. Sally's shareholding will fall to 27.5%.

The conditions appear to be met in Sally's case. **The relief is also available where a company purchases shares to enable the vendor to pay any inheritance tax arising on a death.** The 'benefit to the trade' test and the conditions in (i) - (iv) above do not then apply.

(b) (i) INCOME TAX

	Non-savings £
Schedule E income	
Salary £24,000 × 9/12	18,000
Pension £950 × 3	2,850
Bonus	5,700
Ex gratia payment (first instalment)	40,000
STI	66,550
Less personal allowance	(4,385)
Taxable income	62,165

	£
Income tax on non-savings income	
£1,520 × 10%	152
£26,880 × 22%	5,914
£33,765 × 40%	13,506
Tax liability	19,572

Notes

(1) Bonuses are taxed in the year of receipt. However, for directors the definition of 'receipt' is very wide. An amount not actually received is treated as received as soon as the company's period of account ends (if the amount has already been determined by then), or when the amount is determined (if that is after the end of the period of account). The first of these alternatives applies here, making the bonus to be received on 30 April 2001 taxable in 2000/01.

(2) Ex gratia payments may qualify for a £30,000 exemption. However, that exemption is denied when a payment is regarded as a lump sum payment under an unapproved pension scheme. The payment to Sally is almost certain to be so regarded, because she has reached an age at which she might reasonably retire and there is no indication that she will be taking up any other employment.

Ex gratia payments on the termination of employment are taxed in the year they are received.

(ii) CAPITAL GAINS TAX

Zen Ltd is Sally's personal trading company, and retirement relief is available, based on a six year qualifying period.

	£	£
Gain		170,000
Less retirement relief		
Full relief £150,000 × 60%	90,000	
Partial relief £(170,000 – 90,000) × 50%	40,000	
		(130,000)
Chargeable gain		40,000

Taper relief is available as the shares are a business asset that has been owned for two years.

Gain after taper relief (75% × £40,000)	£30,000
CGT: £(30,000 – 7,200) × 40%	£9,120

(c) Zen Ltd will be able to deduct the following amounts in computing its taxable profits.

(i) Sally's monthly salary, plus employer's National Insurance contributions. of 12.2% of the amount by which the salary exceeds the lower limit of £4,385. This is deductible in the period of account in which the salary is charged in the accounts (since none will be paid more than nine months later than the end of that period).

(ii) Sally's bonus, deductible in the period of account in which the bonus is treated as received by Sally. Thus the bonus determined before 31 March 2001 will be deductible in the year ended 31 March 2001. (Note that if Sally had been treated as receiving the bonus at any time up to nine months after the end of that year, it would still have been deductible in that year.) Employer's National Insurance contributions of 12.2% of the full amount will also be due and deductible.

(iii) The ex gratia payment paid on 31 March 2001 is deductible in the year ended 31 March 2001 because it was all paid in that year or within the subsequent nine months. This deduction is, however, subject to its being shown that the payment was made wholly and exclusively for the purposes of the company's trade (a test which applies to all the payments, but which may be harder to satisfy in the case of the ex gratia payment). Employer's National Insurance contributions are not due on genuinely ex gratia payments.

30   TUTORIAL QUESTION: REGISTRATION AND ACCOUNTING

> **Tutor's hint**. Any discussion of partial exemption or of overseas trade was clearly ruled out by the question, and would have earned no marks.

ABC Certified Accountants
6 Somewhere Road, London, EC4Y 1SX

The Managing Director
XYZ Ltd
1 Anywhere Street
London, WC2 5SJ

Date: 23 October 2000
Our ref: Misc 1
Your ref: 123

Dear Sir,

Thank you for your recent letter.

We set out below the main points which you need to be aware of in respect of VAT.

Registration

If the company makes taxable supplies of goods or services, it must register with HM Customs & Excise if its taxable turnover in any period of up to 12 months to the end of a calendar month has exceeded the registration limit, or if you anticipate that it will exceed the registration limit in the 30 day period starting on any day.

The registration limit is currently £52,000.

Accounts

You should **record all income and expenditure exclusive of any VAT. The VAT should be recorded in a separate account showing the balance due to or from HM Customs & Excise.**

The only exception (when expenditure should be recorded inclusive of VAT) is expenditure, the VAT on which is irrecoverable. The main categories are cars with some non-business use and business entertaining.

Accounting for VAT

VAT is normally accounted for on a **quarterly basis,** the months which end the quarters depending on the type of business. A business may, however, arrange for its VAT quarters to coincide with its own accounting quarters. If VAT repayment claims normally arise (because input VAT normally exceeds output VAT), **a business can apply for monthly accounting in order to improve its own cash flow.** All VAT returns and payments must be made within one month of the end of the relevant period, and you should note that substantial penalties can be imposed on any business which is persistently late in paying VAT.

The normal accounting system for VAT ignores the time when cash is received from debtors and paid to suppliers. Small businesses, in particular, can suffer cash flow problems from the need to account for VAT before receiving payment from customers. Consequently, **taxable persons with an annual taxable turnover of up to £350,000 are entitled to use the cash accounting scheme. Users of the scheme account for VAT on the basis of cash receipts and payments**. This ensures that automatic bad debt relief is given and that VAT never has to be accounted on a supply before a customer has paid for it. Once in the cash accounting scheme a business will only have to leave if it's turnover in a particular year exceeds the built-in tolerance limit of £437,500 and also exceeds £350,000 in the following twelve months.

An entirely **separate scheme, available when annual taxable turnover does not exceed £300,000, is the annual accounting scheme. This is designed to reduce the compliance burden on small businesses by requiring only one VAT return each year. However, throughout the year they make payments on account of the ultimate liability under direct debits.** If annual turnover is £100,000 or more, the business must pay 90% of the previous year's net VAT liability during the year by means of nine monthly payments starting at the end of the fourth month of the year. If taxable turnover in the previous year was up to £100,000, four quarterly payments are required, each of 20% of the previous year's net VAT liability, starting at the end of the fourth month of the year. However, if the sum due does not exceed £400, the trader need not make the quarterly interim payment.

At the end of the year the trader completes an annual VAT return which must be submitted to HM Customs and Excise along with any payment due by two months after the end of the year.

Records

You will have to **keep VAT records for up to six years** including:

(a)   details of all input and output VAT together with invoices (copies of invoices issued);

(b)   details of all credits given or received together with credit notes (copies of credit notes issued);

(c)   details of errors or corrections;

(d)   details of any self-supplies;

(e)   a detailed VAT ledger account.

(f)   all other documentation relating to purchases and sales, such as day books.

Finally, we enclose copies of the relevant VAT booklets which you will need. We hope that you have found the information in this letter helpful but if you have any queries, please let us know.

Yours faithfully

ABC Certified Accountants

31 SCHOONER LTD

> **Tutor's hints.** Take care with written questions to answer all parts of the question.
>
> **Examiner's comments.** Many candidates failed to score high marks in part (b) because they did not deal with each aspect of the question separately.

(a) The deemed time of supply of goods is known as the tax point. The **basic tax point** is **the date on which the goods are removed or made available to the customer**. If a VAT **invoice** **is issued or payment is received** before the basic tax point, the earlier of these dates automatically becomes the tax point. If the earlier date rule does not apply and if the **VAT invoice is issued within 14 days after the basic tax point, the invoice date becomes the tax point** (although the trader can elect to use the basic point for all his supplies if he wishes).

Basic T.P

Actual T.P

Schooner will account for output tax on the deposit of £50,000 and on the payment on account of £100,000 on the quarterly return for the period during which the payments are received. The total output tax to be accounted for on this return will be £22,340 (17.5/117.5 × £150,000). Output VAT on the balance of the payment £38,910 (£350,000 × 17.5% – £22,340) will be accounted for on the following quarterly return.

(b) (i) **The equipment bought outright and the equipment bought on hire purchase will attract first year allowances** of £180,000 (40% (£250,000 + £200,000). These first year allowances will be deducted in computing the Schedule D Case I profits for the year ended 31 December 2001.

The annual charge of £145,000 incurred in respect of the leased equipment will be deducible in computing schedule D Case I profits for the year to 31 December 2001. **In addition, the total financing charge of £76,000 (£276,000 – £200,000) incurred over the life of the hire purchase contract will be deductible in computing schedule D Case I profits.** The amount to be deducted in the year to 31 December 2001 will be the same as the amount that is deducted in computing the profits for accounts purposes on normal accounting principles.

(ii) **VAT of £28,000 (£17.5% × £160,000) will have to be accounted for as output VAT in respect of the equipment which is acquired from other EU countries. However, this VAT may also be treated as input VAT on the same VAT return so there is no overall cash flow effect. VAT** of £15,750 (£90,000 × 17.5%) **will have to be accounted for in respect of the equipment imported from outside the EU at the point of entry into the UK. This amount can then be deducted as input VAT on the next VAT return.**

Deductible input VAT of £35,000 (£200,000 × 17.5%) will be incurred in respect of the hire purchase equipment. In addition, deductible input VAT of £25,375 (£145,000 × 17.5%) per annum will be incurred on the lease rental payments.

158

(c) (i) As the loan from Alex Barnacle will be interest free, it will have no effect on Schooner Ltd's schedule D Case I profits.

As the debenture will be issued for trading purposes, interest of £30,000 (£300,000 × 10%) will be deductible in computing schedule D Case I profits in the year to 31 December 2001. In addition, the 5% discount of £15,000 and the professional fees of £8,000 will be deductible for Schedule D Case I purposes over the life of the debenture. Using the accruals basis this means that £4,600 (£23,000/5) will be deductible in the year to 31 December 2001.

Schooner Ltd will not be able to obtain a Schedule D Case I deduction in respect of any costs associated with the share issue.

(ii) As Schooner Ltd is a close company Alex will be able to obtain tax relief for the interest paid on the loan as a charge on income. This means that the interest will be deductible in computing Alex's statutory total income.

It is assumed that, as Schooner Ltd is an unquoted trading company, the shares will be issued under the Enterprise Investment Scheme (EIS). This means that Chloe Dhow will be entitled to tax relief on the first £150,000 of her investment. The relief will be given as a tax reducer equal to the lower of £30,000 and Chloe's income tax liability for 2000/01. There will be no tax reduction in respect of the additional £30,000 invested.

If the EIS shares are held for three years there will in addition be relief from capital gains tax as any gain arising is exempt.

Marking guide

			Marks
(a)	*Tax point*		
	Goods removed or made available	1	
	Invoice issued or payment received	1	
	Issue of invoice within 14 days	1	
	Output VAT		
	Payments on account	1	
	Balance of output tax	<u>1</u>	
	Maximum/available		5
(b)	*Effect on Schedule D Case I profits*		
	First year allowances	2	
	Lease rental payment	1	
	Finance charge	2	
	VAT		
	EU acquisition	2	
	Non EU importation	2	
	VAT – leasing	1	
	VAT – hire purchase	<u>1</u>	
	Available	11	
	Maximum		9
(c)	*Schedule D Case I profits*		
	Personal loan	1	
	Debenture interest	1	
	Discount/incidental costs	2	
	Shares and incidental costs	2	
	Tax relief		
	Charge on income	2	
	Relief under the EIS	<u>5</u>	
	Available	13	
	Maximum		<u>11</u>
	Maximum		<u>25</u>

32   **HIGHRISE LTD**

> **Tutor's hint**. Your first step should have been to work out the profits that would be included in each set of accounts. Only then should you consider the corporation tax accounting periods.
>
> *Other points*. Schedule A losses for companies are relieved in the same way as management expenses:
>
> - first they are set off against non-Schedule A income and gains of the company for the current period; and any excess
> - is carried forward for set off against future income (of all descriptions); or
> - is available for surrender as group relief
>
> **Examiner's comments**. Many candidates gave away easy marks by not mentioning the due dates of the different mainstream corporation tax liabilities.

(a)   **One set of accounts for the eighteen months to 31 December 2000**

If one set of accounts is prepared, the tax adjusted Schedule D Case I profits before capital allowances arising in the eighteen months to 31 December 2000 will be £432,000 (£141,000 + £126,000 + £165,000).

For corporation tax purposes **there will be two accounting periods, one covering the first twelve months and the other covering the balancing period of six months.** As a result corporation tax will be payable as follows:

	Year to 30 June 2000	*Six months to 31 December 2000*
	£	£
Schedule D profits before capital allowances (12:6)	288,000	144,000
Capital allowances (W1)	(35,000)	(7,500)
	253,000	136,500
Schedule A (W2)	22,000	0
Chargeable gain (£42,000 – £38,000)	4,000	0
PCTCT	279,000	136,500

Corporation tax

	£	£
£279,000 × 20%	55,800	
£136,500 × 20%		27,300

£55,800 will be due and payable by 1 April 2001 and £27,300 will be due and payable by 1 October 2001.

Two sets of accounts

Tax adjusted trading profits included in accounts prepared for the six months to 31 December 1999 will be £141,000 and the tax adjusted profits included in the accounts for the twelve months to 31 December 2000 will be £291,000 (£126,000 + £165,000).

The corporation tax computations resulting from each set of accounts will be

	Six months to 31 December 1999	*Year to 31 December 2000*
	£	£
Schedule D profits before capital allowances	141,000	291,000
Capital allowances (W1)	(2,500)	(34,375)
	138,500	256,625
Schedule A (W2)	30,000	0
Chargeable gain (W3)	42,000	0
	210,500	256,625
Less: Schedule A loss	–	(8,000)
	210,500	248,625

Corporation tax

	£	£
£210,500 × 30% (W4)	63,150	0
Less: (£750,000 – £210,500) × 1/40	(13,488)	0
£248,625 × 20%	0	49,725
Mainstream corporation tax	49,662	49,725

£49,662 will be due and payable by 1 October 2000 and £49,725 will be due and payable by 1 October 2001.

The company should be advised to prepare one set of accounts as the total tax liability is £16,287 (£49,662 + £49,725 – £55,800 – £27,300) smaller.

Workings

1 **Capital allowances**

Separate capital allowance computations are required for each corporation tax accounting period.

One set of accounts

Year to 30 June 2000

			Allowances
	£	£	£
TWDV b/f		20,000	
WDA @ 25%		(5,000)	5,000
		15,000	
Addition qualifying for FYA	75,000		
FYA @40%	(30,000)		30,000
		45,000	
		60,000	35,000

Six months to 31 December 2000

WDA at 25% × 6/12		(7,500)	7,500
		52,500	

Two sets of accounts

Six months 31 December 1999

		£	
TWDV b/f		20,000	
WDA at 25% × 6/12		(2,500)	£2,500
		17,500	

Year to 31 December 2000

WDA at 25%		(4,375)	4,375
Addition qualifying for FYA	75,000		
FYA @ 40%	(30,000)		30,000
		45,000	
		58,125	34,375

2 **Schedule A**

The company's Schedule A profits are computed on an accruals basis. Profits and losses on all properties are pooled.

One set of accounts

12 months to 30.6.00

	£
Bodford (£48,000 × 6/12)	24,000
Ampton (£1,000 × 10)	10,000
Redecoration	(12,000)
Schedule A	22,000

There is no Schedule A income in the six months to 31.12.00 as both buildings have been sold.

Two sets of accounts

Six months to 31.12.99

The building at Ampton will be let until 31 December 1999 so the schedule A income accruing in the six months to 31 December 1999 will be £48,000 × 6/12 = £24,000 and there was no income accruing after this.

The building at Bodford will be let for £1,000 a month, so the rental income accruing in the six months to 31.12.99 is £1,000 × 6 = £6,000.

	£
Ampton	24,000
Bodford	6,000
Schedule A	30,000

Year ended 31.12.00

	£
Ampton (sold)	-
Bodford	
Rent accruing (£1,000 × 4)	4,000
Redecoration	(12,000)
Schedule A loss	(8,000)

A company's Schedule A loss can be set against its non-Schedule A income and gains arising in the same period.

3 **Allowable loss**

Capital losses can be set against gains in the same or future accounting periods only. They can not be carried back.

4 **Rate of tax**

Six months to 31 December 1999

Upper limit is £1,500,000 × 6/12 = £750,000.
Lower limit is £300,000 × 6/12 = £150,000
PCTCT = £210,500
'Profits' = £210,500

As profits are between the small company lower and upper limits, small companies' marginal relief applies.

(b) Highrise Ltd's acquisition of Shortie Ltd will mean that it will be possible for Shortie Ltd to group relieve some of the loss forecast for the year to 31 March 2001. The maximum loss available for group relief will be the lower of:

(i) £38,750 (£155,000 × 3/12)

(ii) 3/12 of Highrise Ltd's PCTCT for the year to 31 December 2001.

If within three years of the acquisition of Shortie Ltd there is a major change in the nature or conduct of Shortie Ltd's trade it will not be possible for Shortie Ltd to carry forward any schedule D Case I losses that arose before the change in ownership.

Shortie Ltd's capital loss of £37,000 is a pre-entry loss. It will also be necessary to ascertain the amount of the unrealised pre-entry loss attributable to the investment in Minute Ltd. This can either be done on a time basis when the shareholding is disposed of, or based on the market value of the shareholding as at 1 January 2001. It will not be possible for Highrise Ltd to utilise the pre-entry capital losses against any gain arising on the disposal of its 5% shareholding in Tiny Ltd, by transferring the shareholding to Shortie Ltd (no gain no loss) prior to disposal outside of the group.

33   EASY-SPEAK LTD

> **Tutor's hints.** It was important to read this question carefully.
>
> **Examiner's comments.** Part (b) was well answered provided that candidates read the question carefully. If not, the deduction for either the rent/premium or the industrial buildings allowance was given in the wrong part of the answer.

(a)   The Courts consider the following **badges of trade** in deciding whether or not an isolated sale transaction should be treated as an adventure in the nature of trade.

The subject matter

Whether a person is trading or not may sometimes be decided by examining the subject matter of the transaction. Some assets are commonly held as investments for their intrinsic value: an individual buying some shares or a painting may do so in order to enjoy the income from the shares or to enjoy the work of art. Any subsequent disposal, even at a profit, may produce a gain of a capital nature rather than a trading profit. But **where the subject matter of a transaction is such as would not be held as an investment, it is to be presumed that any profit on resale is a trading profit.**

The frequency of transactions

Transactions which may be treated in isolation as being of a capital nature will be interpreted as trading transactions where their **frequency indicates the carrying on of a trade.**

The length of ownership

The courts may infer adventures in the nature of trade where items purchased are sold soon afterwards.

Supplementary work and marketing

When work is done to make an asset more marketable, or steps are taken to find purchasers, the courts will be more ready to ascribe a trading motive.

A profit motive

The absence of a profit motive will not necessarily preclude a Schedule D Case I assessment, but its presence is a strong indication that a person is trading.

The way in which the asset sold was acquired

If goods are acquired deliberately, trading may be indicated. If goods are acquired unintentionally, for example by gift or inheritance, their later sale is unlikely to constitute trading.

The taxpayer's intentions

Where a transaction clearly amounts to trading on objective criteria, **the taxpayer's intentions are irrelevant.** If, however, a transaction has (objectively) a dual purpose, the taxpayer's intentions may be taken into account. An example of a transaction with a dual purpose is the acquisition of a site partly as premises from which to conduct another trade, and partly with a view to the possible development and resale of the site.

This intentions test is not one of the traditional badges of trade, but it may be just as important.

The managing director is probably correct in her understanding that the sale of the land in its existing state is likely to be treated as a capital gain because Easy-Speak Ltd purchased the land with a view to building a factory on it and the company will not have carried out any supplementary work on the land. These are both strong indications that the company is not trading.

The managing director is also probably correct in her understanding that the development of the land would appear to establish an adventure in the nature of a trade.

The sale of the industrial units soon after their completion, and the financing of the development by way of a bank loan, support this conclusion, Although the disposal is an isolated transaction, this does not prevent it being treated as an adventure in the nature of a trade. A profit motive is indicated by factors such as developing the land, although the absence of a profit motive will not prevent the sale from being treated as trading.

(b) Corporation tax liability

Sale of land in its existing state

	£	£
Forecast profits		270,000
Less: Annual rent (6/12 × £27,600)		(13,800)
Premium (W2)		(6,720)
		249,480
Capital gain (W)	96,000	
Less: loss b/f	(61,600)	
		34,400
Profits chargeable to corporation tax		283,880
Corporation tax @ 20%		56,776

Development of the plot of land

	£
Forecast profits	270,000
Additional net profits on sale of industrial units (W5)	172,250
Less: industrial buildings allowances (W3)	(9,380)
first year allowance (W4)	(11,400)
Schedule D Case I	421,470

	£
Corporation tax @ 30%	126,441
Less: Small companies marginal relief 1/40 (1,500,000 – 421,470)	(26,963)
	99,478

Advice on undertaking the development

The development of the plot of land by Easy-Speak Ltd will mean that the company makes additional profits of £76,250 (172,250 – 96,000). However, this alternative results in an increased corporation tax liability for the year ended 31 March 2001 of £42,702 (99,478 – 56,776), so the overall benefit is only £33,548 (76,250 – 42,702). Given the high risk of developing the plot of land compared to a sale in its existing state, Easy-Speak Ltd may prefer to forego this potential additional profit. The company's preference between outright purchase of the new factory and the acquisition of a leasehold interest may be the deciding factor.

Workings

1   *Capital gain on sale of land*

	£
Proceeds	320,000
Less: cost	(224,000)
	96,000

Tutorial note. You were instructed by the question to ignore the indexation allowance.

2   *Lease premium*

Amount of premium assessable on the landlord under Schedule A.

	£
Premium	280,000
$2\% \times (15 - 1) \times £280,000$	(78,400)
	201,600

∴ The amount deductible by Easy-Speak Ltd in the year to 31 March 2001 is

$£201,600 \times 1/15 \times 6/12 = £6,720$

3   *Industrial buildings allowances*

		£
Cost		430,000
Less:	Land	(80,000)
	Heating and ventilation systems	(28,500)
		321,500
Less:	general office	(87,000)
Qualifying for industrial buildings allowances		234,500

IBA @ 4% = £9,380

Tutorial note. The general offices do not qualify for IBAs as their cost exceeds 25% of £321,500.

4   *First year allowance*

The heating and ventilation system is plant and machinery which will qualify for a FYA of 40%.

$40\% \times £28,500 = £11,400$

5   *Profits on sales of industrial units*

		£
Proceeds		550,000
Less:	interest on bank loan ($4/12 \times 12.5\% \times £150,000$)	(6,250)
	cost of land	(224,000)
	construction costs	(147,500)
Additional net profits		172,250

Marking guide

		Marks	
(a)	The subject matter of the transaction	1	
	The length of ownership	1	
	Frequency of similar transactions	1	
	Work done on the property	1	
	Taxpayer's intention	1	
	Motive	1	
	The way in which goods acquired	1	
	Sale of land in existing state	2	
	Development of land	_2_	
	Available	11	
	Maximum		9
(b)	**Sales of plot of land in its existing state**		
	Lease premium	2	
	Rent payable	1	
	Capital gain	1	
	Capital loss	1	
	Corporation tax	1	
	Development of the plot of land		
	Industrial buildings allowance	2	
	Office building	1	
	First year allowance	1	
	Sales proceeds/cost of land	1	
	Construction costs	1	
	Loan interest	1	
	Corporation tax	1	
	Advice on undertaking the development		
	Additional profits	1	
	Corporation tax implications	1	
	Conclusion	1	
	Other factors	_1_	
	Available	18	
	Maximum		_16_
	Maximum		_25_

34   BARGAINS LTD

Tutor's hint. The rules treating benefits to participators in close companies as distributions only apply when the normal Schedule E rules taxing benefits do not apply.

Examiner's comment. Many candidates ignored the fact that the cars were only provided for nine months.

(a) (i) The company's first accounting period will run from the start of trade on 1 April 2000 to its accounting date, 31 December 2000. **Any deductible pre-trading expenditure will be treated as incurred on the first day of trading,** and will therefore be deductible in this accounting period.

(ii) The **pre-trading expenditure on advertising will be deductible** for corporation tax purposes. The **expenditure on refurbishment will also be deductible except to the extent that it is capital expenditure**. Expenditure needed to make the premises fit for use will be capital expenditure (*Law Shipping Co Ltd v CIR 1923*). Expenditure leading to significant improvements, such as the installation of a heating system where there was none before, will also be capital expenditure.

Expenditure on routine repairs and redecoration, on the other hand, will be revenue expenditure.

The VAT incurred on both the advertising expenditure and the refurbishment expenditure will be recoverable, because it is VAT on services supplied not more than six months before registration.

(b) Rodney and Reggie will be taxed under Schedule E as follows.

Rodney: £10,575 × 25% × 9/12 = £1,983 (annual business mileage 2,100 × 12/9 = 2,800)

Reggie: £10,575 × 15% × 9/12 = £1,190 (annual business mileage 14,400 × 12/9 = 19,200)

There will be no Schedule E charge on Del, but the provision of a car to him will be treated as a distribution of £10,575 × 35% × 9/12 = £2,776 net. Del will be taxed as if he had received a dividend of this amount, giving him gross income of £2,776 × 100/90 = £3,084, a tax credit of £308 and no further tax liability unless he is a higher rate taxpayer. The actual cost of providing the car will be a disallowable expense for the company. The company will be treated as though it had paid a dividend of £3,084. Any motor expenses incurred by the company in respect of Del's car will be disallowable.

The VAT on the cars will not be recoverable because of the private use. Capital allowances will be available on the full cost (including VAT) of the cars provided for Rodney and Reggie, but not on the cost of the car provided for Del because its provision is treated as a distribution. The annual writing down allowances will be 25% on a reducing balance basis. Because the first accounting period is only 9 months long, the allowance in that period will be 2 × £10,575 × 25% × 9/12 = £3,966. Any motor expenses incurred by the company in respect of servicing, insurance and general running of both Rodney and Reggie's cars will be tax deductible for the company.

(c) **On making the loan to Del, the company will become liable to account for an amount of tax** of £42,000 × 25% = £10,500. This is, in general, due nine months after the end of the accounting period, so it is due by 1 October 2001. However, if the company becomes a large company the tax will be subject to the quarterly payments on account regime. This tax is recovered when the loan is repaid.

Del will only be taxed on the loan as income to the extent that it is written off. He will then be treated as receiving a net dividend equal to the amount written off.

Del will, however, be treated as receiving (and the company will be treated as paying) a dividend equal to the Schedule E benefit for interest-free loans. This will be the interest which Del would have had to pay at the official rate. The tax consequences will be the same as for the deemed distribution in respect of Del's car.

(d) **The company will use the VAT secondhand scheme. The input VAT on an item bought for resale will not be recovered, but the output VAT on its sale will be (gross selling price - gross purchase price) × 7/47. There is no output VAT when an item is sold at a loss.**

35   **TARGET LTD**

> **Tutor's hint.** In parts (a) and (b) it was important to spot that Target Ltd would become a consortium company.
>
> **Prizewinner's point.** Note that under FRS 4 *Capital instruments* the debenture interest, discount and incidental costs should have been written off so as to achieve a constant rate on the outstanding balance in each period. However, the calculations below were those expected from candidates.
>
> **Examiner's comments.** The loan relationship aspects were generally not well answered. This was disappointing since this topic was dealt with in the Finance Act article published in the Students' Newsletter written specifically for this paper.

(a)   **One third of Target Ltd's ordinary share capital acquired**

Target Ltd	£
Schedule D Case I	nil
Capital gain	51,300
Less s 393A Loss relief (W1)	(51,300)
PCTCT	-

Expansion Ltd	£
Schedule D Case I	214,000
Schedule D Case III (£120,000 × 8% × 8/12)	6,400
	220,400
Less: consortium relief (W)	(14,400)
PCTCT	206,000

Corporation tax	£
£206,000 × 20%	41,200
Less: Income tax suffered (£6,400 × 20%)	(1,280)
MCT	39,920

Capital loss c/f	£9,600

Working

If Expansion Ltd acquires one third of Target it will become a consortium member on 1 July 2000 since Target Ltd is a consortium company. Target Ltd is able to surrender one third of its trading loss to Expansion Ltd. Target Ltd must take into account its own current year profits when calculating the surrender. Only the current year loss can be surrendered, and this is restricted to the corresponding period of 1 July 2000 to 31 December 2000.

	£
Target Ltd's loss	137,700
Utilised itself under S 393A	(51,300)
	86,400
Available to consortium members (one third per member)	28,800

Time apportion £28,800 × 6/12 in order to calculate share of loss for Expansion Ltd in the year to 31.12.00.

Brought forward trading losses can not be surrendered or set against chargeable gains. Trading losses of £9,200 will remain to be carried forward.

(b)   **Two thirds of Target Ltd's ordinary share capital acquired**

Target Ltd will become an associated company of Expansion Ltd and the small companies' lower and upper limits for corporation tax purposes are therefore £150,000 and £750,000 respectively. Starting rate is clearly not in point.

Target Ltd

Target Ltd's mainstream corporation tax position will be the same as in part (a) above.

Expansion Ltd	£
Schedule D Case I profit	214,000
Schedule D Case III	6,400
	220,400
Less: Consortium relief (£28,800 × 2 × 6/12)	(28,800)
PCTCT	191,600
Corporation tax at £191,600 × 30%	57,480
Less: marginal relief: 1/40 (750,000 – 191,600)	(13,960)
	43,520
Less: income tax suffered	(1,280)
MCT	42,240
Capital loss c/f	£9,600

(c) **All of Target Ltd's ordinary share capital acquired**

Target Ltd and Expansion Ltd will be members of the same group relief group and also of the same capital gains group.

Target Ltd

Target Ltd's mainstream corporation tax position will be the same as in part (a) above.

Expansion Ltd	£
Schedule D Case I (W2)	199,225
Schedule D Case III	6,400
Capital gain (W1)	3,225
	208,850
Less group relief (£137,700 × 6/12)	(68,850)
PCTCT	140,000
	£
Corporation tax	
£140,000 × 20%	28,000
Less: Income tax suffered	(1,280)
MCT	26,720

1 **Chargeable gains**

Target Ltd and Expansion Ltd should make an election that the office building is treated as if it were being transferred between them immediately before the disposal. The gain of £51,300 will the be treated as made by Expansion Ltd. Election by 31.12.02. £38,475 (£51,300 × ¾) of this gain can be rolled over into the base cost of the new factory to be acquired in January 2001.

	£
Capital gain	51,300
Less rolled over (75% business use)	(38,475)
	12,825
Capital losses b/f	(9,600)
Gain remaining chargeable	3,225

Tutorial note. There is full reinvestment of the sale proceeds relating to the business part of the office £105,000 (£140,000 × ¾), so all of the gain on this part of the building is rolled over.

2 **Schedule D Case I**

The loan relationship legislation does not define 'trading purposes'. If the debenture issue is for trading purposes, then the debenture interest, the 3% discount and the incidental costs of obtaining the finance will be deductible Schedule DI expenses. Expansion Ltd's Schedule D Case I profit for the year ended 31 December 2000 will be:

	£
Previous Schedule DI profit	214,000
Debenture interest (£250,000 at 10% × 6/12)	(12,500)
Discount (£250,000 × 3% = £7,500) × 6/60	(750)
Incidental costs (£15,250 × 6/60)	(1,525)
Revised Schedule DI profit	199,225

Tutorial note. If the issue of debentures is not for trading purposes, then there will be a net loss on loan relationships of £8,375 (£6,400 – £12,500 – £750 – £1,525). Expansion Ltd's PCTCT would (as above) be:

	£
Schedule DI profit	214,000
Capital gain	3,225
	217,225
Less loss on loan relationships	(8,375)
	208,850
Less group relief (£137,700 × 6/12)	(68,850)
PCTCT	140,000

Either of these approaches would be acceptable. The former is followed in this answer.

Marking guide	Marks
One third of ordinary share capital acquired	
Target Ltd	1
Schedule DI/Schedule DII	2
Consortium relief	3
Corporation tax	1
Income tax	1
Two thirds of ordinary share capital acquired	
Schedule DI/Schedule DIII	1
Consortium relief	1
Corporation tax	2
Income tax	1
All of ordinary share capital acquired	
Election re building	1
Rollover relief	2
Calculation of gain	2
Issue of debentures	3
Schedule DI profit	2
Group relief	1
Corporation tax	1
Available/Maximum	25

36 APPLE LTD

Tutor's hint. When using losses, consider the marginal rates of tax of each company.

Examiner's comments. In the second section of part (b), although most candidates correctly explained the reliefs that could be claimed, the calculation of the actual tax saving caused problems.

(a) (i) **Schedule D Case I losses can be surrendered between UK companies that are members of a 75% group.**

Two companies are members of a 75% group where one is a 75% subsidiary of the other, or both are 75% subsidiaries of a third company.

For one company to be a 75% subsidiary of another, the holding company must have:

- at least a 75% effective interest in the ordinary share capital of the subsidiary;

- a right to at least 75% of the distributable income of the subsidiary; and

- a right to at least 75% of the net assets of the subsidiary were it to be wound up.

Assets can be transferred between members of a capital gains group without incurring a chargeable gain/loss.

Companies are in a capital gains group if:

(a) **at each level, there is a 75% holding;** and

(b) **the top company has an effective interest of over 50% in the group companies.**

(ii)   **The most important factor that should be taken into account when deciding which group companies the Schedule DI trading losses should be surrendered to is the rate of corporation tax applicable to those companies.** Surrender should be made initially to companies subject to corporation tax at the marginal rate of 32.5%. The amount surrendered should be sufficient to bring the claimant company's profits down to the small companies lower limit. Surrender should then be to those companies subject to the full rate of corporation tax of 30%, then to companies subject to tax at the marginal rate of 22.5% then to companies subject to corporation tax at the small company rate of 20% and lastly to companies subject to the starting rate of 10%. The ability of companies with minority interests to compensate for group relief surrenders will be another factor.

(iii)   *Chargeable assets*

It would probably be beneficial for all the eligible subsidiary companies to elect to deem the transfer of chargeable assets to Apple Ltd prior to their disposal outside of the group, because capital losses cannot be group relieved. Such deemed transfers would therefore allow chargeable gains and allowable losses to arise in the same company. These losses can then either be offset against chargeable gains of the same period, or carried forward against future chargeable gains. Such elections must be made within 2 years of the end of the accounting period in which the disposal is made.

(b)   (i)   *Apple Ltd*

	Years ended		
	31.3.00	*31.3.01*	*31.3.02*
	£	£	£
Schedule D Case I	620,000	250,000	585,000
Capital gain	-	120,000	80,000
PCTCT	620,000	370,000	665,000

Bramley Ltd

	Years ended		
	31.3.00	*31.3.01*	*31.3.02*
	£	£	£
Schedule D Case I	-	52,000	70,000
Less: s393 (I) ICTA 1988	-	(52,000)	(12,000)
PCTCT	-	-	58,000

Cox Ltd

		Years ended	
	31.3.00	*31.3.01*	*31.3.02*
	£	£	£
Schedule D Case I	83,000	-	40,000
Less: s393A ICTA 1988	(58,000)	-	-
PCTCT	25,000	-	40,000

Delicious Ltd

		Years ended	
	31.3.00	*31.3.01*	*31.3.02*
	£	£	£
Schedule D Case I	-	90,000	-
S393A (I) ICTA 1988	-	(15,000)	-
PCTCT	-	75,000	-

(b) (ii) *Apple Ltd*

		Years ended	
	31.3.00	*31.3.01*	*31.3.02*
	£	£	£
Schedule D Case I	620,000	250,000	585,000
Chargeable gain	-	20,000	36,000
Less: group relief	(64,000)	(58,000)	
PCTCT	556,000	212,000	621,000

In the year to 31.3.00 group relief has been claimed for Bramley Ltd's loss. This saves Apple Ltd corporation tax of £19,200 (£64,000 × 30%). If the loss had been carried forward as shown above it would have saved Bramley Ltd tax of £12,800 (20% × £64,000). The overall tax saving to the group arising as a result of the group relief claim is £6,400.

Rollover relief has been claimed to defer £100,000 of the chargeable gain arising in the year to 31.3.01. **The £20,000 gain remaining chargeable is equal to the amount of proceeds not reinvested by Cox Ltd in the freehold factory.** The small companies' rate lower limit for the year to 31.3.01 is £75,000 so the rollover relief saves Apple Ltd corporation tax of £32,500 (£100,000 × 32.5%).

It is assumed that Delicious Ltd and Apple Ltd will make an election to deem the transfer of the leasehold factory between them immediately before sale. If this occurs, the loss on the sale of the factory will arise on Apple Ltd in the year to 31.3.02. Apple Ltd will be able to relieve the £40,000 loss by setting it against its chargeable gain for the year, saving tax of £13,200 (£44,000 × 30%)

In the year to 31.3.01 group relief has been claimed for Cox Ltd's loss. This saves corporation tax of £18,850 (£58,000 × 32.5%). If the loss had been carried back as shown above, it would have saved Cox Ltd corporation tax of £11,600 (£58,000 × 20%). The overall tax saving to the group of a group relief claim is therefore £7,250 (£18,850 – £11,600).

Delicious Ltd could surrender its loss of £15,000 in the year to 31.3.02 to Cox Ltd. The starting rate lower and upper limits will be £2,500 and £12,500. Therefore, this would not be beneficial as the tax saving would be at 20% whereas the tax saving will be at 32.5% if the s393A ICTA 1988 claim shown in (b) (i) above is made.

Marking guide		Marks	
(a) *Group relationships*			
75% subsidiary		1	
Ordinary share capital		1	
Distributable profits/Net assets		1	
Effective interest		1	
Chargeable gains		1	
Surrender of Schedule D1 trading losses			
Rate of corporation tax		1	
Order of set off		1	
Minority interests		1	
Chargeable assets			
Capital losses cannot be group relieved		1	
Optimum use of capital losses		<u>1</u>	
	Available	<u>10</u>	
	Maximum		9
(b) *Profits chargeable to corporation tax*			
Schedule DI Profits		1	
Capital gains		1	
Bramley Ltd's Loss		1	
Cox Ltd's loss		1	
Delicious Ltd's loss		<u>1</u>	
			5
(c) *Corporation tax saving*			
Delicious Ltd - Transfer leasehold		1	
Capital loss - use		2	
Rollover relief - Proceeds not reinvested still chargeable		1	
Freehold office building		1	
Corporation tax saving		1	
Bramley Ltd's loss		2	
Cox Ltd's loss		2	
Delicious Ltd's loss		1	
Corporation tax savings		<u>3</u>	
	Available	<u>14</u>	
	Maximum		<u>11</u>
	Maximum		<u>25</u>

37 ONGOING LTD

Tutor's hint. A loss can normally be carried back to set against profits of the previous twelve months. However, a loss and any trade charges arising in the twelve months prior to the cessation of trade can be carried back to set against the profits of the previous 36 months.

Examiner's comment. In part (a) too many candidates did not know how to deal with the loss relief claim under s 393A ICTA 1988 where there were two trading losses.

(a) (i)

	Year to 30.6.96 £	Year to 30.6.97 £	6 mths to 31.12.97 £	Year to 31.12.98 £	Year to 31.12.99 £	Year to 31.12.00 £
Schedule D Case I	88,500	59,000	62,500	47,000	0	0
Schedule A	6,000	0	1,500	0	0	0
Capital gain (W1)	0	0	0	0	0	58,800
	94,500	59,000	64,000	47,000	0	58,800
Less: s 393 A current (W2)	0	0	0	0	0	(58,800)
Less: trade charges	(12,000)	(12,000)	(6,000)	(12,000)	0	0
	82,500	47,000	58,000	35,000	0	0
Less: s 393A carryback (W3)	0	(29,500)	(58,000)	(35,000)	0	0
	82,500	17,500	0	0	0	0
Less: non-trade charges	0	0	0	0	0	0
PCTCT	82,500	17,500	0	0	0	0
MCT @ 24.75%	£20,419					
MCT @ 23.25%		£4,069				

(ii) The following corporation tax refunds will be due resulting from the s 393A loss relief claims.

Original MCT before loss relief

	Period ended 30.6.97 £	Period ended 31.12.97 £	Period ended 31.12.98 £
Schedule D Case I	59,000	62,500	47,000
Schedule A	-	1,500	-
Trade charges	(12,000)	(6,000)	(12,000)
Non-trade charges	-	(1,000)	(1,000)
PCTCT	47,000	57,000	34,000
MCT 24%	8,460		
MCT 21%	2,468	11,970	7,140
Original MCT	10,928	11,970	7,140
MCT after s 393A relief	(4,069)	-	-
Tax refund due	6,859	11,970	7,140

(iii) **Ongoing Ltd - year ended 31 March 2001**

	£
Schedule D Case I (£93,000 – £12,000)	81,000
Less: s 393(1) relief	(14,500)
	66,500
Schedule D Case III	3,500
	70,000
Less: Group relief (W4)	(52,500)
PCTCT	17,500

Starting rate limits   £50,000 ÷ 3 = £16,667

£10,000 ÷ 3 = £3,333

CT @ 20%   £3,500

(b) (i) For accounting periods ending after 30 June 1999 **companies that are subject to the full rate of corporation tax will have to pay their corporation tax liability in quarterly instalments.** For the second accounting period to which this applies, 72% of the corporation tax liability is due by instalments with the remaining 28% being due nine months after the end of the period. The position for Hazell Ltd is as follows.

Year ended 30 June 2001

CT liability
£2,000,000 × 30% (FY00)   £600,000

Due instalments (£600,000 × 72%)   £432,000

The instalments will be £432,000 × ¼ = £108,000 and were due for payment on:
14 January 2001
14 April 2001
14 July 2001
14 October 2001

The balance of £168,000 is due on 1 April 2002.

(ii)   **As a notice requiring a return was received in good time, Hazell Ltd will, under self assessment, be required to submit its return and accounts to the Revenue within twelve months of the end of the accounting period, ie by 30 June 2002.** Assuming that the return is filed on time, **the Revenue will have until 30 June 2003 to give written notice that they are going to enquire into it.**

Workings

1   **Chargeable gains**

	y/e 31.12.98	y/e 31.12.00
	£	£
Gain	10,800	72,000
Less: loss b/f	(10,800)	(13,200)
Chargeable gain	nil	58,800

2   **Loss relief y/e 31.12.99**

		£
Loss		68,000
S 393A relief	y/e 31.12.99	-
	y/e 31.12.98	(35,000)
Unrelieved on cessation of trade		33,000

All charges paid in the year to 31.12.99 are also unrelieved on the cessation of trade.

3   **Loss relief - y/e 31.12.00**

		£
Loss		140,000
Less: S 393A relief y/e 31.12.00		(58,800)
Add: unrelieved charges of final period		11,250
		92,450
Less: s 393A carryback	y/e 31.12.99	0
	y/e 31.12.98	0
	6 m/e 31.12.97	(58,000)
	6/12 of y/e 30.6.97	(29,500)
Unrelieved		4,950

In addition, the non-trade charges paid in the final year remain unrelieved on cessation.

Tutorial note. As the trade has ceased trade charges paid in this period are added to the loss carried back.

4   **Group relief**

Ongoing Ltd can claim to reduce profits in the year ended 31 March 2001 by any of Goodbye Ltd's losses that arose in the 'corresponding period'. The 'corresponding period' in respect of Goodbye Ltd's loss for the year to 31 December 2000 is 1.4.00 to 31.12.00. Therefore, the maximum group relief claim is the lower of:

(i)   Available profits   £70,000 × 9/12 =   £52,500

(ii) Available losses   £140,000 × 9/12 =   £105,000

Marking guide		Marks	
(a)	(i) Schedule A/Chargeable gains	1	
	Use of y/e 31.12.99 loss	1	
	y/e 31.12.99 trade charges not used	1	
	y/e 31.12.00: current period relief	1	
	Add final period charges to loss	1	
	6 m/e 31.12.97 relief	1	
	y/e 30.6.97 (50% relief)	2	
	CT liabilities	2	
	Available/Maximum		10
	(ii) PCTCT for each year	1	
	Refunds: y/e 30.6.97	1	
	6 m/e 31.12.97	1	
	y/e 31.12.98	1	
	Available/Maximum		4
	(iii) Schedule D I	½	
	S 393(1) relief	½	
	Schedule D III	½	
	Group relief	1½	
	Corporation tax	1	
	Available/Maximum		4
(b)	Estimated CT liability	1	
	Large companies pay by instalments for		
	periods ending after 30.6.99	1	
	72% due by instalments	1	
	Due dates for instalments	1	
	Due date for balance	1	
	Filing date	1	
	Enquiries	1	
	Available/Maximum		7
			25

38   OCEAN PLC

Tutor's hint. When a question specifies a structure for your answer, you should use it. The structure will make your task a lot easier.

Examiner's comment. Several candidates did not appreciate the difference between selling a subsidiary and selling its assets.

(a)   **Tax implications for Ocean plc**

(i)   **Capital gains**

Ocean plc will have chargeable gains on its disposals of shares in Tarn Ltd and Loch Ltd. It is not selling its shares in Pool Ltd, so will not have a chargeable gain there.

(ii) **Group status**

Tarn Ltd will cease to be a subsidiary for all purposes from the date of disposal. Group relief should be available to Ocean plc for Tarn Ltd's losses up to the date of disposal, unless there were arrangements to sell Tarn Ltd before that date. The losses up to the date of disposal will be computed on a time-apportioned basis unless the result would be unfair or unreasonable.

Loch Ltd's position in relation to the Ocean plc group will be the same except that it will become a consortium-owned company, giving Ocean plc access to 60% of Loch Ltd's post-disposal losses.

Tarn Ltd and Pool Ltd (dormant) will cease to count as associated companies from the end of the accounting period of disposal.

(iii) **VAT**

Loch Ltd will be able to remain in any Ocean plc VAT group. Tarn Ltd will have to leave any such VAT group.

(b) **Tax implications for Tarn Ltd, Loch Ltd and Pool Ltd**

(i) **Capital gains**

Tarn Ltd will have chargeable gains on shops transferred to it from Ocean plc within the six years before the sale of shares. The gains will be computed as if it had sold the shops at the times of transfer for their then market values. The gains will, however, be included in Tarn Ltd's chargeable profits for the accounting period of the sale of shares.

Pool Ltd will have chargeable gains or allowable losses in respect of the sale of its assets. Rollover relief against acquisitions by other members of the Ocean plc group may be available. Alternatively, if other companies in that group have allowable losses, gains could be routed through those other companies by election. This would enable the group to use the losses.

(ii) **VAT**

Pool Ltd, being dormant, will have to de-register. If it transfers it business as a going concern and Sea plc is registered for VAT, that transfer will be outside the scope of VAT.

(iii) **Trading losses**

Tarn Ltd and Loch Ltd will be able to carry forward their losses against future profits from the same trade. However, in the case of Tarn Ltd (the control of which is changing) the carry-forward of losses will be denied if, within three years before or after the transfer, there is a major change in the nature or conduct of its trade.

Pool Ltd will lose the benefit of any losses which it cannot use against profits of the current period or earlier periods.

(iv) **Capital allowances**

Pool Ltd will have balancing adjustment (allowances or charges) on the assets it sells where it has had capital allowances on those assets.

(c) **Tax implications for Sea plc**

(i) **Capital gains**

Sea plc will have base costs for the shares and assets equal to the price its pays.

(ii) **Group status**

Tarn Ltd will become a subsidiary for all tax purposes. Sea plc will be able to claim group relief for Tarn Ltd's losses from the date of purchase. Tarn Ltd will also count as an associated company from the start of the accounting period.

Loch Ltd will become a consortium-owned company, allowing Sea plc to claim relief for 40% of Loch Ltd's loss.

(iii)   **VAT**

Tarn Ltd will be able to join any Sea plc VAT group.

(iv)   **Capital allowances**

Sea plc will be able to claim capital allowances on the qualifying assets which it buys from Pool Ltd.

39   STAR LTD

> **Tutor's hints**. This is a very common type of question. Ensure that you can answer it well.
>
> **Examiner's comments**. This was a popular question and most candidates had few problems with parts (a) and (b).

(a)

	Star Ltd £	Zodiac Ltd £	Exotic Ltd £
Schedule D Case I	-	650,000	130,000
Capital gain	130,000	-	-
Charges on income	(10,000)		
	120,000	650,000	130,000
Less: S393A relief	(20,000)		
Less: group relief (W)		(60,000)	(45,000)
Profits chargeable to corporation tax	100,000	590,000	85,000
Dividends plus tax credit (FII)			15,000
'Profits'	100,000	590,000	100,000
CT @ 20%	20,000		17,000
CT @ 30%		177,000	

Star Ltd's brought forward trading losses of £7,500 remain to be carried forward.

Working

1.   There are three associated companies so the small companies' rate lower and upper limits are £100,000 and £500,000 respectively. The starting rate upper and lower limits are £16,667 and £3,333. Star Ltd's loss should initially be set against its own profits to relieve the £20,000 that would otherwise be taxed at the marginal rate of 32.5%. Next £45,000 should be surrendered to Exotic Ltd, to bring profits down to the lower limit. The balance of the loss should be surrendered to Zodiac Ltd where it will save tax at the full rate.

(b)   (i)   **As the proceeds of the sale of the warehouse will be reinvested within 36 months of sale rollover relief will potentially be available.** Part of the gain equal to the proceeds not reinvested, £90,000, will be immediately chargeable if the freehold office is acquired. The remaining gain of £40,000 could be rolled over by deducting it from the base cost of the office.

None of the gain will be immediately chargeable if the leasehold office is acquired as all of the proceeds will be reinvested. However, as the leasehold is a depreciating asset the gain will not be deducted from the base cost of the new asset. Instead, it will be deferred or held over until the earlier of:

(1)   10 years after acquisition of the leasehold

(2)   the date the leasehold ceases to be used in the trade

(3)   the date of sale of the leasehold.

Zodiac Ltd and Star Ltd are members of the same capital gains group so rollover relief will be available if Zodiac Ltd purchases a freehold warehouse. As all of the sale proceeds would be reinvested, no gain would be immediately chargeable but the base cost of Zodiac Ltd's warehouse will be reduced by £130,000.

(ii) Whichever of the claims are made, Star Ltd's profits will fall below the small companies' limit. This means that Star Ltd should not relieve any of its loss under s393A ICTA 1988 but that it should increase the amount of the loss surrendered to Zodiac Ltd by £20,000 where 30% relief will be obtained.

If none of the gain is immediately chargeable, Star Ltd will also have unrelieved trade charges of £10,000. These can be added to the amount of loss surrendered as group relief.

(c) **The inclusion of Exotic Ltd in the group VAT registration results in the group being partially exempt, thus restricting the recovery of input tax on the overhead expenditure of £450,000.**

$$\frac{\text{Taxable supplies}}{\text{Total supplies}} = \frac{1,900,000+1,800,000}{1,900,000+1,800,000+950,000} = 79.57\% = 80\%$$ (round up to nearest whole number).

The irrecoverable input is therefore £15,750 (£450,000 × 17.5% = £78,750 × 20% (100 − 80)).

If Exotic Ltd is excluded from the group VAT registration, Star Ltd will have to charge output tax on its management fee of £50,000. Exotic Ltd cannot register for VAT (it does not make any taxable supplies), and so will be unable to recover this as input tax. The additional VAT cost is £8,750 (£50,000 × 17.5%).

The exclusion of Exotic Ltd from the VAT group throughout the year ended 31 March 2001 would therefore have reduced the group's overall VAT liability by £7,000 (£15,750 − £8,750).

Marking guide

		Marks
(a)	Schedule DI profit	1
	Capital gain/Charge on income	1
	Lower and upper limits	1
	Loss relief- S 393A	1
	Group relief	2
	FII/profit	1
	Corporation tax	1
	Losses carried forward	1
	Available/Maximum	9
(b)	Reinvestment within three years	1
	Freehold office building	
	Immediate gain	1
	Base cost	1
	Leasehold office building	
	Whole gain rolled over	1
	Depreciating asset	1
	Date of sale/Ten years/ceasing to be used	1
	Freehold warehouse	
	Same capital gains group	1
	Rollover/deduct from base cost	1
	Loss relief	
	Profits less than £100,000	1
	Additional surrender	1
	Charge on income	1
	Available	11
	Maximum	10
(c)	Partially exempt group	1
	Calculation of irrecoverable VAT	2
	VAT on £50,000 fee	1
	VAT on management fee irrecoverable	1
	Conclusion	1
	Maximum	6
	Maximum	25

40 TUTORIAL QUESTION: DOUBLE TAXATION RELIEF FOR INDIVIDUALS

(a) MR POIROT: UK INCOME TAX LIABILITY

Mr Poirot is UK resident and ordinarily resident for 2000/01 but he is not UK domiciled. His 2000/01 income tax liability is as follows.

	Non-savings	Savings (excl dividend)
	£	£
Schedule E	45,000	
Bank deposit interest £800 × 100/80		1,000
	45,000	1,000
Less personal allowance	(4,385)	
Taxable income	40,615	1,000

		£
Income tax on non savings income		
£1,520 × 10%		152
£26,880 × 22%		5,914
£12,215 × 40%		4,886
Income tax on savings (excl dividend) income		
£1,000 × 40%		400
Tax liability		11,352

(b) MR WAIN: UK INCOME TAX LIABILITY

	Non-savings £	Savings (excl dividend) £	Dividend £	Total £
Schedule E	31,644			
Schedule D Case III		1,490		
Schedule D Case V £2,400 × 100/60			4,000	
STI	31,644	1,490	4,000	37,134
Less personal allowance	(4,385)			
Taxable income	27,259	1,490	4,000	32,749

	£
Income tax on non-savings income	
£1,520 × 10%	152
£25,739 × 22%	5,663
Income tax on savings (excl dividend) income	
£1,141 × 20%	228
£349 × 40%	140
Income tax on dividend income	
£4,000 × 32.5%	1,300
	7,483
Less double taxation relief (W)	(1,300)
Tax liability	6,183

Working: double taxation relief	
Overseas tax suffered on dividends £4,000 × 40%	£1,600
UK tax on £4,000 of dividends £4,000 × 32.5%	£1,300

Double taxation relief is therefore restricted to £1,300.

41 TUTORIAL QUESTION: DOUBLE TAX RELIEF FOR COMPANIES

Calculation of mainstream corporation tax liability

Stripe Ltd y/e 31.3.01

	£
Schedule DI - UK	800,000
overseas	600,000
Schedule DV (W1)	244,622
Capital gains	95,000
Less: Charges paid	(85,000)
PCTCT	1,654,622

	£
Corporation tax @ 30%	496,387
Less: DTR (W2) (£180,000 + 59,822)	(239,822)
MCT	256,565

Workings

1   Schedule DV - Stripe Ltd

	£
Dividend income (withholding tax @ 12% = £25,200)	210,000
Underlying tax £305,000 × $\dfrac{210,000}{1,850,000}$	34,622
	244,622

Total foreign tax suffered: £25,200 + £34,622 = £59,822

2   Double tax relief - Stripe

		UK profits £	DI - overseas £	DV £
PCTCT		810,000	600,000	244,622
CT @ 30%		243,000	180,000	73,387
Less: DTR				
(i)	DI overseas lower of UK CT - £180,000 overseas tax - £222,000 £600,000 × 37%		(180,000)	
(ii)	DV lower of UK CT - £73,387 overseas tax - £59,822 (W1)		-	(59,822)
		243,000	-	13,565

42   OLIVER SEAS

> **Tutor's hint.** Do not mix up the rules for income tax and CGT when a person leaves the UK.
>
> **Examiner's comments.** In part (a) many candidates failed to mention that the period overseas must be in respect of full time employment in order for non-residence to apply for the period of the contract.

(a) **As Oliver is leaving the UK to work abroad under a full time contract of employment and the time spent overseas will include a complete tax year (2001/02), for income tax purposes he will be treated as not resident and not ordinarily resident in the UK from the date of his departure until the date of return.**

(b)   (i)

	Non Savings £	Savings (excl dividends) £	Dividend £	Total £
Schedule E (£2,600 × 5)	13,000			
Schedule A (£825 × 4)	3,300			
Dividends (× 100/90)			6,600	
Schedule D Case V (£800 × 8)	6,400			
Schedule D Case V (£510 × 100/85 × 8)		4,800		
	22,700	4,800	6,600	34,100
Less: Personal allowance	(4,385)			
	18,315	4,800	6,600	29,715

	£
Income tax on non savings income	
£1,520 × 10%	152
£16,795 × 22%	3,695
Income tax on savings (excl dividend) income	
£4,800 × 20%	960
Income tax on dividend income	
£5,285 × 10%	529
£1,315 × 32.5%	427
	5,763
Less: double tax relief (W1)	
Interest	(720)
Rent	(1,408)
Less: tax credit on dividends	(660)
Tax payable	2,975

Tutor's hint. Oliver is subject to UK tax on his worldwide income until 1 December 2000. From this date he is only subject to UK tax on his UK income.

(ii)   *Sale 5.10.00*

This sale was made whilst Oliver was still resident and ordinarily resident in the UK. **It is initially matched with the 2,000 shares purchased in the next 30 days.**

	£
Proceeds (2,000/6,500 × £58,500)	18,000
Less: cost	(18,400)
Allowable loss	(400)

The remaining 4,500 shares sold are matched to the 12.5.00 purchase.

	£
Proceeds (4,500/6,500 × £58,500)	40,500
Less: cost	(27,450)
Gain before taper relief	13,050

Sale 3.4.01

The 5,000 shares sold on 3.4.01 are charged to CGT in 2000/01 (the tax year of departure) because Oliver is treated as resident and ordinary resident in the UK for the whole of the tax year for CGT purposes. The sale is matched with the FA 1985 pool shares.

	£
Proceeds	54,000
Less: indexed cost (£46,400 × $\frac{5,000}{10,000}$)	(23,200)
Untapered gain	30,800

Net gains

	5.10.00 gain £	3.4.01 gain £
Gains	13,050	30,800
Less: loss	(400)	
Net gains before taper relief	12,650	30,800
Gains after taper relief		£
£12,650 × 100%		12,650
£30,800 × 95%		29,260
Total gains £(12,650 + 29,260)		41,910
Less: annual exemption		(7,200)
		34,710

Oliver's CGT liability is £13,884 (£34,710 × 40%).

(c) (i) If Oliver had reinvested his capital in an overseas bank account he would not be subject to UK tax on the interest arising whilst he remained abroad under his contract of employment.

(ii) The chargeable gain would be chargeable in 2000/01 (the year of departure) if it accrued on 3.4.01. However, if it accrued in 2001/02, the year following departure, it will not be chargeable until the tax year in which Oliver resumes his residence or ordinary residence in the UK. This is because Oliver will be temporarily non resident in the UK. This will give Oliver a cash flow advantage plus the fact that he will be able to set a later year (and presumably greater annual exemption) against the gain.

Workings

1   *Double tax relief*

The interest is the *only* source of savings (excl dividend) income so DTR is the lower of:

UK tax	£4,800 × 20% = £960
Overseas tax	£4,800 × 15% = £720

ie £720

The rental income is treated as the top slice of non-savings income. DTR is the lower of:

UK tax	£6,400 × 22% = £1,408
Overseas tax	£6,400 × 35% = £2,240

ie £1,408

The salary from Overseas Aid is not assessable from 1 December 2000 so the Changan tax paid from this date is irrelevant.

Tutorial note. Strictly the above method of calculating UK tax on overseas income is incorrect (the UK tax with and without the overseas income should be calculated). However, the examiner indicated that he would accept the above simplified treatment as correct.

Marking guide			Marks	
(a)	Working full-time abroad		2	
	Complete tax year		2	
		Available	4	
		Maximum		3
(b)	*Income tax liability*			
	Schedule E/Schedule A/Dividends		2	
	Schedule D Case V		2	
	Personal allowance/income tax liability		2	
	DTR on bank interest		1	
	DTR on rental income		2	
	Explanation		1	
	Tax suffered on dividends		1	
	CGT liability			
	Matching rules		1	
	Disposal on 5 October 2000		2	
	Disposal on 3 April 2001 - chargeable to CGT		1	
	- calculation		2	
	Annual exemption/CGT liability		1	
		Available	18	
		Maximum		16
(c)	*Reinvestment of capital from bank deposit account*			
	Income arising overseas		1	
	No UK income tax liability		1	
	Delaying the disposal of the shares in Medusa plc			
	Gains charged in year of return		2	
	Cash flow advantage		1	
	Annual exemption		1	
		Maximum/available		6
		Maximum		25

43 BARNEY HALL

> **Tutor's hint.** This question has been amended to reflect changes in the syllabus.
>
> **Examiner's comments.** In part (b) it was often not apparent which aspect of the question was being answered. When answering a question of this nature it is essential that each section is clearly labelled with a heading.

(a) *Residence in the UK during a tax year*

A person will be resident in a given tax year if, in that year he either:

(i) **is present in the UK for 183 days or more** (excluding days of arrival and departure); or

(ii) **he makes substantial visits to the UK.** Visits averaging 91 days or more a year for each of four or more consecutive years will make the person resident for each of these tax years (for someone emigrating from the UK, the four years are reduced to three).

If days are spent in the UK because of exceptional circumstances beyond the control of the individual's control (eg illness), those days are ignored for the purposes of the 91 day rule (but not the 183 day rule).

A person who is **leaving the UK permanently after being resident** in the UK who can produce evidence to that effect (eg sale of UK house, setting up permanent home abroad), **will be treated as being non-UK resident from the date of departure.** In other cases, the decision will be postponed for three years and then retrospective adjustments will be made.

If a person goes abroad for full-time service under a contract of employment such that:

(i) **his absence from the UK is for a period which includes a complete tax year;** and

(ii) **interim visits to the UK do not amount to six months or more in any one tax year or three months or more per tax year on average;**

he is normally regarded as **being not resident and not ordinarily resident for the whole of the period of the contract.**

A person **coming to the UK to take up permanent residence or with the intention of staying for at least three years is treated as resident in the UK from the date of arrival. A person who comes to the UK to work for a period of at least two years is treated as resident for the whole period from arrival to departure.**

Someone who comes to the UK for 'temporary' purposes (such as for a brief spell of employment) **is not UK resident unless he spends 183 days or more in the UK in that year.**

(b) (i) *Working overseas for a period of fifteen months*

Barney will be resident and ordinarily resident in the UK for 2000/01 and 2001/02, as he will not be abroad for a complete tax year. He will therefore be assessable in 2000/01 on his worldwide income which will consist of the following:

	Non-savings Income £	Savings (excl dividend) Income £	Total £
Schedule E Case I	33,600		
Benefits: travel for self	2,400		
Subsistence £850 × 5	4,250		
Travel for spouse	700		
	40,950		
Less: allowable deduction (benefits – see below)	(7,350)		
	33,600		
Schedule A	2,600		
Schedule D Case V (£5,460 × 100/30)		7,800	
Statutory total income	36,200	7,800	44,000

Barney will be able to claim a deduction for the following amounts paid or reimbursed by his employer from his Schedule E benefits:

(i) Cost of travel from any place in the UK to take up the overseas employment, and travel back to any place in the UK on its termination.

(ii) Board and lodging outside the UK provided for the purpose of enabling him to perform the duties of the overseas employment.

(iii) The cost of up to two return journeys for his spouse and children under the age of 18, provided that he is absent from the UK for a continuous period of at least 60 days, as is the case here.

Barney will be able to claim double taxation relief of the lower of the tax in the UK on the bank interest (ie £7,800 × 40% = £3,120) and the tax in Yalam (ie £7,800 × 30% = £2,340), that is £2,340.

Barney is liable to CGT on the disposal of assets situated anywhere in the world because he is UK resident. His gain on the land is:

	£
Proceeds $180,000/8	22,500
Less: Cost $84,000/6	(14,000)
Unindexed gain	8,500
Less: Indexation allowance to April 1998	

$$\frac{162.6 - 154.4}{154.4} (= 0.053) \times £14,000 \qquad (742)$$

Indexed gain	7,758
Gain after taper relief (95% × £7,758)	
This gain will be taxable in 2000/01.	£7,370

His gain on the gift of the shares is estimated to be:

	£
	16,960

$$\text{Deemed proceeds (MV)} \frac{218 - 210}{4} = 2 + 210 = 212p \times 8,000$$

Less: Cost	(9,450)
Unindexed gain	7,510
Less: Indexation allowance to April 1998	

$$\frac{162.6 - 154.4}{154.4} \times £9,450 \qquad (502)$$

Indexed gain	7,008

Gift relief is not available on small holdings of quoted shares.

Gain after taper relief (90% × £7,008)	£6,307

This gain will be taxable in 2001/02

(ii) *Working overseas for a period of eighteen months*

Barney will be working abroad for a period which includes the whole tax year of 2001/02. He should therefore be treated as not resident or ordinarily resident in the UK for the whole of the period between 1 November 2000 to 30 April 2002, provided that he does not make interim visits as described in (a) above.

For income tax he will only be taxable on UK source income during his absence. He will also be liable to tax on his worldwide income up to his departure. His 2000/01 statutory total income will therefore be:

	Non-savings Income £	Savings (excl dividend) Income £	Total £
Schedule E Case I (£33,600 × 7/12)	19,600		
Schedule A	2,600		
Schedule D Case V £5,460 × 100/70 × 7/12		4,550	
Statutory total income	22,200	4,550	26,750

In this case, double taxation relief will be restricted to the UK tax payable on the interest, as the UK tax rate (20%) is less than the Yalamese tax rate. The DTR will therefore be £4,550 × 20% = £910.

For capital gains tax purposes, it is not possible for Barney to treat 2000/01 as a split year as he has previously always been resident in the UK. Therefore the gain made in 2000/01 will still be taxable in that year.

The gain on the gift of shares to his daughter is made during a period when Barney is treated as not resident and not ordinarily resident. It is therefore not taxable in the year 2001/02. **However, since there are less than five tax years**

between the year of Barney's departure (2000/01) and his rearrival in the UK (2002/03), the gain will be caught by the temporary non-residence provisions. This means that the gain will be taxable in 2002/03, as a gain of that year.

(c) *Inheritance tax on gift to daughter*

This gift to Barney's daughter will be a potentially exempt transfer:

		£
Value of shares (as in (b))		16,960
Less:	AE 2001/02	(3,000)
	AE 2000/01 b/fwd	(3,000)
Potentially exempt transfer		10,960

No lifetime tax is payable. If Barney dies within seven years of the transfer, there will be no tax to pay on the PET as it is within the nil rate band. However, it will use up £10,960 of the nil rate band available on later transfers and the death estate.

It does not matter if Barney gives shares situated in Yalam to his daughter, instead of the UK shares. This is because Barney will remained domiciled in the UK and, as such is subject to IHT on assets situated anywhere in the world.

Marking guide			
		Marks	
(a)	*Residence in the UK*		
	183 day rule	1	
	91 day rule	1	
	Exceptional circumstances	1	
	Leaving the UK permanently	2	
	Coming to the UK permanently/three years	1	
	Coming to the UK for 2 years/temporary purposes	2	
	Available	8	
	Maximum		6
(b)	*Working overseas for 15 months*		
	Assessed on worldwide income	1	
	Calculation of STI	2	
	Benefits/Deduction of expenses	2	
	DTR	1	
	Plot of land gain	1	
	Shares gain	1	
	Taxation of gains in year of disposal	1	
	Working overseas for 18 months		
	Not resident or ordinarily resident	1	
	Liability to UK income tax	1	
	STI/DTR	1	
	Capital gains tax on land	1	
	Capital gains tax on shares	2	
	Available/maximum		15
(c)	*Inheritance tax on gift*		
	Value of transfer	1	
	Treatment of PET	1	
	UK Domicile – liability to IHT on worldwide assets	2	
	Available/maximum		4
	Maximum		25

44 EYETAKI INC

> **Tutors hint**. To score well you needed to be able to answer all parts of this question.
>
> **Examiner's comments**. This was the least popular question on the paper and was generally answered quite badly.

(a) (i) Eyetaki Inc **will be liable to UK corporation tax if it is trading through a branch or agency in the UK (trading within the UK).** The company will **not be liable to UK corporation tax if it is merely trading with the UK.**

From 1 January 2001 to 28 February 2001, Eyetaki Inc employed a UK agent, and maintained a stock of cameras in the UK. **Provided that contracts for the sale of cameras were concluded in Eyeland, Eyetaki Inc will probably not be liable to UK corporation tax on** profits made during this period.

On 1 March 2001, Eyetaki Inc appears to have opened a **permanent establishment** in the UK by renting an office and showroom, and it is likely that the sales managers will be empowered to **conclude contracts in the UK.** Eyetaki Inc will therefore be liable to UK tax on the profits made in the UK from 1 March 2001 to the date that the trade is transferred to Uktaki Ltd (presumably 31 July 2001).

Corporation tax will be at the full rate regardless of the level of profits made in the UK, or by Eyetaki Inc, since there is no double taxation treaty between the UK and Eyeland.

(ii) **Uktaki Ltd's accounting periods**

Uktaki Ltd's first chargeable accounting period starts when the company commences trading on 1 August 2001 and ends 12 months later on 31 July 2002. The next period runs from 1 August 2002 to the end of Uktaki Ltd's period of account, 31 December 2002.

(b) Each part of the building must be considered separately.

(i) The part to be used to assemble cameras from components imported from Eyeland will qualify for industrial buildings allowance (IBA) since it is to be used in a **trade consisting of a subjection of goods to a process.**

(ii) The part used to **store goods which are to be subjected to a process, and to store manufactured goods not yet delivered** will also qualify for IBAs. Whether the cameras are sold wholesale or retail should not affect the building's classification as an industrial building.

(iii) The **showroom and general offices will only qualify for allowances if they represent 25% or less of the total cost of the building.** Otherwise, the industrial buildings allowance will be restricted to the other qualifying proportion of the building.

Allowances

A writing-down allowance at the rate of 4% on a straight-line basis will be given, commencing with the accounting period that the building is brought into use.

Enterprise zone

If the building is in an enterprise zone, the full cost of the building (excluding the land) will qualify for industrial buildings allowance, regardless of the proportion of the cost represented by the showroom and general offices.

Allowances

If the building is in an enterprise zone, a 100% initial allowance is available. If the initial allowance is not taken in full, a writing-down allowance at the rate of 25% of cost on a straight-line basis is given.

(c) **Eyeland is not a member of the European Union (EU)**

Uktaki Ltd will have to account for VAT on the value of goods imported from outside the EU at the time of their importation. The value of the goods will include carriage costs, and all taxes, dues and other charges levied on importation. An input VAT deduction will be given on the company's next VAT return.

If Uktaki Ltd arranges for a guarantee to be given, the VAT due on importation can be accounted for on a monthly basis rather than on importation.

Eyeland becomes a member of the European Union

No VAT will have to be paid on importation if goods are purchased from a supplier in another EU state to whom Utaki Ltd has supplied its VAT registration number. Instead, output VAT will be accounted for in the period which includes the date of acquisition of the goods. The date of acquisition is the earlier of the date of issue of a VAT invoice or the 15th of the month following the removal of the goods. **This VAT payable (output tax) is also input VAT which can be deducted in the normal way on that same VAT return.**

(d) As goods are purchased at an over valuation from an overseas holding company, the UK transfer pricing legislation will apply. This means **Utaki Ltd will have to substitute a market price for the transfer price when calculating its profit chargeable to UK corporation tax. The market price will be an 'arm's length' one that would be charged if the parties to the transaction were independent of each other.**

(e) The director is to come to the UK in order to take up employment for a period in excess of two years, and so will be treated as UK resident for the entire period. The director will only be treated as ordinarily resident in the UK if there is the intention to stay in the UK for three years or more, or if he actually remains for three years.

   (i) **Emoluments for UK duties**

      The director will be subject to UK tax on emoluments for duties performed in the UK regardless of his residence status.

   (ii) **Emoluments for duties performed in Eyeland**

      The director will be subject to UK tax on emoluments for duties performed in Eyeland if he is both resident and ordinarily resident in the UK. If the director is resident, but not ordinarily resident in the UK, only such emoluments remitted to the UK will be taxable in the UK.

   (iii) **Investment income arising in Eyeland**

      The director is domiciled in Eyeland, and so will only be subject to UK tax on investment income arising in Eyeland if it is remitted to the UK.

Marking guide		Marks
(a) *Liability to corporation tax*		
Trading within the UK/Trading with the UK	1	
1 January 2001 to 28 February 2001	2	
1 March 2001 to 31 July 2001	2	
Rate of corporation tax	1	
Accounting periods	2	
Available	8	
Maximum		7
(b) Qualification as an industrial building		
Camera assembly	1	
Storage of goods	2	
Showroom and general offices	1	
Writing-down allowance	1	
Designated enterprise zone	1	
Available/Maximum		6
(c) Not a member of the European Union	2	
Member of European Union	2	
Available/Maximum		4
(d) Substitution of market price in calculating PCTCT	2	
Market price = arms length price	1	
Maximum/Available		3
(e) Resident status of director	2	
Emoluments for duties performed in the UK	1	
Emoluments for duties performed in Eyeland	1	
Investment income arising in Eyeland	1	
Available/Maximum		5
Maximum		25

45   MAGEE PLC

Tutor's hint. Your answer to part (b) should have quantified the tax saving obtained by making a distribution.

(a) (i)   **A company incorporated in the UK is UK resident.** Gavin Ltd should therefore not be incorporated in the UK.

     (ii)   **UK residence would depend on whether central management and control is exercised in the UK.** Superficially it would appear likely since the board will meet in the UK. However, the place of exercise of central management and control is a matter of fact and if the directors (or others) actually exercised control outside the UK, Gavin Ltd would not be UK resident.

     (iii) Gavin Ltd would not be UK resident for corporation tax purposes as it would be neither incorporated in the UK nor controlled from the UK. Thus the final option would meet Magee plc's requirements.

(b) (i)   **A controlled foreign company (CFC) is one which is controlled by UK resident persons, and which is resident in a country with a lower level of tax. A lower level of tax is defined as less than three quarters of the amount which would have been payable had the company been resident in the UK.** Legislation includes a list of countries which are not regarded as low tax countries.

            For the rules to apply, a UK company together with connected or associated persons **must have at least a 25% stake** in the overseas company.

A CFC's profits may be apportioned among the persons having an interest in it, and corporation tax charges may then be levied on UK corporate shareholders. However, no tax charge arises if the CFC distributes 90% of its profits.

(ii) (1) If no dividend is paid, the effect on Magee plc's corporation tax liability will be as follows.

	£
Tax on apportioned profits £420,000 × 30%	126,000
Less foreign corporation tax £450,000 × 8%	36,000
Increase in corporation tax liability	90,000

(2) If a dividend of 90% of Gavin Ltd's profits is paid (the minimum to avoid an apportionment), the position will be as follows.

	£
Gavin Ltd's tax adjusted profits	420,000
Less tax thereon £450,000 × 8%	(36,000)
Gavin Ltd's distributable profits	384,000

	£
Dividend received by Magee plc	
£384,000 × 90%	345,600
Underlying tax	
£345,600 × 36,000/364,000	34,180
Schedule D Case V income	379,780
Corporation tax £379,780 × 30%	113,934
Less underlying tax relief	(34,180)
Increase in corporation tax liability	79,754

The distribution would save corporation tax of £(90,000 − 79,754) = £10,246, so it should be made.

(c) If Alex only stays abroad for 14 months, he will leave the UK in 2001/02 (in December 2001) and return in 2002/03 (in February 2003). There is therefore no possibility of his becoming non-UK resident, and so his earnings will be taxable in full.

If the period abroad is 18 months, it will include a complete tax year (2002/03), and Alex will be treated as not UK resident for the whole of the period abroad. This will ensure that his earnings are not within the scope of Schedule E, so they will escape UK income tax. However, non-resident status will be lost if visits to the UK amount to six months or more in any one tax year or three months or more a year on average. Alex should take care that his visits to the UK do not break the three months rule.

(d) The reimbursements will be taxable emoluments. **If Tony Smith's duties of employment are performed wholly abroad, he may claim a Schedule E deduction equal to the reimbursement by Magee plc of his own travelling expenses** from the UK to Ruritania at the start of his employment abroad, and back to the UK at its end. If Tony Smith's duties of employment are performed partly abroad, the same deduction is available provided that the duties performed abroad can only be performed abroad and the journey is made wholly and exclusively to perform them or to return to the UK after performing them.

Provided that Tony Smith is **absent from the UK for a continuous period of at least 60 days the same deduction will also be available in respect of the reimbursed cost of up to two return trips per tax year to visit him by his wife and his 15 year old child. However, this deduction will not be available in respect of visits by his 20 year old child, as the age limit is 18.**

46   PADDINGTON LTD

> **Tutor's hints**. The examiner has said that you can expect questions to require knowledge of open ended investment companies.
>
> **Examiner's comments**. In part (a) the inclusion of information for the UK resident subsidiary confused many candidates.

(a) **Mainstream corporation tax liability**

	Total £	UK £	Overseas £
Schedule D Case I	79,000	79,000	
Trading loss brought forward	(7,000)	(7,000)	
	72,000	72,000	
Capital gain	6,000	6,000	
Schedule D Case V (W1)	246,400		246,400
	324,400	78,000	246,400
Charge on income	(12,000)	(12,000)	
PCTCT	312,400	66,000	246,400
Corporation tax (W2)	89,030	18,809	70,221
Double taxation relief (W3)	(70,221)	-	(70,221)
Mainstream corporation tax liability	18,809	18,809	Nil

Workings

1   **Dividend from Waterloo Ltd**

Paddington Ltd owns 10% or more of Waterloo Ltd, so relief for the underlying tax paid in Westoria is available.

	£
Dividend received £213,400 × 80%	170,720
Withholding tax at 3%	5,280
	176,000
Underlying tax $176,000 \times \dfrac{117,600}{294,000}$	70,400
Schedule D Case V income	246,400

2   **Corporation tax**

The small companies' rate upper limit of £1,500,000 are lower limit of £300,000 is divided by three, since both Victoria Ltd and Waterloo Ltd are associated companies.

	£
£312,400 at 30%	93,720
Marginal relief 1/40 × (£500,000 – £312,400)	(4,690)
	89,030
UK income £89,030 × 66,000/312,400	18,809
Overseas income £89,030 × 246,400/312,400	70,221

3   **Double taxation relief**

Double taxation relief is restricted to the lower of:

		£
(i)	Overseas tax (£5,280 + £70,400)	75,680
(ii)	UK corporation tax on overseas income	70,221

(b) As a result of its reduction in corporation tax rates from 30% to 10%, Westoria will become a 'low tax country', since its rate of tax will be **less than three quarters of that payable on the equivalent profits in the UK.** Waterloo Ltd will therefore be classified as a controlled foreign company unless it meets one of the following exclusion tests.

(i)   It is **quoted on a recognised Stock Exchange**.

(ii)   Its **profits are less than £50,000.**

(iii) It has an **acceptable distribution policy** (90% of taxable profits must be distributed.)

(iv)   The **exempt activities test**. This test is unlikely to be satisfied because Waterloo Ltd appears to be engaged in the non-qualifying business, of dealing in goods for delivery from a connected person (Paddington Ltd).

(v)   **The motive test.** (Waterloo Ltd must not exist for the main purpose of avoiding UK tax. The fact that Waterloo Ltd was set up prior to the reduction in the rate of Westoria's corporation tax, supports this argument.)

If Waterloo Ltd is classified as a controlled foreign company, then Paddington Ltd will be assessed to UK corporation tax on its share (80%) of the profits of Waterloo Ltd, rather than on the dividends remitted to the UK. Relief would be given for tax paid in Westoria.

(c) Unit trusts and OEICs are similar in nature but, as the name suggests, **OEICs are incorporated companies rather than trusts. OEICS are easier to market overseas. Dividends from OEICs are treated in exactly the same way as any other company dividend.**

(d) **ISAs are available to anyone who is resident and ordinarily resident in the UK and aged 18 or over.**

No income tax arises on ISAs. Tax credits are paid on dividends from shares held in the account before 5 April 2004 and no CGT arises on disposals. Withdrawals may be made at any time without penalty.

There is an annual subscription limit of £7,000 of which a maximum of £3,000 can be in cash and £1,000 in life insurance. A husband and wife will each have their own limits.

47   GLOBAL PLC

> **Tutor's hints.** It was important to read this question carefully. You were not required to calculate Global plc's corporation tax liability for the year ending 31.3.01 but you were required to support your answer with calculations.
>
> **Examiner's comments.** Many candidates tried to answer this question in general terms without providing any of the required supporting calculations.

(a) **Acquisition of Nouveau Inc**

Northia is not a low tax country since its corporation tax rate of 25% is higher than 22.5% (30% × 75%). Therefore, Nouveau Inc will not be classed as a controlled foreign company.

The dividend received from Nouveau Inc will be included as Schedule D Case V income when calculating Global plc's corporation tax liability for the year ended 31 March 2001. **Global plc owns 10% or more of the share capital of Nouveau Inc, so relief will be given for the underlying tax paid in Northia.**

		£
Dividend received	£300,000 × 90%	270,000
Underlying tax	£270,000 × 25/(100 − 25)	90,000
		360,000

The total tax paid in Northia is £103,500 (£90,000 + (£270,000 at 5%)). This is less than the UK corporation tax on the Schedule D Case V income (£360,000 at 30% = £108,000), and so can be relieved in full as a tax credit.

Transfer pricing

As Nouveau Inc is a non-resident group company and sales have been made to it at an undervalue the transfer pricing rules apply. This means that Global plc will have to substitute the arms length market price of the product for the actual price charged when completing its self assessment corporation tax return for the year to 31 March 2001.

The transfer pricing adjustment will increase Global plc's profits chargeable to corporation tax by £42,500.

Branch in Eastina

As the branch in Eastina is controlled from there, Global plc will be taxed under Schedule D Case V on the branch profits. All of the branch profits will be subject to UK corporation tax regardless of the amount remitted here.

UK double tax relief will be available for the lower of:

(i)   UK tax on branch profits £52,500, (£175,000 × 30%), and
(ii)   Overseas tax on branch profit £70,000 (£175,000 × 40%)

That is £52,500. There will be no relief for the remaining overseas tax suffered.

Middleman Inc

Controlled foreign company

Westonia is a low tax country since its corporation tax rate of 10% is less than 75% of the rate that would have been payable in the UK 22.5% (75% × 30%). Also Middleman Inc does not meet the following exclusion tests.

(i)   It is not quoted on a recognised stock exchange

(ii)   Its profits are not less than £50,000 pa

(iii)   It does not have an acceptable distribution policy, since less than 90% of taxable profits are distributed.

(iv)   The exempt activities test. Middleman Inc would appear to be engaged in a non-qualifying business, since it is dealing in goods for delivery from a connected person (Global plc).

Unless the motive test can be satisfied in that Middleman Inc does not exist for the purpose of avoiding UK tax, it will be classed as a controlled foreign company. Global plc will then be assessed to UK corporation tax on apportioned profits of £450,000 in the year ended 31 March 2001, rather than on the dividend remitted to the UK in the following year. Double taxation relief will be given for the tax paid in Westonia of £45,000 (£450,000 at 10%). Global plc will have to include details of the apportioned profits in its self assessment corporation tax return.

Sale of Surplus Ltd

As the sale of Surplus Ltd is to take place within six years of the transfer of the factory from Global plc, the following gain will be charged on Surplus Ltd in the accounting period during which it is sold.

	£
Value of factory June 1996	630,000
Less: cost	(260,000)
	370,000
Less: indexation	(48,620)
Chargeable gain	321,380

Surplus Ltd's corporation tax liability arising as a result of the above gain is £321,380 × 30% = £96,414.

Global plc's proceeds from the sale of Surplus Ltd will, therefore, be reduced by £96,414 and the chargeable gain arising on the sale of Surplus Ltd will be £743,586 (£840,000 – £96,414).

Acquisition of Wanted Ltd

Wanted Ltd will become a member of the same group relief group as Global plc. However, as Wanted Ltd did not join the group until 1 August 2000 it will only be able to surrender up to 8/12 × £240,000 = £160,000 of its loss for the year to 31.3.01 to set against the profits of the fellow group members arising in the corresponding accounting period.

Wanted Ltd's loss of £170,000 is a pre-entry capital loss as it arose before Wanted Ltd joined Global plc's capital gains group. This means that it will not be possible for Global plc to utilise this loss against the gain arising on the disposal of the shares in Surplus Ltd, by transferring the shareholding to Wanted Ltd prior to disposal outside of the group (or by electing that the shareholding was transferred to Wanted Ltd).

(b) **As Global plc pays the full rate of corporation tax it must make quarterly payments of its CT liability.** It will have to pay 72% of its corporation tax liability for the year to 31.3.01 by instalments, with the remaining 28% being due on 1 January 2002. An exception will apply if profits do not exceed £10 million (reduced according to the number of associated companies), and Global plc was not a large company for the year ended 31 March 2000.

The four quarterly instalments will be due on 14 October 2000, 14 January 2001, 14 April 2001 and 14 July 2001. Instalments will be based on the expected corporation tax liability for the year ended 31 March 2001, and so Global plc will have to produce an accurate forecast of its corporation tax liability for the year.

Marking guide

		Marks
(a)	**Shareholding in Nouveau Inc**	
	Rate of corporation tax	1
	Not classified as a controlled foreign company	1
	Relief for underlying tax	1
	Calculation of Schedule D Case V income	2
	Double taxation relief	1
	Transfer pricing	
	Transfer pricing rules apply/market price	1
	Adjustment under self assessment	1
	Calculation	1
	Branch in Eastina	
	UK corporation tax/Schedule D Case V income	1
	Double taxation relief	1

Controlled foreign company		
Low tax country	1	
Quoted on stock exchange/limit of £50,000	1	
Acceptable distribution policy/exempt activities	1	
Motive test	1	
Tax implications	2	
Sale of shareholding		
Transfer within six years	1	
Chargeable gain/corporation tax liability	2	
Implications for Global plc	1	
Trading loss and capital loss		
Group relief	1	
Restriction	1	
Pre-entry loss	<u>1</u>	
Available	<u>24</u>	
Maximum		21

(b)	Large company	1	
	Implications	1	
	Exception	1	
	Due dates	<u>1</u>	
	Maximum/available	<u>4</u>	
			<u>4</u>
	Maximum		<u>25</u>

48   LUCY LEE

Tutor's hint. This question has been amended to take changes in the syllabus into account.

Examiner's comment. The mistake made by some candidates was to waste time writing at length about tax avoidance and the related decided cases, despite there only being two marks available.

(a)   **Tax avoidance**

Tax avoidance is the reduction of tax by legal, although possibly artificial means. Thus tax avoidance is using the existing law to reduce your tax bill.

Artificial arrangements may be limited by the courts and statutory provisions exist to counteract specific forms of tax avoidance.

Tax evasion

Tax evasion is the attempted reduction of tax liabilities by misrepresenting the facts or by concealing information and it is illegal. Thus tax evasion means you have deliberately not paid the tax due.

(b)   (i)   **Employment of husband**

If Lucy employs her husband, paying him £28,000 pa, her income tax liability will be reduced as follows.

	£
Salary	28,000
Employers' NIC (£28,000 – 4,385) × 12.2%	<u>2,881</u>
	30,881
Income tax saved at 40%	<u>12,352</u>

Her NIC will not be affected as her profits will not be reduced to below the upper limit of £27,280.

As a result of the salary, additional income tax and NIC will be payable by Lucy's husband and also the business:

	£
Schedule E	28,000
Less: personal allowance	(4,385)
Taxable income	23,615

Income tax on non-savings income	£
£1,520 at 10%	152
£22,095 at 22%	4,861
	5,013

Employees' NIC	
(£27,820 – £3,952) × 10%	2,387
Payable by husband	7,400
Employer's NIC (payable by business)	2,881
	10,281

This results in an overall tax saving of £2,071 (£12,352 – £10,281).

The salary paid to Lucy's husband is only deductible if it is wholly and exclusively for business purposes. As the previous personal assistant was paid less, it is unlikely that the additional salary will be deductible unless it can be justified.

(ii) **New business venture**

(1) The **partnership is a separate taxable person from Lucy's own business for VAT purposes** and as its taxable supplies are below the registration threshold it is not liable to register for VAT.

However, **disaggregation rules exist whereby if the partnership is effectively an extension of Lucy's own business, then the two will be classed as one taxable person**, and the partnership will then have to account for VAT. As both businesses are engaged in similar activities, and the partnership uses Lucy's office premises, equipment and employees, the disaggregation rules are likely to apply.

(2) **Accounting for output VAT**

The tax point is normally the date the service is completed.

However **if an invoice is issued or payment is received earlier than the above date, then this earlier date becomes the tax point.**

If **an invoice is issued in the 14 days after the date the service is completed, then the 'normal' tax point is replaced by the invoice date.**

Deposit of £500

The VAT point is the date the deposit is received

Output VAT of £74.47 (500 × 7/47) must be accounted for in the return period in which the deposit is received. VAT is payable to Customs one month after the end of the return period.

Balance of contract price

The VAT point is the date the contract is completed (as an invoice is not issued within the next 14 days).

Output VAT of £74.47 must be accounted for in the return period in which this occurs.

VAT is due one month after the end of the return period.

(iii) **Wedding gift to daughter**

The gift by Lucy to her daughter will be a PET, but exemptions are available as follows.

		£
Gift		12,500
Marriage exemption		(5,000)
Annual exemption	2001/02	(3,000)
	2000/01	(3,000)
PET		1,500

The £1,500 will be fully exempt if Lucy survives seven years from the date of the gift.

Lucy's gift of £12,500 to her husband will be exempt as it is a transfer to a spouse.

The same exemptions will be available to Lucy's husband when he makes a gift of £12,500 to his daughter.

If Lucy's gift to her husband is conditional upon him giving it to their daughter, her gift may be caught under the associated operations rule. The associated operations rule is a piece of anti-avoidance legislation used by the Inland Revenue to attack schemes set up to avoid inheritance tax by using several transactions instead of just one transaction.

(c) (i) If the company continues trading the loss could be:

(1) carried forward to set against future schedule D Case I profits arising from the same trade.

(2) set against other profits (before the deduction of charges) incurred in the nine months to 31.12.01. Any trade charges that become unrelieved as a result of this set off can be carried forward to set against future Schedule D profits.

(3) Once the set off described in (2) above has been made any remaining loss could be carried back to set against total profits (after the deduction of trade charges) incurred in the previous twelve months.

(ii) If the company ceases trading the loss could be set against other profits (before the deduction of charges) incurred in the same period.

Any remaining loss could then be carried back to set against total profits (after the deduction of trade charges) incurred in the previous 36 months. Any unrelieved trade charges arising in the final 12 months of trading may be added to the loss carried back.

49 GEWGAW LTD

Tutor's hints. As part (c) was worth 3 marks only, you should have been careful not to waste time on this part of the question.

Examiner's comments. In part (b) the main problem was that candidates either ignored or incorrectly identified the amount of business mileage driven.

BPP PUBLISHING

(a)   **VAT payable for the quarter to 31 March 2001**

	£	£
Output VAT		
Standard rated sales (£62,500 × 97½% × 17 ½%)		10,664
Fuel scale charge (£325 × 7/47)		48
		10,712
Less: Input tax		
Standard rates purchases (£21,000 × 17½ %)	3,675	
Bad debts (£2,000 × 17½ %)	350	
Expenses (£14,640 – £480) × 17½ %	2,478	
		(6,503)
VAT payable		4,209

Tutorial notes.

1   **VAT is calculated on sales net of any prompt payment discount whether or not the discount is taken up.**

2   **Bad debts must be at least six months and before VAT relief can be claimed.**

3   **VAT on business entertaining is non-deductible.**

4   **Input VAT cannot be reclaimed on the purchase of the car or the sunroof as this was not fitted subsequent to the purchase and invoiced separately.**

5   **The managing directors private use of the car does not affect the input tax recovery on repairs.**

Implications of not paying above VAT until 20 May 2001

Gewgaw Ltd's first VAT return due on 31 July 2000 was submitted late, so HM Customs & Excise will have issued a **surcharge liability notice specifying a surcharged period running to 30 June 2001.** Although the second and third returns were submitted by the due dates of 31 October 2000 and 31 January 2001 respectively, **the VAT due was paid late in each case. Surcharges of 2% and 5% will therefore have been charged. VAT for the quarter to 31.3.01 is due on 30.4.01. If it is not paid until 20 May 2001, a surcharge of £421 (4,209 × 10%) will arise. In addition, the surcharge period will be extended to 31 March 2002.**

Gewgaw Ltd can use the cash accounting scheme if:

(i)   **its expected taxable turnover for the next 12 months does not exceed £350,000 (excl VAT), and**

(ii)   **it is up to date with its VAT returns and VAT payments.**

The scheme will result in the tax point becoming the date that payment is received from customers. This may be advantageous since it delays the payment of output VAT, and also provides for **automatic bad debt relief should a customer not pay.** In the quarter ended 31 March 2001 the company would have accounted for output VAT on sales of £9,485 (£54,200 × 17.5%) instead of £10,664 but the recovery of input VAT on purchases would have been reduced from £3,675 to £3,395 (£19,400 × 17.5%). Overall, using the cash accounting scheme would have been advantageous.

Annual accounting scheme

Gewgaw Ltd can apply to use the annual accounting scheme if:

(i)   **it has been VAT registered for 12 months;**

(ii)   **its expected taxable turnover for the next 12 months does not exceed £300,000 (excl VAT); and**

(iii) **it is up to date with its VAT returns.**

Under the scheme only **one VAT return is submitted each year, with nine monthly payments being made on account. The balancing payment is due two months after the end of the year.** It should be beneficial for Gewgaw Ltd to join the scheme, since the reduced administration required should mean that default surcharges are avoided.

(b) **Managing director's motor car**

Managing director

Income tax

The managing director will be assessed under Schedule E on the following car and fuel benefits.

	£
Car benefit (£17,300 × 25% (W1) × 3/12)	1,081
Fuel benefit (£2,170 × 3/12) (exactly 2,000cc)	543
	1,624

The tax on these benefits will be collected under the PAYE system. There will be no NIC implications of the benefits for the managing director.

Gewgaw Ltd

For corporation tax purposes, Gewgaw Ltd can claim capital allowances on the VAT inclusive cost of the motor car of £17,300, with the writing-down allowance for the year ended 31 March 2001 being restricted to £3,000. The company can deduct the cost of fuel and repairs in calculating its Schedule D Case I trading profit without any adjustment for private use.

The company will have to pay Class 1A NIC's on the benefits of £198.13 (£1,624 × 12.2%) for the period to 31 March 2001.

(c) The annual cost of using the bookkeeping agency is £6,300 (525 × 12), since the VAT charge is reclaimed as input VAT.

The employee required £5,200 pa (£100 × 52) net of income tax at the rate of 22% and employee Class 1 NIC at the rate of 10%, so additional gross salary of £7,647 (5,200 × 100/(100 – 22 – 10)) will have to be paid. Employers Class I NIC will increase the annual cost to £8,580 (£7,647 × $\frac{112.2}{100}$).

It is therefore beneficial, all other factors being equal, for Gewgaw Ltd to continue to use the bookkeeping agency, since this results in an overall annual savings of £2,280 (8,580 – 6,300).

Workings

1 *Mileage*

The following is private mileage:

	£
Ordinary commuting (85 × 60)	5,100
Commuting at weekends (85 × 3)	255
Travel to dinner party	105
Private miles	1,100
	6,560

This means that in the three months to 31.3.01, 4,440 business miles were travelled. This is equivalent to business miles at the rate of 17,760 per annum.

Marking guide

		Marks
(a)	**VAT return**	
	Output VAT on sales	1
	Scale charge	1
	Purchases	1
	Bad debts	1
	Motor car/sunroof	1
	Expenses	1
	The default surcharge	
	Surcharge liability notice	1
	Surcharges	1
	Implications for VAT return to 31 March 2001	1
	Cash accounting scheme	
	Use of scheme	1
	Tax point	1
	Bad debt relief	1
	Quarter ended 31 March 2001	1
	Annual accounting scheme	
	Use of scheme	1
	VAT return/payments on account	1
	Balancing payment/advantages	1

Available	16
Maximum	14

		Marks
(b)	**Managing director**	
	Car benefit	1
	Fuel benefit	1
	Annual mileage rate	1
	Ordinary commuting	1
	Private mileage	1
	NIC implications	1
	Gewgaw Ltd	
	Capital allowances	1
	Fuel and repairs	1
	Class 1A NIC	1

Available	9
Maximum	8

		Marks
(c)	Bookkeeping agency	1
	Employee	2
	Conclusion	1

Available	4
Maximum	3
Maximum	25

50 DELIA JONES

Tutor's hint. A gain arising on the transfer of a business as a going concern is automatically rolled over if the consideration is in shares and all the assets are transferred.

Examiner's comments. It was disappointing that very few candidates appreciated that the disposal of the business would result in a balancing charge for plant and machinery and many, therefore wasted time preparing unnecessarily detailed capital allowances computations.

(a) (i)   **2000/01 Schedule D Case I profits**

2000/01 (1.9.99-31.3.01)

	£
Y/e 31.8.00	77,200
1.9.00 – 31.3.01 (W2)	153,500
Less: overlap profits b/f	(24,200)
Schedule D Case I assessment	206,500

(ii)   *Capital gains*

	£
Total net gains (W3)	279,350
Less: Annual exemption	(7,200)
	272,150

Capital gains tax at 40% is £108,860.

(iii)   **The transfer of a business as a going concern is outside the scope of VAT** so Delia will not have to charge any VAT on the sale. Delia will have to inform Customs and Excise by 30 April 2001 that she has ceased to trade and **her VAT registration will be cancelled** with effect from 31.3.01.

(b) (i)   If the sale is delayed until 30 April 2001 Schedule D Case I assessments will be:

	£
2000/01 (y/e 31.8.00)	77,200
2001/02 (1.9.00 – 30.4.01) (W4)	138,300

Delaying the assessment of some of the Schedule D Case I profits until 2001/02 will delay the due date for the payment of some of Delia's income tax liability. The final payment for 2001/02 will be due on 31 January 2003 with payments on account being due on 31 January 2002 and 31 July 2002.

Maximum Class 4 NICs will be due for 2001/02 as well as for 2000/01. This is an additional cost of $7\% \times (27,820 - 4,385) = £1,640$.

Taper relief on the disposal of the goodwill and property (2) will be increased leaving the following gains chargeable.

	£
Property (1) (50 %)	116,000
Goodwill (50 %)	62,500
Property (2) after loss b/f	11,600
	190,100

This is a reduction of £89,250 in the gains chargeable leads to a decrease of £35,700 in the capital gains tax payable. In addition the capital gains tax liability will be due on 31 January 2003 rather than on 31 January 2002.

In conclusion delaying the sale until 30 April 2001 is beneficial in tax terms.

(ii)   **If the consideration is taken wholly in shares, the gains arising on the disposal of the business of £381,000 (£232,000 + £125,000 + £24,000) (before taper or loss relief) will be rolled into the base cost of the shares and no CGT will be immediately payable.** The shares will be a business asset for taper relief purposes as the company is unlisted (AIM does not count as listing), but for taper relief purposes Delia will only be treated as owning the shares from the date of sale. If Delia sells her shares in several different tax years she will be able to make use of several years annual exemptions. She will be able to set the loss brought forward against any gain on the sale of the shares. If she retains the shares for at least four years, she will be entitled to full business asset taper relief.

Workings

1   *Capital allowances*

	£
TWDV b/f	114,000
Addition	31,000
Less: Disposal proceeds	(240,000)
	(95,000)
Balancing charge	95,000

Tutorial note. Delia and Fastfood Ltd are not connected persons and so they cannot elect for the transfer to be made at TWDV.

2   *Schedule D Case I profits for period to 31.3.01*

	£
Trading profits	58,500
Balancing charge (W1)	95,000
	153,500

3   *Chargeable gains*

	£
Proceeds property (1)	462,000
Less: cost	(230,000)
Gain before taper relief	232,000

	£
Proceeds property (2)	118,000
Less: cost	(94,000)
Gain before taper relief	24,000

Goodwill – gain before taper relief	125,000

The unused loss brought forward should be set against the gain on property (2) as taper relief is not available to reduce this gain.

	£
Gain on property (2)	24,000
Less: loss b/f	(12,400)
	11,600
Gain after taper relief on property (1) (75%)	174,000
Gain after taper relief on goodwill (75%)	93,750
Total net gains after taper relief	279,350

4   *Cessation 30.4.01*

	£
1.9.00 – 31.3.01	58,500
April 2001	9,000
Balancing charge (W1)	95,000
	162,500
Less: overlap profits	(24,200)
	138,300

Marking guide

			Marks
(a)	**Schedule D Case I assessment**		
	Balancing charge		2
	Year ended 31 August 2000		1
	Period ended 31 March 2001		1
	Relief for overlap profits		<u>1</u>
		Maximum/Available	5
	Capital gains tax liability		
	Goodwill		1
	Freehold properties		1
	Capital loss brought forward		1
	Taper relief		2
	Annual exemption/CGT liability		<u>1</u>
		Maximum/Available	6
	VAT		
	Transfer as a going concern		1
	VAT registration		<u>1</u>
		Maximum/Available	2
(b)	**Disposal on 30 April 2001**		
	2000/01 assessment		1
	2001/02 assessment		2
	Due dates		1
	Class 4 NIC		1
	Taper relief		2
	CGT due date		1
	Conclusion		<u>1</u>
		Available	<u>9</u>
		Maximum	7
	Consideration as ordinary shares		
	Gain rolled over into base cost of shares		2
	Taper relief		2
	Business asset		1
	Several annual exemptions		<u>1</u>
		Available	<u>6</u>
		Maximum	<u>5</u>
		Maximum	<u>25</u>

51   FRED BARLEY

> **Tutor's hint**. Question like this are very common. This means you must ensure that you are fully aware of all the tax aspects arising on the transfer of a business.
>
> **Examiner's comments**. Candidates who confuse the different reliefs available such as retirement relief and BPR cannot expect to pass this paper.
> _{¹ for CGT.   ↳ for IHT.}

(a)   **Income tax implications of sale of business**

The sale of the business to Simon will result in a cessation for Fred and a corresponding commencement for Simon. In the absence of any election, plant and machinery will be transferred to Simon for capital allowance purposes at its market value on 31 May 2001 resulting in the following allowances and balancing charge.

	£
Seven months to 31.12.97	
Addition	34,000
WDA at 25% × 7/12	(4,958)
	29,042

205

Year to 31.12.98
WDA at 25%   (7,261)
                                                             ─────
                                                             21,781

Year to 31.12.99
WDA at 25%   (5,445)
                                                             ─────
                                                             16,336

Year to 31.12.00
WDA at 25%   (4,084)
                                                             ─────
                                                             12,252

Five months to 31.5.01
Less: disposal (limited to cost)   (34,000)
Balancing charge   21,748
                                                             ─────

However, since Simon and Fred are connected persons, the balancing charge can be avoided by electing for the plant and machinery to be transferred to Simon at its tax written down value of £12,252. Such an election must be made jointly by 31 May 2003.

Assuming this election is made Fred's Schedule D Case I profits/(loss) will be:

	£
Seven months to 31.12.97 (£70,000 –£4,958)	65,042
Year to 31.12.98 (£122,000 – £7,261)	114,739
Year to 31.12.99 (£81,000 – £5,445)	75,555
Year to 31.12.00 (£34,000 – £4,084)	29,916
Five months to 31.5.01	(36,000)

The taxable profits in each year will be:

	£
1997/98 (1.6.97 – 5.4.98) (£65,042 + 3/12 × £114,739)	93,727
1998/99 (y/e 31.12.98)	114,739
1999/00 (y/e 31.12.99)	75,555
2000/01 (y/e 31.12.00)	29,916
2001/02 (five months to 31.5.01)	-

A claim could be made under s 380 ICTA 1988 for the loss to be set against Fred's total income of £29,916 in 2000/01. As Fred has no income in 2001/02, a s 380 ICTA 1999 claim will not be possible in 2001/02. The loss available for relief under s 380 ICTA 1988 is:

	£
Schedule D Case I	36,000
Overlap relief	28,685
	─────
	64,685

Alternatively, a claim could be made to relieve the loss of the last twelve months of trading under s 388 ICTA 1988. The loss of the last twelve months is:

	£	£
1.6.00 - 5.4.01		
7/12 × £29,916	17,451	
3/5 × (£36,000)	(21,600)	
	─────	
		(4,149)
6.4.01 - 31.5.01		
2/5 × (£36,000)	(14,400)	
Overlap relief	(28,685)	
	─────	
		(43,085)
		─────
		47,234

This would be relieved against Schedule D Case I income of £29,916 in 2000/01 and against £17,318 of income in 1999/00.

Clearly a S 388 ICTA 1988 claim will be worthwhile, resulting in a tax refund of £12,361 (£5,434 + £6,927).

Simon will take over the plant and machinery at its tax written down value of £12,252 on 1 June 2001. His capital allowances for the year to 31 May 2002 will be £3,063 and his Schedule D Case I loss will be £15,063 (£12,000 + £3,063). The loss available for relief under s 381 in each of the opening years will be:

2001/02 (1.6.01 – 5.4.02)
    (£15,063 × 10/12)   £12,553
2002/03 (y/e 31.5.02)
    £15,063 – £12,553 (already relieved in previous year)   £2,510

The loss could be carried forward for relief under s 385 ICTA 1988 but as this would not result in relief until at least 2003/04 a claim under s 381 ICTA 1988 would be better. A s 381 claim would result in £12,553 being set against income of 1998/99 and £2,510 being set against income of 1999/00.

These claims should result in immediate tax refunds totalling £6,025 ((£12,553 + £2,510) × 40%)

A s 381 claim must be made by the 31 January which is nearly two years after the end of the year in which the relevant loss was made.

(b) **Capital gains implications - Fred**

Since Fred and Simon are connected persons, the market value of the assets transferred will be used, rather than the sale proceeds.

Farm land and farm buildings

As Fred is 50 years old, he qualifies for retirement relief. As he ran the business for four years the upper and lower limits are multiplied by 4/10. Provided that Fred and Simon jointly elect, gift relief will also be available.

	£	£
Deemed proceeds		600,000
Cost		(115,000)
Unindexed gain		485,000
Indexation to April 1998 $£115,000 \times \dfrac{162.6 - 157.5}{157.5}$ (0.032)		(3,680)
		481,320
Retirement relief		
(4/10 × £150,000) × 100%	60,000	
(£240,000 (*Note 2*) – £60,000) × 50%	90,000	
		(150,000) ✓
		331,320
Gain held over (*Note 3*)		(221,320)
Chargeable gain		110,000

The farmland and buildings are business assets that have been owned for three years since 6.4.98 so the gain chargeable after taper relief is:

£110,000 × 50% = £55,000

Note 2. The retirement relief upper limit is £240,000 (£600,000 × 4/10). We are using the upper and lower limits for 2000/01 as instructed by the question. As retirement relief is being phased out, the limits are actually lower in 2001/02.

Note 3. The consideration paid by Simon exceeds the cost of the land and buildings and the retirement relief available by £110,000 (£375,000 – £115,000 – £150,000). Therefore only £271,320 (£331,320 – £110,000) of the gain qualifies to be held over as a gift of business assets.

Investments	£
Deemed proceeds	250,000
Cost	(35,000)
Gain before taper relief	215,000

No taper relief available – held less than 3 years.

Fred's chargeable gain	£
Chargeable gains £55,000 + £215,000	270,000
Annual exemption	(7,200)
	262,800

CGT liability		£
£1,520 × 10%		152
£26,880 × 20%		5,376
£234,400 × 40%		93,760
262,800		99,288

The CGT of £99,288 will be due on 31 January 2003. It would be beneficial if at least £110,000 of the consideration paid by Simon was allocated to other assets. The hold over of the gain on the farm land and farm buildings would then not be restricted.

Capital gains tax - Simon

Simon will take over the farm land and farm buildings at a base cost of £378,680 (£600,000 – £221,320), and the investments at a base cost of £250,000.

(c) **Inheritance tax**

The transfer of value to Simon on 31 May 2001 will be a PET that will only become chargeable to IHT if Fred dies within seven years of the transfer. If Fred dies within three years of the transfer the IHT payable will be:

	£
Value transferred (£1,000,000 – £375,000)	625,000
Less: Business property relief (*Note 4*) (£625,000 – £250,000)	(375,000)
	250,000
Less: Annual exemptions	
2001/02	(3,000)
2000/01	(3,000)
	244,000

		£
IHT		NIL
£234,000 × 0%		4,000
£10,000 × 40%		4,000

The IHT of £4,000 will be reduced by taper relief if Fred survives for at least three years after making the transfer of value. Simon will have to pay any IHT due within six months of the end of the month of Fred's death.

Note 4. BPR is only available to set against the value of business assets transferred. It will not be available if Simon has sold the business or the business has ceased to qualify at the date of Fred's death. APR is not available because Simon purchased the farmland and farm buildings at their agricultural value.

It would be beneficial if Simon purchased the investments, plus other assets worth £125,000 at full value, and the farm land and buildings were gifted. That way APR/BPR would be available @ 100% on the full gift.

Tax Planning
BPP Mock Exam: June 2001

Question Paper:	
Time allowed	**3 hours**
FOUR questions ONLY to be answered	

Disclaimer of liability

Please note that we have based our predictions of the content of the June 2001 exam on our long experience of the ACCA exams. We do not claim to have any endorsement of the predictions from either the examiner or the ACCA and we do not guarantee that either the specific questions, or the general areas, that are forecast will necessarily be included in the exams, in part or in whole.

We do not accept any liability or responsibility to any person who takes, or does not take, any action based (either in whole or in part and either directly or indirectly) upon any statement or omission made in this book. We encourage students to study all topics in the ACCA syllabus and the mock exam in this book is intended as an aid to revision only.

paper 11

DO NOT OPEN THIS PAPER UNTIL YOU ARE READY TO START

UNDER EXAMINATION CONDITIONS

FOUR questions ONLY to be attempted.

1   Moon Ltd is the holding company for a group of companies. The group structure is as follows.

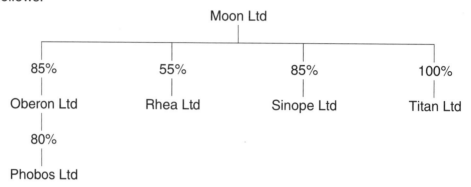

Each percentage holding represents a holding of ordinary share capital. The shareholdings were all held throughout the year ended 31 March 2001 except for Moon Ltd's 100% shareholding in Titan Ltd that was acquired on 1 October 2000. All of the companies have an accounting date of 31 March. The results of each company (except Titan Ltd) for the year ended 31 March 2001 are as follows:

	Tax adjusted *Schedule D Case I profit* £
Moon Ltd	278,000
Oberon Ltd	47,000
Rhea Ltd	124,000
Sinope Ltd	72,000
Phobos Ltd	4,000

Sinope Ltd's tax adjusted profit of £72,000 is entirely in respect of an overseas branch. Overseas taxation of £25,920 has been paid on the branch profits.

Titan Ltd previously had an accounting date of 30 September, but has produced accounts for the six month period to 31 March 2001 to make its accounting date coterminous with the other group companies. Due to a reorganisation following its takeover by Moon Ltd, Titan Ltd made a tax adjusted Schedule D Case I loss of £95,000 for the six month period to 31 March 2001. On 31 December 2000 the company received bank interest of £1,500, and on 15 February 2001 it paid a patent royalty of £4,000 (gross). For the year ended 30 September 2000, Titan Ltd has profits chargeable to corporation tax of £8,000. It did not pay any charges in this year.

Required:

(a) (i)   **Explain the possible ways that Titan Ltd can relieve its Schedule D Case I trading loss for the six month period to 31 March 2001.**

(5 marks)

(ii)   **State, giving appropriate reasons, the companies to which Titan Ltd can surrender its Schedule D Case I trading loss.**   (3 marks)

(iii) **Advise the Moon Ltd group as to which loss relief claims as specified in (a) and (b) above would be the most beneficial. Your answer should be supported by appropriate calculations.**   (7 marks)

You are not expected to calculate the mainstream corporation tax liabilities for any of the companies.

(b) **Moon Ltd, Rhea Ltd and Oberon Ltd are registered as a group for VAT purposes but, the inclusion of Rhea Ltd in the group is now being reconsidered. The forecast sales and purchases of the companies for the year to 31 March 2002 are:**

	Moon Ltd	*Oberon Ltd*	*Rhea Ltd*
	£	£	£
Sales			
Standard rated	400,000		
Zero rated		50,000	
Exempt			150,000
Purchases	(50,000)	(10,000)	(10,000)
Overheads	(80,000)		
Management fee	20,000	(10,000)	(10,000)

The purchases, overhead expenditure and management fees are all standard rated. Each of the company's purchases relate to its own sales. The overhead expenditure cannot be attributed to any of the three companies sales. All of the above figures are exclusive of VAT.

Required:

(i) **State what the consequences of VAT group registration are** (4 marks)

(ii) **Advise whether it would be beneficial for Rhea Ltd to leave the VAT group.** (6 marks)

(25 marks)

2   Albert Bone, a widower aged 64, died on 31 March 2001. The main beneficiary under the terms of Albert's will is his son Harold, aged 37. At the date of his death Albert owned the following assets.

(a) 76,000 £1 ordinary shares in Hercules plc. On 31 March 2001 the shares were quoted at 139-147, with bargains on that day of 137, 141 and 143.

(b) Building society deposits of £115,900.

(c) A life assurance policy on his own life. Immediately prior to the date of Albert's death, the policy had an open market value of £42,000. Proceeds of £55,000 were received following his death.

Albert was a beneficiary of two trusts.

(a) Under the terms of the first trust, Albert was entitled to receive all of the trust income. The trust owned 50,000 units in the Eureka unit trust, which was quoted at 90-94 on 31 March 2001. Accrued distributable income at 31 March 2001 was £800 (net).

(b) Under the terms of the second trust, Albert was entitled to receive the income at the discretion of the trustees. The trust's assets were valued at £95,000 on 31 March 2001.

Until 15 March 1992, Albert owned his main residence. On that date, he had made a gift of the property to Harold. Albert continued to live in the house with Harold, rent free, until the date of his death. On 15 March 1992 the property was valued at £65,000, and on 31 March 2001 it was valued at £180,000.

Albert has also made the following gifts during his lifetime.

(a) On 3 December 1993, he made a gift of £95,000 into a discretionary trust.

(b) On 18 October 1996, he made a gift of £39,500 to a granddaughter as a wedding gift.

(c) On 20 April 1997, he made a gift of ordinary shares (a 52% holding) in a quoted trading company, into a discretionary trust. The shareholding was valued at £302,000, and had been owned for 10 years. The trust still owned the shares at 31 March 2001.

Any inheritance tax arising from the above gifts was paid by Albert.

At the date of his death, Albert owed £900 in respect of credit card debts, and he had also verbally promised to pay the £750 hospital bill of a neighbour. Albert's funeral expenses came to £1,200.

Under the terms of his will, Albert left specific gifts to his grandchildren totalling £40,000. The residue of his estate was left to Harold.

Required:

(a) Calculate the IHT that will be payable as a result of Albert's death. Your answer should show who is liable to pay the tax, and by what date. You should also include an explanation as to your treatment of Albert's main residence, and a calculation of the amount of the inheritance that Harold will receive.

You should ignore Albert's income tax liability for 2000/01, and should assume that the tax rates and allowances for 2000/01 apply throughout.   (17 marks)

(b) Harold is to make a gift of some of his inheritance to his son, aged 8, so as to utilise his son's personal allowance. Advise Harold of whether or not such a gift would be effective for income tax purposes. Your answer should include any tax planning advice that you consider to be appropriate.   (4 marks)

(c) Harold plans to invest the balance of his inheritance so as to achieve capital growth, since he already has sufficient income. He will require the capital in five years time when he is to purchase a new house. Briefly advise Harold of investments that would be appropriate for such an investment strategy.   (4 marks)

(25 marks)

3   (a) Ming Khan and Nina Lee are in partnership running a music recording studio. The partnership commenced trading on 1 May 1999, and their first accounts for the 15 month period to 31 July 2000 show a tax adjusted Schedule D Case I trading loss (*before* capital allowances) of £71,250. On 12 May 1999 the partnership purchased a freehold building and converted it into a recording studio during May and June of 1999 at a cost of £211,500, made up as follows.

	£
Land and building	69,500
Recording equipment	70,300
Installation of electrical system for the recording equipment	19,400
Sound insulation	13,200
Replacement doors and windows	2,500
Heating system	5,100
VAT	31,500
	211,500

Ming and Nina decided not to claim first year allowances in respect of any or the above expenditure. They did, however, claim writing down allowances for the fifteen month period to 31.7.00.

Profits and losses are shared 60% to Ming and 40% to Nina. The partnership is registered for VAT, and all of its supplies are standard rated.

Required:

(i) **Show how the partnership's Schedule D Case I trading loss for the 15 month period to 31 July 2000 will be allocated between Ming and Nina for 1999/00 and 2000/01. Your calculations should be made on a monthly basis.** (4 marks)

(ii) **State the possible ways of relieving the Schedule D Case I trading loss.** (3 marks)

(b) Ming was previously employed by a music company at an annual salary of £42,000. she was made redundant on 28 February 1999, and received an *ex gratia* redundancy payment of £60,000.

Nina was previously a student. She had inherited an investment property on the death of her parents, and sold this for £125,000 on 31 March 1999 in order to finance her partnership capital. The disposal resulted in a chargeable gain of £39,200. Until March 1999 Nina received Schedule A income of £6,250 pa.

Required

(i) **Advise Ming and Nina as to which loss relief claims would be the most beneficial for them.** (4 marks)

(ii) **Calculate the tax refunds that will be due to Ming and Nina. You should ignore the possibility of any repayment supplement being due.**

You should use the tax rates and allowances for 2000/01 throughout. Ignore taper relief. (7 marks)

(c) Ming and Nina are concerned about the partnership's financial position. They have asked for your advice on the following matters.

(i) One of the partnership's clients owes the partnership £23,500, and this amount is now four months overdue. Ming and Nina want to know how relief for bad debts can be obtained.

(ii) The partnership needs to purchase computer equipment costing £61,100, but does not have sufficient funds to do so outright. The computer equipment can either be leased for three years at a cost of £28,200 pa or can be bought on hire-purchase for an initial payment of £11,100 (including VAT of £9,100), followed by 35 monthly payments of £2,000.

The computer equipment will be replaced after three years use, at which time it will be worthless. Ming and Nina want to know the tax implications of each alternative method of financing the computer equipment.

All figures are inclusive of VAT where appropriate.

Required:

Advise Ming and Nina in respect of the matters they have raised. Your answer should cover both the income tax and the VAT implications. You

should ignore the implications of SSAP 21: *Accounting for leases and Hire-Purchase Contracts.* (7 marks)

(25 marks)

4   Benny Fitt is the managing director of Usine Ltd, an unquoted trading company. Usine Ltd is a small company for the purposes of the Companies Acts. Benny, aged 39, is paid a salary of £45,000 per annum. You should assume that today's date is 20 December 2000. Benny has asked for your advice on the following matters.

(a) On 1 October 2000 Usine Ltd provided Benny with a new 2,600 cc petrol powered motor car with a list price of £28,400. The motor car was subsequently fitted with a sun-roof costing £700. Benny made a capital contribution of £2,500 towards the cost of the motor car. During 2000/01 Benny will drive 1,100 business miles. He has a business meeting planned for 8 April 2001, which is a round trip of 220 miles from his home. The round trip from work to the meeting would be 190 miles, and Benny drives a total of 45 miles each day to work and back. It may be possible to bring this meeting forward to 4 April 2001. Benny has the use of a company credit card. During 2000/01 this will be used to pay for motor repairs of £460, business accommodation of £380, entertaining of customers £720 and petrol of £425. Included in the figure for petrol is £180 in respect of private mileage which is not reimbursed to Usine Ltd.

On 6 April 2000 Usine Ltd provided Benny with a lap-top computer at a cost of £3,000, for private use and occasional business use.

Required:

Advise both Benny and Usine Ltd of the tax implications arising from the provision of the company motor car, the company credit card and the computer. Your answer should include an explanation of why it would be beneficial if Benny:

(i)   brought his business meeting forward to 4 April 2001; and
(ii)   paid Usine Ltd £180 for his private petrol.

You should ignore VAT, and confine your answer to the implications for 2000/01. (11 marks)

(b) On 10 December 2000 Usine Ltd dismissed their sales director, and paid him a lump sum redundancy payment of £45,000. This consisted of the following.

	£
Statutory redundancy pay	2,100
Payment in lieu of notice	3,100
Holiday pay	2,800
Ex gratia compensation for loss of office	34,000
Agreement not to work for a rival company	3,000
	45,000

A new sales director is to commence employment on 1 January 2001. She is to be paid a lump sum payment of £10,000 upon the commencement of employment. The new director currently lives 120 miles from Usine Ltd's head office, so the company has offered her two alternative arrangements.

(i)   Usine Ltd will pay £9,500 towards the cost of the director's relocation, and will also provide an interest free loan of £50,000 in order for the director to purchase a property.

(ii)   Usine Ltd will provide accommodation for the director. The company owns a house which it purchased in 1989 for £86,000, and improved at a cost of £8,000 during 1998. The house has a rateable value of £4,400, is currently valued at £105,000, and has recently been furnished at a cost of £10,400. Usine Ltd will pay for the annual running costs of £3,200.

Required:

Explain the income tax implications of the lump sum payments of £45,000 and £10,000, and the two alternative arrangements offered to the new sales director.

You are not expected to consider the tax implications of Usine Ltd, and you should confine your answer to the implications for 2000/01.   (9 marks)

(c)   Usine Ltd runs an occupational pension scheme for its employees. Employees contribute 4% of their salary, and the company contributes a further 8%. The benefits on retirement are based upon final salary. At present the scheme is not approved by the Inland Revenue, but Usine Ltd is planning to amend the conditions of the scheme so that Inland Revenue approval can be obtained.

Required:

Advise Usine Ltd of the tax advantages for both itself and for its employees if Inland Revenue approval is obtained for the occupational pension scheme.   (5 marks)

(25 marks)

5   Yaz Pica commenced trading as a self-employed printer on 1 January 2001. He is to make up his accounts to 31 December 2001, and has produced the following quarterly profit forecast:

	Quarter ending 31.3.01 £	Quarter ending 30.6.01 £	Quarter ending 30.9.01 £	Quarter ending 31.12.01 £	Total for year £
Sales					
Standard rated	19,400	28,600	40,200	51,200	139,400
Zero rated	5,100	7,500	9,700	12,500	34,800
	24,500	36,100	49,900	63,700	174,200
Purchases	(14,900)	(16,700)	(18,400)	(20,600)	(70,600)
Opening stock	(3,600)	(3,800)	(4,400)	(5,700)	(3,600)
Closing stock	3,800	4,400	5,700	7,200	7,200
Subcontractor costs	-	(3,100)	(8,800)	(12,400)	(24,300)
Expenses					
Standard rated	(9,900)	(5,200)	(5,600)	(6,100)	(26,800)
Exempt	(1,100)	(1,300)	(1,600)	(1,800)	(5,800)
Profit/(Loss)	(1,200)	10,400	16,800	24,300	50,300

Yaz registered for VAT on 1 January 2001, even though the VAT registration turnover limit was not exceeded until May 2001. All of Yaz's sales are to members of the general public. The purchases are all standard rated. Because of the pressure of work, Yaz was late submitting his first VAT return due on 30 April 2001.

The opening stock of £3,600 represents purchases made during December 2000. On 10 December 2000 Yaz purchased printing equipment for £18,000, and spent £1,400 on an advertising campaign that ran throughout December. All the expenses included in the profit forecast are allowable for tax purposes, but do not include capital allowances or the cost of the advertising campaign.

The above figures are all net of VAT.

On 1 May 2001 Yaz started sub-contracting some of his work to another printer, Albert Elite. As a result of the continued expansion of the business it is likely that as from 1 October 2001 Albert will work for Yaz on a full-time basis. Yaz considers Albert to be self-employed because he issues invoices for the work done. Albert is not registered for VAT.

Until 30 November 2000 Yaz was employed on a salary of £42,000 pa, and PAYE of £6,927 has been deducted during 2000/01. He is single and has no other income or outgoings.

Required:

(a) (i)   **Calculate the amount of income tax that Yaz will have to pay on 31 January 2002 if he makes up his accounts for the year ended 31 December 2001.**   (6 marks)

(ii) **Advise Yaz of whether it will be beneficial to make up his accounts for the three month period to 31 March 2001, rather than for the year ended 31 December 2001.**   (4 marks)

You are only expected to calculate Yaz's income tax liability for 2000/01. NIC should be ignored.

(b) (i)   **With hindsight, it is evident that Yaz should not have registered for VAT until 1 July 2001. Explain why this is the case, and calculate the additional profit that Yaz would have made if he had registered for VAT as from 1 July 2001 rather than from 1 January 2001.**   (5 marks)

(ii) **State the implications of Yaz being late in submitting any further VAT returns during 2001.**   (2 marks)

(iii) **Advise Yaz of the advantages of using the annual accounting scheme, and explain when he will be permitted to join.**   (3 marks)

(c) **Briefly explain the criteria that will be used in deciding whether Albert should be treated as employed or self-employed. State the implications for Yaz if Albert is incorrectly treated as self-employed rather than employed.**   (5 marks)

(25 marks)

6   (a) Velo Ltd manufactures bicycles, making up its accounts to 31 March. The company is planning to move into new business premises during March 2001 (you should assume that today's date is 15 February 2001). The company's plans are as follows.

(i)   On 25 March 2001 Velo Ltd is to sell its existing freehold factory for £920,000. The factory was purchased from a builder on 1 April 1990 for £326,000, and was immediately brought into use. The cost and selling price are made up as follows:

	Cost £	Selling price £
Land	95,000	180,000
Factory	160,000	575,000
General office	71,000	165,000
	326,000	920,000

(ii)   On 1 March 2001 Velo Ltd is to purchase a freehold factory at a cost of £725,000, and this will be brought into use immediately. The factory was originally constructed between 1 January and 31 March 1992 at a cost of £640,000, and was bought into use on 1 July 1992. The original cost and purchase price are made up as follows:

	Original cost	Purchase price
	£	£
Land	132,000	154,000
Factory	478,000	531,000
Drawing office	30,000	40,000
	640,000	725,000

Velo Ltd will immediately install a new overhead crane in the factory at a cost of £53,000. The crane is a long-life asset.

(iii)   On 1 March 2001 Velo Ltd is to pay a premium of £80,000 for the grant of a 15 year lease on an office building. An annual rental of £16,200 will be payable quarterly in advance. The company will immediately install new computer equipment in the office building at a cost of £14,000. The computer equipment will probably be replaced in three years time.

The tax written down value of Velo Ltd's plant and machinery at 1 April 2000 is £38,000. The company is registered for VAT, and all of the above figures are net of VAT. Velo Ltd is a medium-sized company as defined by the Companies Acts.

Required:

Advise Velo Ltd of the tax implications arising from each aspect of its proposed plan. Your answer should be supported by appropriate calculations. Assume the RPI figure for March 2001 is 174.5.   (17 marks)

(b)   Following further enquiries regarding Velo Ltd's proposed plan, the following additional information is now available in respect of the factory that is to be sold on 25 March 2001.

(i)   On 10 March 1998 Velo Ltd installed heating and ventilation systems in the factory at a cost of £54,000. All of the expenditure qualified as plant and machinery. The tax written down value of these systems at 1 April 2000 is £28,000. This figure is included in the pool tax written down value of £38,000 above.

(ii)   On 31 January 2001 Velo Ltd installed an overhead crane in the factory at a cost of £64,000. The crane is a long-life asset, and has a current market value equivalent to its cost.

The market value of each of these assets is included in the value of the factory of £575,000.

Required:

Advise Velo Ltd of the tax implications arising from this additional information, and how it affects your answer to part (a) above. You should include tax planning advice in your answer as appropriate.   (8 marks)

(25 marks)

MOCK EXAM: ANSWERS

DO NOT TURN THIS PAGE UNTIL YOU
HAVE COMPLETED THE MOCK EXAM

WARNING! APPLYING OUR MARKING SCHEME

If you decide to mark your paper using our marking scheme, you should bear in mind the following points.

1   The BPP solutions are not definitive: you will see that we have applied the marking scheme to our solutions to show how good answers should gain marks, but there may be more than one way to answer the question. You must try to judge fairly whether different points made in your answers are correct and relevant and therefore worth marks according to our marking scheme.

2   If you have a friend or colleague who is studying or has studied this paper, you might ask him or her to mark your paper for you, thus gaining a more objective assessment. Remember you and your friend are not trained or objective markers, so try to avoid complacency or pessimism if you appear to have done very well or very badly.

3   You should be aware that BPP's answers are longer than you would be expected to write. Sometimes, therefore, you would gain the same number of marks for making the basic point as we have shown as being available for a slightly more detailed or extensive solution.

It is most important that you analyse your solutions in detail and that you attempt to be as objective as possible.

1

> **Tutor's hint.** As instructed by the question you should not have calculated the mainstream corporation tax liability for any of the companies.
>
> **Examiner's comments.** Most candidates had few problems with part (a), although some confused the income and corporation tax loss reliefs.

(a) *Loss relief*

 (i) The Schedule D Case I trading loss of Titan Ltd can be relieved in the following ways:

 • Under s 393(1) ICTA 1988, it can set off its trading loss against income from the same trade in future accounting periods. Relief is available against the first available profits.

 S 393(I): 1 mark

 • Under s 393A(1) ICTA 1988 the loss can be set against total profits (before deducting any charges) of the current accounting period ie the six months to 31 March 2001. The only other income is the bank interest of £1,500, so such a claim would not be beneficial as it would merely result in unrelieved patent royalties of £4,000. However, if the carryback claim discussed below is to be made, this claim must be made first. The unrelieved patent royalties can be added to the loss carried forward under s 393(1) ICTA 1988.

 S 393A: current: 1 mark

 • After a s 393A(1) ICTA 1988, described above has been made relief can be given for any remaining loss against total profits (after deducting trade charges but before deducting non-trade charges) of an accounting period falling wholly or partly within the 12 months of the start of the period in which the loss was incurred ie y/e 30.9.00.

 S 393A (I): carryback: 1 mark

 A claim for relief against current or prior period profits must be made within two years of the end of the accounting period in which the loss arose ie by 31.3.03.

 However, no relief is available against profits made in accounting periods on one side of (in this case before) a change of ownership of a company where the loss making period is on the other side of (in this case, after) the change in ownership and there has been a major change in the nature or conduct of the trade within three years before or after the change. On 1 October 2000, there was such a change in ownership of Titan Ltd, and therefore the carry back of loss relief may be restricted. It is possible that the reorganisation mentioned would be treated as a major change in the conduct of the business.

 Restriction: 1 mark

 • Group relief enables Titan Ltd to surrender trading losses and excess charges on income to other group companies. Since the accounting periods of Titan Ltd and the claimant company will not be the same, only relief for the period of overlap can be given ie 6/12 of the claimant company's profits chargeable to corporation tax in y/e 31.3.01 can be relieved.

 Group relief: 2 marks

 (ii) *Group relief*

 Group relief applies between UK companies within a 75% group. Members of a 75% group are the holding company and its 75% subsidiaries so in this case the 75% group will be:

 Group definition: 1 mark

221

(1) Moon Ltd
(2) Titan Ltd (100% holding by Moon Ltd)
(3) Sinope Ltd (85% holding by Moon Ltd)
(4) Oberon Ltd (85% holding by Moon Ltd)

Phobos Ltd is not in the group (80% × 85% = 68% holding only) nor is Rhea Ltd (55% holding only).

This means that Titan Ltd will be able to surrender its loss to Moon Ltd, Sinope Ltd and Oberon Ltd but not to Phobos Ltd or Rhea Ltd

(iii) *Choice of loss reliefs*

In making a choice between loss reliefs the most important factor is the rate at which relief will be obtained. If relief is claimed under s 393A(1) against the profits of the twelve months to 30 September 2000, the rate of relief will be at 10% and 20%. In addition additional trade charges will become unrelieved in the six months to 31.3.01 and will have to be carried forward.

A group relief claim will be more beneficial. The amount that can be relieved is:

	£
Schedule D Case I loss	95,000
Excess trade charges £(4,000 – 1,500)	2,500
	97,500

Relief should, in general, be given first to companies whose profits fall within the small companies' rate marginal relief band. The associated companies here are Moon Ltd and all the subsidiaries (Oberon, Rhea, Sinope and Titan) and subsidiary (Phobos Ltd). The limits for small companies are therefore:

Lower: £300,000 ÷ 6 =   £50,000
Upper: £1,500,000 ÷ 6 =   £250,000

Only Sinope Ltd is currently affected by marginal relief. However, it should also be taken into account that Sinope Ltd has paid overseas taxation at the rate of 36% (25,920/72,000 × 100) and so would lose DTR if group relief were surrendered to it. Therefore, the best use of the relief would be against Moon Ltd profits which are just above the upper limit. The maximum relief would be 6/12 × £278,000 = £139,000, so a full group relief claim can be made, as the actual loss to be surrendered is only £97,500. The first £(278,000 – 250,000) = £28,000 will be relieved at 30% and the remaining £(97,500 – 28,000) = £69,500 relieved at 32.5%.

(b) (i) **Companies under common control may apply for group registration.** The effects and advantages of group registration are as follows.

- Each VAT group must appoint a representative member which must **account for the group's output VAT and input VAT, thus simplifying VAT accounting** and allowing payments and repayments of VAT to be netted off. However, all members of the group are jointly and severally liable for any VAT due from the representative member.

- **Any supply of goods or services by a member of the group to another member of the group is, in general, disregarded for VAT purposes,** reducing the VAT accounting work. However, VAT does have to be accounted for on certain services supplied to a UK group company via an overseas group member.

- Any other supply of goods or services by or to a group member is in general treated as a supply by or to the representative member but any special status of the representative member (eg charitable status) is ignored unless the member by or to whom the supply was made also has that special status.

- Any VAT payable on the import of goods by a group member is payable by the representative member.

(ii) The inclusion of Rhea Ltd in the VAT group makes the group partially exempt. The following proportion of non-attributable input VAT on overhead expenditure will be recoverable:

Partial exemption: 1 mark

$$\frac{\text{Taxable supplies}}{\text{Total supplies}} = \frac{450,000}{600,000} = 75\%$$

Non-attributable VAT
£80,000 × 17.5% = £14,000

Irrecoverable VAT 2 marks

Irrecoverable amount
25% × £14,000 = £3,500

However, as the total irrecoverable input VAT of £5,250 (£3,500 + $17\frac{1}{2}\%$ × £10,000) is below the de minimis limit of £625 per month on average and is less than 50% of all input VAT incurred, it is in fact recoverable.

Deminimis: 1 mark

Thus group registration does not result in any irrecoverable VAT.

If Rhea Ltd is not included in the group registration VAT will have to be charged on the management fee of £10,000. As Rhea Ltd does not make taxable supplies it cannot register for VAT and it would not be able to recover this VAT. If Rhea Ltd is included in the group registration VAT does not have to be charged on the management fee. This means inclusion within the group is recommended.

Management fee: 1 marks

Conclusion: 1 mark

PET: 1 mark

Marking guide

				Marks
(a)	(i)	*Loss relief*		
		S 393(1) ICTA 1988	1	
		S 393A(1) ICTA 1988 – current year	1	
		S 393A(1) ICTA 1988 – previous 12 months	1	
		Restriction on carry back	1	
		Group relief	2	
		Available	6	
		Maximum		5
	(ii)	*Group relief*		
		Group definition	1	
		Companies qualifying	1	
		Companies not qualifying	1	
		Available/Maximum		3
	(iii)	*Loss relief claims*		
		S 393A(1) claim	1	
		Group relief claim amount	1	
		Associates/limits	2	
		Sinope Ltd	2	
		Moon Ltd	2	
		Available	8	
		Maximum		7
(b)	(i)	*VAT*		
		Consequences of group registration	4	
		Partial exemption group	1	
		Calculate irrecoverable VAT	2	
		De minimis limit	1	
		VAT on Management charge	1	
		Conclusion	1	
		Available/Maximum		10
		Maximum		25

2

Tutor's hint. The £nil band of £234,000 has been used throughout this question as that is what was required by the examiner.

Examiner's comment. There was confusion as to the seven year cumulation period, with some candidates ignoring the chargeable lifetime transfer made more than seven years before death altogether, despite this having an impact on subsequent transfers.

(a) **Lifetime tax on lifetime gifts**

Gift with reservation: 1 mark

    (i)   Main residence - 15.3.92

This was a PET so no lifetime tax was due.

CLT: 1 mark

    (ii)   CLT - 3.12.93

	£
Gift	95,000
Less: Annual exemption (93/94)	(3,000)
Annual exemption (92/93)	(3,000)
	89,000

This falls within the £nil band so the lifetime tax is:

£89,000 × 0% = £nil

PET: 1 mark

    (iii)   PET - 18.10.96

No lifetime tax due on PET

(iv)   CLT - 20.4.97

The gift was a CLT on which IHT would have been due:

CLT: 2 marks

	£
Gift	302,000
BPR @ 50%	(151,000)
Annual exemption (97/98)	(3,000)
	148,000

BPR at 50% is available for controlling interests in quoted shares.

In the previous seven years, £89,000 of the £nil band had been used, leaving £145,000:

	£
£145,000 × 0%	Nil
£3,000 × ¼	750
	750

The gross value of this chargeable transfer is therefore £148,750 (£148,000 + £750).

Death tax

As a result of Albert's death IHT will, in addition, be due on gifts made after 31 March 1994 and on the value of his chargeable estate at death.

IHT on death: 2 marks

Gifts made after 31 March 1994

		£
PET 18.10.96		39,500
Marriage exemption		(2,500)
Less: Annual exemption	(96/97)	(3,000)
	(95/96)	(3,000)
		31,000

In the seven years before 18.10.96, £89,000 of the £nil band had been used leaving £145,000.

There is therefore no IHT due on the PET as it falls within the £nil band.

CLT 20.4.97 £148,750 (see above).

In the previous seven years, £120,000 (£89,000 + £31,000) of the £nil band had been used leaving £114,000:

£		£
114,000 × 0%		Nil
34,750 × 40%		13,900
148,750		13,900
Less: taper relief (20%)		(2,780)
		11,120
Less: lifetime tax paid		(750)
		10,370

£10,370 must be paid by the trustees of the discretionary trust by 30 September 2001. Alternatively, as the trust property consisted of a shareholding in a company that was controlled by Albert immediately prior to the transfer, the trustees could pay the IHT in ten equal annual instalments commencing on 30 September 2001.

Due date/ instalment option: 1 mark

Chargeable estate on 31 March 2001

	£	£
Free estate		
76,000 shares in Hercules plc at lower of		
(i) $139 + \frac{1}{4}(147 - 139) = 141p$		
(ii) $\frac{137 + 143}{2} = 140p$		106,400
Building society deposit		115,900
Life assurance policy		55,000
Accrued trust income		800
Less: Funeral expenses		(1,200)
Credit card debts		(900)
Net free estate		276,000
Settled property (W2)		
Eureka unit trust (50,000 × 90p (W1))	45,000	
Less: accrued trust income (800 × $^{100}/_{80}$)	(1,000)	
		44,000
Gift with reservation		180,000
Chargeable estate		500,000

In the seven years before death £179,750 of the £nil band had been used leaving £54,250:

	£		£
54,250 × 0%			Nil
445,750 × 40%			178,300
500,000			178,300

IHT of £178,300 is payable in respect of the chargeable estate of £500,000. The estate rate is, therefore, 35.66%.

IHT of £15,690 (£44,000 × 35.66%) will be payable by the trustees of the interest in possession trust by 30 September 2001. Harold will have to pay IHT of £64,188 (£180,000 × 35.66%) in respect of the gift with reservation. This IHT is also payable by 30 September 2001 although Harold may elect to pay it in ten equal annual instalments commencing on 30 September 2001.

IHT of £98,422 (£276,000 × 35.66%) will be payable by the executor's of Albert's estate by the earlier of 30 September 2001 and the date of the delivery of the account.

Harold will receive an inheritance of £137,578 (£276,000 – £40,000 – £98,422).

Treatment of main residence

As Albert continued to live **rent free** in the main residence, the gift in March 1992 was a **gift with a reservation of benefit. The gift is treated in the same way as any other gift** (ie as a PET when made). **In addition, as the reservation still existed at the date of Albert's death, the residence is included in Albert's chargeable estate at its value on the date of his death.**

The **IHT due** on the main residence **as a result of Albert's death is the higher of:**

(i) **any additional IHT due as a result of treating the gift as a PET;**
(ii) **the IHT due as a result of including the residence in the death estate.**

As the PET was made more than seven years before Albert's death, there is no additional tax due under (i). This means the IHT due is the IHT that will be due as a result of including the main residence in Albert's death estate.

Workings

1   Units in unit trust

   Units in a unit trust are always valued at the lower of the quoted prices.

2   An interest in a discretionary trust is never part of a chargeable estate at death.

(b) There is a legislation to prevent the parent of a minor child transferring income to the child in order to use the child's personal allowance. **Income which is derived from capital transferred by the parent remains income of the parent for tax purposes.** There is a **de-minimis limit where the income does not exceed £100** so it could be effective for Harold to transfer a very small amount of capital in order to generate income below this threshold.

Income: 2 marks

It would be better for a deed of variation to be used to vary the terms of Albert's will so that the capital passes directly to Harold's son and any income arising from the capital is treated as that of his son. There would be no effect on the IHT due on Albert's estate. A deed of variation must be signed by all of the beneficiaries under a will and must be entered into within two years of Albert's death.

Deed: 2 marks

(c) As Harold wishes to achieve capital growth rather than income he could consider investing in the following.

Each valid investment: 1 mark

   (i)   **Gold and antiques.**

   (ii)   **National saving certificates**. These must normally be held for five years but the return is tax free

   (iii) **Zero coupon bonds**. These bonds have no income. Investor's get their return by buying the bond for less than its redemption value

   (iv)   **Certificates of deposit**. These work in a similar way to zero coupon bonds

   (v)   **Equity shares**. The potential for capital growth is unlimited, (depending on the share). However, shares may be a high risk investment as their value can fall as well as rise

   (vi)   **Unit trust and investment trusts**. These offer a number of options for growth

   (vii) **Individual savings account (ISA)**. £7,000 can be invested in an ISA. This investment can be made up of cash, life insurance and stocks and shares. A fund specifically aimed at capital growth can be chosen. No income tax or capital gains tax will arise on ISAs.

Marking guide		Marks
(a)	*Lifetime transfers*	
	Gift with reservation	1
	Chargeable transfer 3.12.93	1
	PET 18.10.96	1
	Chargeable transfer 20.4.97	2
	Additional IHT on death	2
	Due date/instalment option	1
	Estate at death	
	Ordinary shares	1
	Other assets/debts and funeral expenses	2
	Settled property	1
	Gift with reservation	1
	Cumulative total	1
	IHT liability	1
	Rate of IHT on estate	1
	IHT due by estate/due date	1
	Other IHT liabilities/due dates	1
	Harold	1
	Gift with reservation	1
	Available	20
	Maximum	17
(b)	Income tax treatment	2
	Variation of terms of will	2
	Maximum/Available	4
(c)	Each valid investment 1 mark per investment	4
	Available/Maximum	4
	Maximum	25

3

> **Tutor's hint.** Chargeable gains are taxed at 10% if they fall within the starting rate band and at 20% if they fall within the basic rate band. They are, however, taxed at 40% to the extent that, when added to taxable income, they are at or above the higher rate threshold.
>
> **Examiner's comment.** A common mistake in part(a) was not to restrict the loss relief for the second year of assessment to the balance remaining.

(a) **Period to 31.7.00**

Capital allowance:
2 marks

Capital allowances	*Pool*
	£
Recording equipment	70,300
Electrical system	19,400
Sound insulation	13,200
Heating system	5,100
	108,000
WDA (25% × 15/12)	33,750
TWDV carried forward	74,250

The building is not an industrial building hence no IBAs are due on its cost.

The Schedule D Case I loss is therefore £105,000 (71,250 + 33,750): This is allocated as to Ming, £63,000 (60%) and Nina, £42,000, (40%) as follows.

The losses for the tax years are:

Allocation of
loss: 2 marks

	Ming (60%)	Nina (40%)
	£	£
1999/00 (1.5.99 to 5.4.00)		
£63,000/£42,000 × 11/15	46,200	30,800
2000/01 (Balance of loss)	16,800	11,200
	63,000	42,000

The assessments for 1999/00 and 2000/01 will be nil.

The trading loss can be relieved in the following ways.

(i) **Carrying it forward under s 385 ICTA 1988 to set against future trading profits.**   S385: 1 mark

(ii) **Claiming relief against total income under s 380 ICTA 1988.** The loss for 1999/00 can be set against total income for 1999/00 and/or 1998/99. The loss for 2000/01 can be set against total income for 2000/01 and/or 1999/00. Provided, in any particular year, that a s 380 claim is made first, a claim could also be made under s 72 FA 1991 to extend the set off to chargeable gains of the same year.   S380: 1 mark

S72: 1 mark

(iii) **Claiming relief under s 381 ICTA 1988 against total income of the three years preceding the year of the loss, earliest year first.** Thus the 1999/00 loss can be carried back to; 1996/97, 1997/98 and 1998/99 and the 2000/01 loss can be carried back to 1997/98, 1998/99 and 1999/00.   S381: 1 mark

(b) **Ming Khan**

Ming should claim under s 380 ICTA 1988 to set the loss of £46,200 for 1999/00 against her total income for 1998/99.   S380: 1 mark

		£	£
Schedule E -	Salary (£42,000 × 11/12)		38,500
	Compensation	60,000	
	Exemption	30,000	
			30,000
			68,500
Less: Loss relief (S 380)			46,200
			22,300
Personal allowance			(4,385)
Taxable income			17,915

Sch E: 1 mark

Taxable: 1 mark

This will result in a tax repayment of:

£		£
10,485 (£28,400 – £17,915) × 22%		2,307
35,715 × 40%		14,286
46,200		16,593

Tax repayment;
1 mark

Ming does not have any income for 1999/00 or 2000/01, and so a claim under s 380 ICTA 1988 in respect of her loss for 1999/00 is not available. She should therefore make a claim under s 381 ICTA 1988 against her total income for 1997/98.   S381: 1 mark

	£
Schedule E - Salary	42,000
Loss claim (s 381)	(16,800)
	25,200
Personal allowance	(4,385)
Taxable income	20,815

Taxable: 1 mark

This will result in a tax repayment of:

Tax repayment:
1 mark

	£		£
7,585 × 22%			1,669
9,215 × 40%			3,686
16,800			5,355

Nina Lee

S381: 1 mark

Nina's taxable income for 1996/97 and 1997/98 is £1,865 (£6,250 − £4,385). A claim under s 381 ICTA 1988 is not beneficial as it would waste personal allowances in these years and only save a small amount of tax.

Nina should utilise her loss of £30,800 for 1999/00 by claiming under s 380 ICTA 1988 against her total income for 1998/99. Although this does waste personal allowances it allows Nina to also set the loss against her chargeable gain and obtain an immediate repayment of CGT:

Sch A: 1 mark

	£
Schedule A rental income	6,250
Less: Loss relief (S 380)	(6,250)
	nil
Tax refund: £1,520 at 10% + £345 at 22%	£228

Capital gain:
1 mark

	£
Chargeable gain	39,200
Less: Loss relief (£30,800 − £6,250)	(24,550)
	14,650
Annual exemption	(7,200)
	7,450

Capital gains tax due:	£
£1,520 × 10%	152
£5,930 × 20%	1,186

Previously paid on £32,000 (£39,200 − £7,200):

Repayment:
1 mark

£26,535 (£28,400 − £1,865) @ 20%	(5,307)
£5,465 @ 40%	(2,186)
Repayment due	(6,155)

S385: 1 mark

Nina's loss of £11,200 for 2000/01 should be carried forward under s 385 ICTA 1998 against her Schedule DI trading profits for 2001/02 (year ended 31 July 2001).

(c) (i) **Bad debts**

IT: 1 mark

For income tax purposes, relief will be given in the period of account when the bad debt is either written off or provided for by specific provision. No relief is available for a general provision. The relief will be for £20,000 (£23,500 × 100/117.5) less any amount that is recoverable.

VAT: 2 marks

For VAT purposes, relief will be given on the appropriate VAT return when the debt is over six months old, and has been written off. The six month time limit starts on the date the debt should have been paid (not the invoice/supply date). The relief will be for £3,500 (£23,500 × 17.5/117.5). However, if the partnership operates the cash accounting scheme, then relief is automatic, since output VAT would not have been accounted for to Customs in respect of the original invoice.

(ii) **Computer equipment - hire-purchase**

CAS: 1 mark
FYA: 1 mark

The partnership will be able to claim capital allowances on the cost of the computer equipment of £52,000 (£61,100 × 100/117.5). A first year allowance of 100% will be available.

The finance charge of £20,000 (36 × £2,000 = £72,000 – £52,000) will be a deductible expense for the partnership, and will be allocated to periods of account using normal accounting principles.

The input VAT of £9,100 will be reclaimed on the VAT return for the period in which the computer equipment is purchased.

Computer equipment - leasing

The lease rental payments of £24,000 pa (£28,200 × 100/117.5) will be a deductible expense for the partnership, and will be allocated to periods of account in accordance with the accruals concept.

The input VAT of £4,200 (£28,200 × 17.5/117.5) included in each lease rental payment will be reclaimed on the tax return for the period during which the appropriate tax point occurs.

No capital allowances can be claimed by the partnership.

Marking guide			Marks	
(a)	Capital allowances		2	
	Allocation of loss		2	
	Section 385 ICTA 1988		1	
	Section 380 ICTA 1988/Section 72		2	
	Section 381 ICTA 1988		1	
		Available	8	
		Maximum		7
(b)	*Ming Khan*			
	Loss relief claims		2	
	Refund 1998/99		3	
	Refund 1997/98		2	
	Nina Lee			
	Loss relief claims		2	
	Refund 1998/99		3	
		Available	12	
		Maximum		11
(c)	*Bad debts*			
	Income tax		1	
	VAT		2	
	Computer equipment – Hire-purchase			
	Capital allowances		1	
	FYA @ 100%		1	
	Finance charge		1	
	VAT		1	
	Computer equipment – Leasing			
	Lease rental payments		1	
	VAT		1	
		Available	9	
		Maximum		7
		Maximum		25

4

Tutor's hint. It was important to answer all parts of this question.

Examiner's comments. This was a popular question although answers were somewhat disappointing given that most of the material being examined was of a Paper 7 level.

(a) **Benny Fitt**

Benefits in kind assessable on Benny are:

	£
Car benefit (£28,400 + £700 − £2,500) × 35% × 6/12	4,655
Fuel benefit (3,200 × 6/12)	1,600
Expense payments (£380 + £720)	1,100
Computer £(3,000 × 20% = £600 − £500 (exempt))	100
	7,455

Car benefit: 2 marks

Other BIK: 2 marks

Benny will be able to claim a deduction under s 198 ICTA 1988 for the expense payments of £1,100. The tax due on these benefits for 2000/01 will be £2,542 (£7,455 − £1,100 = £6,355 at 40%). The tax on the car and fuel benefits will be collected under PAYE, with any remaining liability being due on 31 January 2002.

Expense claim: 1 mark

Tax: 1 mark

Usine Ltd

Capital allowances are available on the cost of the motor car. The writing-down allowance on the car is initially restricted to £3,000 per annum.

Capital allowances: 2 marks

A 100% FYA will be given on the computer as Usine Ltd is a small company.

Expenses: 1 mark

Credit card expenses of £1,265 (£460 + £380 + £425) are allowable for Schedule D Case I purposes. However, the cost of entertaining is not allowable.

Class 1A: 1 mark

Class 1A NIC of £775 (£4,655 + £1,600 + £100 = £6,355 at 12.2%) will be due on 19 July 2001.

Effect of earlier business meeting

Mileage: 2 marks

If the business meeting is brought forward to 4 April 2001 then it falls into 2000/01 rather than 2001/2002. For 2000/01 the 2,500 business mileage limit is 1,250 (2,500 × 6/12). The business mileage for the meeting will be 220 miles, being the actual distance travelled from home to the meeting. If the meeting is brought forward to 4 April 2001, then Benny's business mileage for 2000/01 will be 1,320 (1,100 + 220) and his income tax liability for 2000/01 will be reduced by £532 (£4,655 − £3,325) × 40%).

Tax saving: 1 mark

Usine Ltd's Class 1A NIC liability will be reduced by £162 (£1,330 at 12.2%).

Private petrol

If Benny pays £180 for his private petrol there would be no assessable fuel scale benefit. This would reduce his income tax liability by £640 (£1,600 at 40%). The net saving for Benny is £460 (£640 − £180).

Tax saving: 1 mark

Usine Ltd's Class 1A NIC liability will be reduced by £195 (£1,600 at 12.2%).

(b) **Leaving employee**

Redundancy payment

Any payment that the sales director was contractually obliged to receive is taxable income.

Wages in lieu: 1 mark

Normally wages in lieu of notice are an ex gratia payment (since generally there is no contractual entitlement to receive this). Statutory redundancy pay is exempt. The first £30,000 of ex gratia payments are exempt. However although exempt itself, the statutory redundancy payment reduces the exempt amount of £30,000. The redundancy payment of £45,000 is therefore taxable as follows.

Taxable amount: 2 marks

	£	£
Holiday pay		2,800
Restrictive covenant		3,000
Ex-gratia payment (£34,000 + £3,100)	37,100	
Less: exempt amount (£30,000 − £2,100)	27,900	
		9,200
Taxable		15,000

Lump sum payment on taking up employment

The lump sum payment of £10,000 to the new sales director will be taxable, unless the payment represents compensation for a right or asset given up on taking up employment with Usine Ltd.

Beneficial loan

In 2000/01 there will be a taxable benefit of £1,250 (£50,000 × 10% × 3/12).

Relocation costs

There will be no taxable benefit in respect of eligible removal expenses up to £8,000. The exemption covers such items as legal and estate agents' fees, stamp duty, removal costs, and the cost of new domestic goods where existing goods are not suitable for the new residence.

Accommodation

The benefit in kind in respect of the accommodation in 2000/01 will be as follows.

	£
Rateable value (£4,400 × 3/12)	1,100
Additional benefit (£105,000 – £75,000) = 30,000 at 10% × 3/12	750
Furniture (£10,400 × 20% × 3/12)	520
Running costs (£3,200 × 3/12)	800
	3,170

(c) The following tax advantages will result from Usine Ltd's occupational pension scheme obtaining Inland Revenue approval.

(i) **Contributions paid will be deductible in calculating the company's Schedule D profits.**

(ii) **Usine Ltd's contributions will not be taxable benefits for employees. There will be no NIC liability.**

(iii) **An employee's contributions will be deductible from his Schedule E income.**

(iv) **The pension fund will not be subject to tax on either income or capital gains (although the tax credit attached to dividends cannot be recovered).**

(v) **A tax-free lump sum may be taken by an employee upon retirement.**

(vi) **Provision can be made for a tax-free lump sum to be paid on an employee's death in service.**

Marking guide	Marks	
(a) Benny		
Car benefit	2	
Other benefits	2	
Expense claim	1	
Income tax liability	1	
Usine Ltd		
Capital allowances	2	
Deductible expenses	1	
Class 1A NIC	1	
Business meeting		
Business mileage	2	
Tax saving	1	
Private petrol		
Tax saving	1	
Available	14	
Maximum		11
(b) *Lump sum payments*		
Wages in lieu of notice	1	
Taxable amount	2	
Lump sum on taking up employment	1	
Beneficial loan	1	
Relocation costs	2	
Accommodation		
Additional benefit	2	
Furniture/running costs	1	
Available	10	
Maximum		9
(c) Advantages of approval		
1 mark per advantage		
Available	6	
Maximum		5
Maximum		25

5

> **Tutor's hint.** The VAT aspects of questions such as this are of increasing importance.
>
> **Examiner's comments.** The annual accounting scheme was often confused with the cash accounting scheme.

(a) (i)   *Payments of income tax 31.1.2002*

This payment will be the full payment of income tax for 2000/01. No payments on account will have been made because the 1999/00 liability was met under PAYE. The first payment on account for 2001/02 will also have to be paid.

Income tax 2000/01

	£	Non-savings Income £	
Schedule E (8/12 × £42,000)		28,000	Sch E: 1 mark
Schedule D Case I			
Profits per accounts (y/e 31.12.01)	50,300		
Less: pre-trading expenditure	(1,400)		
First year allowance 40% × £18,000	(7,200)		
	41,700		
2000/01 taxable (41,700 × 3/12)		10,425	Sch D: 3 marks
STI		38,425	
Less: personal allowance		(4,385)	
Taxable income		34,040	

Tax on non-savings income	£	Tax: 1 mark
£1,520 × 10%	152	
£26,880 × 22%	5,914	
£5,640 × 40%	2,256	
	8,322	
Less: PAYE	(6,927)	PAYE: 1 mark
Tax for 2000/01	1,395	
Add: payment on account 2001/02 – 50%	697	Payments: 1 mark
Total tax due 31.1.02	2,092	

(ii)   If accounts are made up to 31 March 2001, there will be a trading loss as follows:

	£	
Loss per accounts	1,200	Loss: 1 mark
Pre trading expenditure	1,400	
First year allowance	7,200	
Loss for 2000/01	9,800	

There will be a *nil* Schedule D Case I assessable amount for 2000/01. Under s 381 ICTA 1988 the loss can be set against the total income of the preceding three years on a first in, first out basis ie against income of 1997/98 first. If Yaz's income was sufficiently high in that tax year, this could result in an income tax refund of £(9,800 × 40%) = £3,920.

In addition, no payment on account will be needed for 2001/02, since the tax in 2000/01 will be covered by the PAYE deducted, and, indeed, there will be a refund position. No income tax will be due until 31 January 2003. Therefore there is a cashflow advantage, although this will be offset by a higher liability in 2001/02 if the profit forecast is correct.

(b) (i)   As Yaz exceeded the VAT registration limit in May 2001, he should have applied to be registered by 30 June 2001 and then would have been registered from 1 July 2001. In this case, as his sales to the general public would have been at the same selling price, output tax would have been additional income. The input tax on the stock purchased in December 2000 (to the extent retained at 1 July 2001) the printing equipment; and the standard rated expenses incurred in the six months before registration, can be recovered. However, the input tax on the advertising campaign could not be recovered as it was incurred more than six months before registration.

Output VAT:
1 mark

The additional profit is therefore:

	£	£
Output VAT		
q/e 31.3.01 £19,400 × 17.5%		3,395
q/e 30.6.01 £28,600 × 17.5%		5,005
		8,400

Input VAT:
2 marks

Less: (1) input tax on goods sold		
q/e 31.3.01 £(14,900 + 3,600 − 3,800) = £14,700		
× 17.5%	2,573	

Advertising/
Pretrading:
2 marks

q/e 31.6.01 £(16,700 + 3,800 − 4,400) = £16,100		
× 17.5%	2,817	
(2) input tax on advertising not recoverable		
£1,400 × 17.5%	245	(5,635)
Increased profit		2,765

Extend period:
1 mark

(ii) **A default arises whenever a trader submits his VAT return late, even if a VAT repayment is due.** As Yaz's VAT return to 31.3.01 was late HM Customs & Excise would have served a surcharge liability notice on him. **This notice would specify a surcharge period running from the date of the notice until the anniversary of the end of the period for which he was in default** (ie until 31 March 2002).

If a further default occurs during the specified surcharge period, the original period will be extended to the anniversary of the end of period in which the new default occurs.

Surcharge: 1 mark

In addition, if there is a late payment of VAT (as opposed to simply a late return), a default surcharge will be incurred as follows:

Default in period	*Surcharge as % of VAT outstanding at due date*
1st	2%
2nd	5%
3rd	10%
4th and over	15%

Return: 1 mark
Payments: 1 mark

(iii) **Under the annual accounting scheme, a trader only has to submit a VAT return once a year. However, throughout the year, the trader makes payments on account of the ultimate liability under direct debit.** If the annual turnover is £100,000 or more, the trader must pay 90% of the previous year's net VAT liability in nine monthly payments starting in the fourth month of the year. At the end of the year, the trader completes an annual return and submits it within two months of the end of the year, together with any balancing payment.

Advantages:
1 mark

Late payments of instalments are not a default for the purposes of the defaults surcharge, although the trader may be expelled from the scheme.

Joining:
1 mark

From an administration point of view, the annual accounting scheme is beneficial and should ensure default surcharges are avoided. However, **Yaz must be registered for at least 12 months before he can apply to join. He must be up-to-date with his returns at that date. His expected taxable turnover for the next twelve months should not be in excess of £300,000.**

(c) *Employed/self employed*

There is no single test as to whether a person is employed rather than self-employed. The following tests have, however, been used as a guideline:

(i) control – if Yaz can tell Albert how to do his work, this is likely to indicate Albert is employed.

(ii)   integration – if Albert's work is integral to Yaz's business, Albert may be an employee.

(iii)   mutuality of obligations – does Yaz have to offer Albert work and does Albert have to accept work offered? If so, Albert may be an employee. Such mutuality may be built up over a period of time.

(iv)   separate business – is Albert in business 'on his own account'? If so, he is more likely to be an independent contractor. Factors here would include taking financial risks; profiting from good management; having his own premises and equipment.

If Yaz incorrectly treats Albert as not employed when he is in fact an employee, Yaz will be liable for loss of tax due to his failure to operate PAYE and Class 1 NIC.

Marking guide

				Marks	
(a)		Schedule E		1	
		Schedule D Case I adjustment		2	
		2000/01 assessment		1	
		PA/Tax liability		1	
		Collected under PAYE		1	
		Final payment/payment on account		1	
		Trading loss		1	
		S 381 ICTA 1988 claim		1	
		Income tax refund		1	
		Tax liability/payment on a/c		1	
		Conclusion		<u>1</u>	
			Available	<u>12</u>	
			Maximum		10
(b)	(i)	*Additional profit*			
		Income		2	
		Input VAT on goods sold		2	
		Pre-trading expenditure		<u>2</u>	
			Available	<u>6</u>	
			Maximum		5
	(ii)	Extend default surcharge period		1	
		Default surcharge level		<u>1</u>	
			Available/maximum		2
	(iii)	VAT return annually		1	
		Payments on account		1	
		Advantages		1	
		Joining scheme		<u>1</u>	
			Available	<u>4</u>	
			Maximum		3
(c)		Control test		1	
		Integration test		1	
		Mutuality of obligations test		1	
		Separate business test		1	
		Incorrect treatment		<u>1</u>	
			Available/maximum		<u>5</u>
			Maximum		<u>25</u>

6

> **Tutor's hints.** There were a number of tricky technical points in this question but even if you did not know how to deal with these you should have still been able to achieve a pass mark in the question by applying your basic knowledge.
>
> **Examiner's comments.** This was the least popular question on the paper and produced very few good answers.

(a) (i) *Sale of factory*

This will result in the following capital gain:

	£
Proceeds	920,000
Less: cost	(326,000)
Unindexed gain	594,000
Less: Indexation allowance	
$£326,000 \times \dfrac{174.5 - 125.1}{125.1} (= 0.395)$	(128,770)
Indexed gain	465,230

Gain: 1 mark

Rollover relief is available to defer the above gain to the extent that the proceeds are re-invested in the following replacement property:

Rollover: 1 mark

	Proceeds reinvested £
(1) Freehold factory	725,000
(2) Leasehold office	80,000
(3) Fixed plant and machinery (overhead crane)	53,000
	858,000

Gain: 1 mark

The balance of the proceeds not reinvested of £(920,000 – 858,000) = £62,000 is chargeable in the year ended 31 March 2001.

Depreciating Assets:1 mark

Allocation: 1 mark

Rollover relief defers the gain reinvested of £(465,230 – 62,000) = £403,230. The leasehold office building and the overhead crane are both depreciating assets, and so any proportion of the gain rolled over against them will only be held over until the earlier of their disposal or ten years from the date of acquisition. However, in this situation the legislation would appear to allow the claim to be effectively made wholly against the value of the freehold factory. The base cost of the freehold factory will be £321,770 (725,000 – 403,230).

There would also be a balancing charge under the IBA regime as follows:

Balacing charge: 2 marks

	£
Original cost (not land or offices (exceeds 25% of cost))	160,000
Less: IBAs given (y/e 31.3.91 – 31.3.00)	
10 × 4% × £160,000	(64,000)
Residue before sale	96,000
Less: proceeds (limited to cost)	(160,000)
Balancing charge	64,000

(ii) *Purchase of new factory and crane*

Qualifying expenditure: 2 marks

Velo Ltd can claim IBAs on the new factory. The eligible expenditure is the lower of the purchase price and the original cost incurred by the person incurring the construction expenditure ie the original cost of £(478,000 + 30,000) = £508,000. The cost of the drawing office is eligible expenditure.

The unexpired tax life of the building remaining on 1 March 2001 is 16 years 4
months. This means Velo Ltd is entitled to IBAs of $\dfrac{£508,000}{16\,^{4}\!/_{12}} = £31,102$ per
annum commencing in the year to 31.3.01 until the expenditure is written off.

Although the crane is a long-life asset, because Velo Ltd has not exceeded   Limit: 1 mark
the £100,000 annual limit, it will be treated as plant and machinery. It will   FYA: 1 mark
therefore quality for a 40% FYA (£53,000 @ 40% = £21,200) in the y/e 31.3.01 as   WDA: 1 mark
Velo Ltd is a medium-sized company. Thereafter a WDA of 25% can be claimed
on the reducing balance.

(iii)   *Leasehold factory and computer equipment*

A Schedule D Case I deduction can be claimed in respect of the leasehold office
as follows:

	£
Premium paid	80,000
Less: £80,000 × (15 – 1) × 2%	(22,400)
Total deductible	57,600

Premium:
2 marks

£57,600/15 = £3,840 deductible per annum

	£
Amount deductible for y/e 31.3.01	
1/12 × £3,840	320
Add: rent paid $\left(\dfrac{16,200}{12}\right)$	1,350
Total deduction	1,670

Rent paid: 1 mark

Normally the amortisation (depreciation) of the lease will be deducted in the
accounts and must be added back as an appropriation.

The computer equipment is a short life asset and a claim should be made to   Short life
'de-pool' the expenditure. This must be made by 31.3.03. If the equipment is   asset: 1 mark
disposed of before 31.3.05, a balancing charge or allowance will be made.
Otherwise, its tax written down value is added to the general pool at that   Balancing
time. It should be noted that the election is not advantageous if the   allowance:
equipment is not sold before 31.3.05 at less than tax written down value.   1 mark

For the y/e 31.3.01, the allowance will be a first year allowance of 40% × £14,000
= £5,600. The 100% allowance is only available for small enterprises.   FYA: 1 mark

(b) (i)   *Heating and ventilation systems*

Election: 1 mark

A joint election can be made by Velo Ltd and the purchaser of the building to
identify the disposal price of the systems and the corresponding amount on   Limits: 1 mark
which the purchaser can claim allowances. The time limit for the election is two
years after the purchaser acquires the interest (ie 25 March 2003). The amount   Balancing
cannot exceed the original cost of the plant (£54,000) and it must not be less than   charge: 1 mark
the tax written down value of £28,000.

It would be beneficial for Velo Ltd, if the price was not to exceed £38,000 (the
pool WDV). The most beneficial figure would be £28,000, giving a WDA on the   WDA: 1 mark
rest of the pool for y/e 31.3.01 of £(38,000 – 28,000) = £10,000 @ 25% = £2,500.

(ii)   *Overhead crane*

The overhead crane is a long-life asset. As it was acquired in y/e 31.3.01 and Velo
Ltd intends to acquire another crane on 1 March 2001 costing £53,000 the   Limit: 1 mark
£100,000 limit regarding long-life assets will be exceeded.

Tax planning:
1 mark

WDA: 1 mark

If both cranes are purchased in y/e 31.3.01, the first crane will not affect the long-life pool calculation as it is bought and sold in the same year. However, there will be no first year allowance on the second crane and the WDA will be 6% instead of 25%. It would therefore be better for the new crane to be acquired after 31.3.2001.

(iii)   *Effect on rollover relief*

Reduction:
1 mark

If the heating and ventilation system and the crane are separately identified, the sale proceeds of the factory will be reduced to:

£(575,000 – 28,000 – 64,000) = £483,000.

This means the full proceeds are reinvested in qualifying assets and so the whole gain can be deferred.

Marking guide

		Marks	
(a)	*Sale of factory*		
	Gain	1	
	Rollover relief/Amount reinvested	1	
	Immediate gain	1	
	Depreciating assets	1	
	Allocation of gain	1	
	Balancing charge	2	
	New factory		
	Expenditure qualifying for IBAs	2	
	25 year life/Balance remaining	2	
	IBAs commencing year to 31.3.01	2	
	New crane		
	Limit - £100,000	1	
	FYA	1	
	Subsequent WDA	1	
	Leasehold offices		
	Premium paid/Amortisation	2	
	Rent paid (deduction)	1	
	Computer equipment		
	Short life asset	1	
	Balancing allowance	1	
	FYA	1	
	Available	22	
	Maximum		17
(b)	*Heating and ventilation systems*		
	Joint election	1	
	Lower and upper limits	1	
	Balancing charge	1	
	WDA	1	
	Overhead crane		
	Limit of £100,000	1	
	Tax planning	1	
	WDA if two cranes purchased	1	
	Rollover relief		
	Reduction in gain immediately chargeable	1	
	Available/maximum		8
	Maximum		25

REVIEW FORM & FREE PRIZE DRAW

All original review forms from the entire BPP range, completed with genuine comments, will be entered into a draw on 31 July 2001. The names on the first four forms picked out will be sent a cheque for £50.

Name: _____   Address: _____

_____

_____

How have you used this Kit?
(Tick one box only)

☐ Home study (book only)

☐ On a course: college _____

☐ With 'correspondence' package

☐ Other _____

Why did you decide to purchase this Kit?
(Tick one box only)

☐ Have used complementary Study Text

☐ Have used BPP Kits in the past

☐ Recommendation by friend/colleague

☐ Recommendation by a lecturer at college

☐ Saw advertising

☐ Other _____

During the past six months do you recall seeing/receiving any of the following?
(Tick as many boxes as are relevant)

☐ Our advertisement in *ACCA Students' Newsletter*

☐ Our advertisement in *Pass*

☐ Our brochure with a letter through the post

Which (if any) aspects of our advertising do you find useful?
(Tick as many boxes as are relevant)

☐ Prices and publication dates of new editions

☐ Information on Kit content

☐ Facility to order books off-the-page

☐ None of the above

Have you used the companion Study Text for this subject?   ☐ Yes   ☐ No

Your ratings, comments and suggestions would be appreciated on the following areas

	Very useful	Useful	Not useful
Introductory section (Advice on revision and practice, Question and Answer checklist, etc)	☐	☐	☐
Interactive checklists	☐	☐	☐
Tutor's hints	☐	☐	☐
Examination-standard questions	☐	☐	☐
Content of answers	☐	☐	☐
Marking schemes	☐	☐	☐
Mock exam	☐	☐	☐
Structure and presentation	☐	☐	☐
Icons	☐	☐	☐

	Excellent	Good	Adequate	Poor
Overall opinion of this Kit	☐	☐	☐	☐

Do you intend to continue using BPP Study Texts/Kits?   ☐ Yes   ☐ No

Please note any further comments and suggestions/errors on the reverse of this page.

Please return to: Katy Hibbert, BPP Publishing Ltd, FREEPOST, London, W12 8BR

REVIEW FORM & FREE PRIZE DRAW (continued)

Please note any further comments and suggestions/errors below

FREE PRIZE DRAW RULES

1   Closing date for 31 July 2001 draw is 30 June 2001.

2   No purchase necessary. Entry forms are available upon request from BPP Publishing. No more than one entry per title, per person. Draw restricted to persons aged 16 and over.

3   Winners will be notified by post and receive their cheques not later than 6 weeks after the draw date. Lists of winners will be published in BPP's *focus* newsletter following the draw.

4   The decision of the promoter in all matters is final and binding. No correspondence will be entered into.

See overleaf for information on other
BPP products and how to order

Mr/Mrs/Ms (Full name)
Daytime delivery address
Postcode
Daytime Tel
Date of exam (month/year)

	6/00 Texts	1/01 Kits	1/01 Psscrds	Tapes	Videos	Master CDs
FOUNDATION						
1 The Accounting Framework	£18.95 ☐	£10.95 ☐	£5.95 ☐	£12.95 ☐	£25.00 ☐	£34.95 ☐
2 The Legal Framework	£18.95 ☐	£10.95 ☐	£5.95 ☐	£12.95 ☐	£25.00 ☐	£34.95 ☐
3 Management Information	£18.95 ☐	£10.95 ☐	£5.95 ☐	£12.95 ☐	£25.00 ☐	£34.95 ☐
4 The Organisational Framework	£18.95 ☐	£10.95 ☐	£5.95 ☐	£12.95 ☐	£25.00 ☐	£34.95 ☐
CERTIFICATE						
5 Information Analysis	£18.95 ☐	£10.95 ☐	£5.95 ☐	£12.95 ☐	£25.00 ☐	
6 The Audit Framework	£18.95 ☐	£10.95 ☐	£5.95 ☐	£12.95 ☐	£25.00 ☐	
7 The Tax Framework (Finance Act 00)	£18.95 ☐	£10.95 ☐	£5.95 ☐	£12.95 ☐	£25.00 ☐	
(8/00 Text, 1/01 P/C, 1/01 Kit, 9/00 Tape, 12/00 Video)						
8 Managerial Finance	£18.95 ☐	£10.95 ☐	£5.95 ☐	£12.95 ☐	£25.00 ☐	£39.95 ☐
PROFESSIONAL						
9 Information for Control and Decision Making	£19.95 ☐	£10.95 ☐	£5.95 ☐	£12.95 ☐	£25.00 ☐	£39.95 ☐
10 Accounting and Audit Practice (Accounting)	£15.95 ☐	£10.95 ☐	£5.95 ☐	£12.95 ☐	£25.00 ☐	£39.95 ☐
10 Accounting and Audit Practice (Auditing)	£13.95 ☐					
11 Tax Planning (Finance Act 00)	£20.95 ☐	£10.95 ☐	£5.95 ☐	£12.95 ☐	£25.00 ☐	
(8/00 Text, 1/01 P/C, 1/01 Kit, 9/00 Tape, 12/00 Video)						
12 Management and Strategy	£20.95 ☐	£10.95 ☐	£5.95 ☐	£12.95 ☐	£25.00 ☐	
13 Financial Reporting Environment	£20.95 ☐	£10.95 ☐	£5.95 ☐	£12.95 ☐	£25.00 ☐	
14 Financial Strategy	£20.95 ☐	£10.95 ☐	£5.95 ☐	£12.95 ☐	£25.00 ☐	
INTERNATIONAL STREAM						
1 The Accounting Framework	£18.95 ☐	£10.95 ☐				
6 The Audit Framework	£18.95 ☐	£10.95 ☐				
10 Accounting and Audit Practice (Accounting)	£15.95 ☐	£10.95 ☐				
10 Accounting and Audit Practice (Audit)	£13.95 ☐					
13 Financial Reporting Environment	£20.95 ☐	£10.95 ☐				

SUBTOTAL £ ☐

POSTAGE & PACKING

Study Texts

	First	Each extra	
UK	£3.00	£2.00	£ ☐
Europe*	£5.00	£4.00	£ ☐
Rest of world	£20.00	£10.00	£ ☐

Kits/Passcards/Success Tapes

	First	Each extra	
UK	£2.00	£1.00	£ ☐
Europe*	£2.50	£1.00	£ ☐
Rest of world	£15.00	£8.00	£ ☐

Master CDs/Breakthrough Videos

	First	Each extra	
UK	£2.00	£2.00	£ ☐
Europe*	£2.00	£2.00	£ ☐
Rest of world	£20.00	£10.00	£ ☐

Grand Total (Cheques to *BPP Publishing*) I enclose
a cheque for (incl. Postage) £ ☐
Or charge to Access/Visa/Switch
Card Number
Expiry date _____ Start Date _____
Issue Number (Switch Only) _____
Signature _____

We aim to deliver to all UK addresses inside 5 working days; a signature will be required. Orders to all EU addresses should be delivered within 6 working days. All other orders to overseas addresses should be delivered within 8 working days. * Europe includes the Republic of Ireland and the Channel Islands.

See overleaf for information on other
BPP products and how to order

ACCA Order – New Syllabus

To BPP Publishing Ltd, Aldine Place, London W12 8AA
Tel: 020 8740 2211. Fax: 020 8740 1184

Mr/Mrs/Ms (Full name)
Daytime delivery address

Postcode

Daytime Tel

Date of exam (month/year)

	2/01 Texts	9/01 Kits	9/01 Psscrds	MCQ cards	Tapes	Videos
PART 1						
1.1 Preparing Financial Statements	£19.95	£10.95	£5.95	£5.95	£12.95	£25.00
1.2 Financial Information for Management	£19.95	£10.95	£5.95	£5.95	£12.95	£25.00
1.3 Managing People	£19.95	£10.95	£5.95		£12.95	£25.00
PART 2						
2.1 Information Systems	£19.95	£10.95	£5.95		£12.95	£25.00
2.2 Corporate and Business Law (6/01)	£19.95	£10.95	£5.95		£12.95	£25.00
2.3 Business Taxation FA 2000 (for 12/01 exam)	£19.95	£10.95	£5.95		£12.95	£25.00
2.4 Financial Management and Control	£19.95	£10.95	£5.95		£12.95	£25.00
2.5 Financial Reporting (6/01)	£19.95	£10.95	£5.95		£12.95	£25.00
2.6 Audit and Internal Review (6/01)	£19.95	£10.95	£5.95		£12.95	£25.00
PART 3						
3.1 Audit and Assurance Services (6/01)	£20.95	£10.95	£5.95		£12.95	£25.00
3.2 Advanced Taxation FA 2000 (for 12/01 exam)	£20.95	£10.95	£5.95		£12.95	£25.00
3.3 Performance Management	£20.95	£10.95	£5.95		£12.95	£25.00
3.4 Business Information Management	£20.95	£10.95	£5.95		£12.95	£25.00
3.5 Strategic Business Planning and Development	£20.95	£10.95	£5.95		£12.95	£25.00
3.6 Advanced Corporate Reporting (6/01)	£20.95	£10.95	£5.95		£12.95	£25.00
3.7 Strategic Financial Management	£20.95	£10.95	£5.95		£12.95	£25.00
INTERNATIONAL STREAM						
1.1 Preparing Financial Statements	£19.95	£10.95				
2.5 Financial Reporting (6/01)	£19.95	£10.95				
2.6 Audit and Internval Review (6/01)	£19.95	£10.95				
3.6 Advanced Corporate Reporting (6/01)	£20.95	£10.95				
SUCCESS IN YOUR RESEARCH AND ANALYSIS PROJECT						
Tutorial Text (9/00)	£19.95					

SUBTOTAL £

POSTAGE & PACKING

Study Texts

	First	Each extra
UK	£3.00	£2.00
Europe*	£5.00	£4.00
Rest of world	£20.00	£10.00

Kits/Passcards/Success Tapes

	First	Each extra
UK	£2.00	£1.00
Europe*	£2.50	£1.00
Rest of world	£15.00	£8.00

Breakthrough Videos

	First	Each extra
UK	£2.00	£2.00
Europe*	£2.00	£2.00
Rest of world	£20.00	£10.00

Grand Total (Cheques to *BPP Publishing*) I enclose a cheque for (incl. Postage) £

Or charge to Access/Visa/Switch

Card Number

Expiry date   Start Date

Issue Number (Switch Only)

Signature

We aim to deliver to all UK addresses inside 5 working days; a signature will be required. Orders to all EU addresses should be delivered within 6 working days. All other orders to overseas addresses should be delivered within 8 working days. * Europe includes the Republic of Ireland and the Channel Islands.